Catacombs

Guillermo O'Donnell

Translated by **Rebecca Wolpin**

Critical Introduction by **John Ackerman**

LASApress

Published by
LASA Press
www.lasapress.org
lasa@lasaweb.org

Originally published in Spanish by Prometeo in 2008.

Chapters I, II, and V were previously translated and published in Guillermo A. O'Donnell, *Counterpoints: Selected Essays on Authoritarianism and Democratization* (University of Notre Dame Press, 1999). Minor revisions have been made, primarily to the footnotes, to adapt and unify these texts with the other newly translated texts in the present volume. They are reprinted here with the permission of the University of Notre Dame Press.

Cover design: Consuelo Parga
Cover image: ©Guillermo Loiácono / Photo Library ARGRA
Print version typesetting: Lara Melamet
Digital versions typesetting: Estudio Ebook
Copy editor: Melina Kervandjian
Index: Florencia Osuna

ISBN (Paperback b&w version): 978-1-951634-66-7
ISBN (PDF): 978-1-951634-67-4
ISBN (EPUB): 978-1-951634-68-1
ISBN (Kindle): 978-1-951634-69-8
DOI: https://doi.org/10.25154/book19

Suggested citation:
O´Donnell, Guillermo. 2026. *Catacombs.* Pittsburgh: LASA Press. DOI: https://doi.org/10.25154/book19. License: CC BY-NC 4.0.

To read the free, open-access version of this book online, visit https://doi.org/10.25154/book19 or scan this QR code with your mobile device:

The dictator Jorge Rafael Videla presides over a military parade,
©Guillermo Loiácono, July, 1977, City of Buenos Aires, Argentina.
Courtesy of Photo Library ARGRA.

Table of Contents

Introduction

Gabriela Ippolito-O´Donnell

In the annals of political science, few scholars have dissected the anatomy of authoritarianism with the precision and moral urgency of Guillermo O'Donnell. A foundational figure in modern Latin American studies, his theories on the bureaucratic-authoritarian state, the nuanced contours of state power, and the fragile—often reversible—nature of democratic transitions reshaped how generations of scholars understand the cycles of repression and resistance that have defined not only Latin America but the broader global struggle for freedom.

To translate and publish *Catacombs* in English today is not merely an act of academic preservation; it is a political and moral imperative—one uniquely urgent in our current global moment.

There are books that illuminate a field of study, and then there are books that emerge from the darkness itself. *Catacombs* is decidedly the latter. For decades, the English-speaking world has known Guillermo O'Donnell as a preeminent political scientist, considered by most "the architect of indispensable theories that provided a rigorous language for understanding Latin America's political milieu." Yet *Catacombs* offers us something different: a glimpse into the intellectual and existential catacombs where that language was forged—not in the halls of academia, but under the crushing weight of state terror.

The title itself provides the first and most vital clue: it refers not to the book's content, but to the circumstances of its creation. The essays collected in *Catacombs* were written during Argentina's last and most brutal military dictatorship (1976–83)—a period described by the author as "tenebrous times of solitude, cold, and fear." To write critically about politics, economics, and the state during such an era was an act of profound courage. To preserve those writings, to hide them, to pass them along—these were acts of resistance.

What readers will discover in this collection is a series of penetrating analyses that capture Guillermo O'Donnell's mind at work in real time. The chapters—ranging from granular studies of political alliances to grand theoretical sketches of the state—are the building blocks of his later, more widely known works.

But *Catacombs* is more than just a precursor. It is a work imbued with a unique and vital tension. On one hand, it offers a stark analysis of power, documenting with chilling clarity how economic and political actors often prefer order to democracy, how they make their peace with terror when terror protects their interests. On the other hand, as Ariel Colombo notes in the preface to the Spanish edition, it is a work that "never closes action in inexorable fatality but leaves the ending or the way out open to the imagination of the protagonists." This conviction—that history is not predetermined, that the future remains contested—runs like a lifeline through these pages, transforming them from a simple record of disaster into a meditation on possibility.

It is here that *Catacombs* speaks most directly to our present. We are living through a global resurgence of authoritarian politics. In this context, *Catacombs* is not a historical artifact. It is a warning. It is a guide. It is a companion for those who find themselves in their own catacombs, wondering whether resistance is possible, whether hope is naive, whether the darkness will ever lift.

Bringing *Catacombs* to an English-speaking audience serves another crucial purpose: it allows students and scholars to understand not just what Guillermo O'Donnell thought, but how he thought under extreme pressure. It reveals the experiential and ethical roots of his theoretical contributions. The book stands as a powerful reminder that the study of politics is not a detached academic exercise, but a discipline born from the urgent need to comprehend and resist the forces that threaten human dignity.

Catacombs offers no false comfort. It does not promise victory. It does not pretend that resistance is easy or that hope is simple. What it offers is something more precious: the example of a mind that refused to surrender, a voice that refused to be silenced, a life that insisted on meaning even when meaning seemed impossible to find.

It is a great joy and honor to present this work to the English-speaking world. I am deeply grateful to LASA Press for their courage and vision in committing to this publication. In an era when scholarly presses face mounting pressures and foundational works risk being forgotten, LASA Press has demonstrated that the life of the mind remains worth nurturing. Their commitment to publishing this text is a service to the entire intellectual community—and a gift to those of us who carry Guillermo O'Donnell's legacy in our hearts.

The editorial team, led by Julieta Mortati, deserves special recognition. Their meticulous work—tracing references, verifying quotations, consulting with those who knew the author and his context—has been indispensable. They have treated this text not as an artifact to be preserved in amber, but as a living document meant to speak to new readers in a new time. Their skill, patience, and dedication are evident on every page.

I am also grateful to Oscar Oszlak for granting permission to reprint his review essay on the Spanish edition of the book.

A special note of thanks is due to my exceptional colleague and good friend John Ackerman, whose insightful critical introduction provides an invaluable framework for understanding *Catacombs* within the broader intellectual trajectory and the historical context from which it emerged. Ackerman's deep engagement with Guillermo O'Donnell's legacy illuminates the continuities and ruptures in O'Donnell's thought, helping readers navigate the complex terrain between the catacombs and the light.

May this English edition carry the echoes of those catacombs out into the world. May it find its way into the hands of students wondering whether their studies matter, of scholars questioning the purpose of their work, of citizens watching their democracies erode and searching for a language to name what they see. May it inform, challenge, and inspire all those who continue to grapple with the complexities of democracy and authoritarianism.

And may it remind us, in the words that echo through these pages, that the ending is not yet written. That history is not fate. That even in the darkest hours, the work of thinking, of witnessing, and of hoping remains an act of resistance.

Taipei, 2026

Critical Introduction
O'Donnell's Legacy of Transformative Democracy

John M. Ackerman[1]

What a delight that the English-speaking world can finally read together in a single volume the seminal early writings of one of Latin America's greatest political scientists. In these essays, written in Argentina during the politically tragic but intellectually fertile 1970s, Guillermo O'Donnell developed many of the key theories and approaches that would distinguish his path-breaking scholarship during the following decades.

This book is not only an essential reference point for those interested in tracing O'Donnell's intellectual trajectory. It also speaks loudly and clearly to the present moment. As we descend into a new stage of authoritarian revival throughout the world, O'Donnell's innovative understanding of the underlying configurations and processes that defined Argentina's bureaucratic-authoritarian (BA) state are a useful guide for contemporary research. Making O'Donnell's essays available in English should help revitalize debates among Anglo-American

---

1 John M. Ackerman is Research Professor at the Institute for Legal Research (Instituto de Investigaciones Jurídicas, IIJ) and Director of the University Program on Democracy, Justice and Society (Programa Universitario de Estudios sobre Democracia, Justicia y Sociedad, PUEDJS) of the Universidad Nacional Autónoma de México (UNAM). The author extends his most profound gratitude to Gabriela Ippolito-O'Donnell for her kind invitation to write this Introduction for the English version of *Catacumbas*.

political scientists by rekindling the flames of twentieth-century Latin American political sociology.

O'Donnell's English-speaking audience may be surprised by the decidedly political economy approach of these texts. Our author is best known for his work on democratic transitions, accountability, citizenship, and the rule of law, topics that are often understood to be strictly political or institutional phenomena. But in these essays, politics and economics are inseparable. For O'Donnell, the key to understanding the brutal authoritarianism that was descending on Argentina at the time was to explore the past and present of the class dynamics embedded in the Argentine state.

Some have argued that O'Donnell's later contributions have little in common with these early writings. For instance, Leonardo Eiff (2022) writes that "our author no longer pursues a conceptualization of the state by delving into its relations with the capitalist social formation" (my translation, 202). But, in fact, O'Donnell always held these early writings close to his heart and explicitly recognized the fundamental role that Latin American political economy and political sociology played not only at the beginning of his scholarly journey but throughout his entire intellectual trajectory. Although he did modify the language he used to speak about the Latin American state during his career, his focus on the impact that "social relations" and "economic orthodoxies" have on political dynamics remained quite consistent.

Given this, it is remarkable that only some of these essays were published sporadically in English during O'Donnell's lifetime. This suggests that their approach was of little interest, or perhaps even bothersome, or "*molesto*," as Guillermo liked to say about the role of academics in general, to the Anglo academic establishment. The publication of this important volume therefore implies a poetic moment of reconciliation and closure. Finally, O'Donnell's English-speaking audience will be able to fully understand and be confronted by the entire depth of his work.

This introductory essay is divided into four sections. In the first section, I highlight O'Donnell's own words about the importance of returning to the key issues and approaches that dominated Latin American social sciences during the 1970s. In the second section, I engage with the robust and provocative general theories of the capitalist state that O'Donnell offers in the present volume, with particular attention to his arguments in Chapter VI, "Notes on the Theory of the State," which appears here for the first time in English. Although O'Donnell's research on the specific dynamics of the bureaucratic-authoritarian state is already well known, the broader theories that undergirded and grew out of this research are still underappreciated in the English-speaking world. I argue that O'Donnell never abandoned the political economy approach developed in these essays. On the contrary, it directly inspired his later writing on democratic consolidation, accountability, and the rule of law.

In the third section, I take on the accusation that O'Donnell's work on democratic transitions is somehow "elitist." The texts contained in this volume, including the original draft he wrote for the project "Transitions From Authoritarian Rule," later published in altered form coauthored with Philippe Schmitter, demonstrate that his thinking has always been accompanied by a firm belief in the power of mobilized civil society and the embeddedness of political institutions. Finally, I close with some "tentative conclusions" about our author's overall intellectual contributions. I argue that O'Donnell's outsized impact on the field of political science is precisely due to the fact that he never abandoned the political project and theoretical approaches first developed during the 1970s. We would all do well to maintain alive and well O'Donnell's distinguished legacy in the present moment of global democratic crisis.

I. Democracy and Dependency

In his acceptance speech for the 2003 LASA Kalman Silvert Award for Lifetime Achievement, O'Donnell made an explicit call to return to the central concerns of 1970s Latin American social sciences. He reminded us that his work on BA was inspired by dependency theory and argued that the issues dealt with at the time are today more relevant than ever.

> Dependency factors and theories have not been a subject for the academy for quite a long time. But I believe that the problems to which these theories pointed to are still alive, arguably stronger and more decisive than ever before. We should be aware that recognizing this

> topic as the problem it is will not be done from a center that greatly benefits from these asymmetric relationships, which it often subsumes under the umbrella of "inter-dependencies." Serious studies on these subjects must be our task, updating the contributions made by ECLAC and the dependency authors. [O'Donnell 2007a, 144]

I remember, as if it were yesterday, the mischievous excitement I felt as a young doctoral student listening to my teacher and mentor in that conference room in Dallas. Instead of using the opportunity for self-aggrandizement or for the intellectual back-slapping of the distinguished colleagues who were in the room, O'Donnell preferred to share thoughts he knew would raise more than a few eyebrows.

The idea that transformative thinking about democracy cannot be done from the "center" directly questioned the utility of a great amount of Anglo-American political science literature on Latin America. And the bold call to recover the key lessons and approaches of dependency theory was an open invitation to break with the institutionalist bias present in much of this same literature.

Political scientists typically try to separate political and economic phenomena. Democracy should be judged on its own merits, without "adjectives" and independently from the economic policies that result from it (Przeworski 1999). Indeed, there is a vast literature whose central purpose is the policing of the barriers between the economic and political spheres, including frequent admonishments to those who mix up or confuse political process and policy outcomes (Linz 1990; Huntington 1991).

In contrast, one of the hallmarks of O'Donnell's long career was that he systematically insisted that it was a mistake to encapsulate democratization within the bubble of strictly political or institutional reform. For instance, in the Kalman Silvert lecture, O'Donnell directly took on neoliberal economic policies:

> [For the improvement of the quality of democracy] to happen it will be necessary to overcome, with professional seriousness and civic passion, the intellectual and political prohibitions springing from the current economic orthodoxy. These necessary advances pose a

> crucial challenge to the creativity and professionalism of the Latin American social sciences. [O'Donnell 2007a, 153]

Although O'Donnell does not employ the word "neoliberalism" (he was always resistant to terms whose excessive use leads to analytical imprecision), his statement that we should remove the blinders of "the current economic orthodoxy" is unequivocal. Political analysis necessarily goes hand in hand with a robust understanding of the economic sphere. If we limit our research on democracy only to those political expressions consistent with neoliberal economic policies, then we are dangerously constraining the "creativity" and "civic passion" necessary to move forward social sciences.

In his acceptance speech for the first Lifetime Achievement Award granted by the International Political Science Association in 2006, O'Donnell hit on similar themes:

> Democracy always projects a horizon of both hope and dissatisfaction. Because it is grounded on the various dimensions of citizenship, and on the notion of intrinsic human dignity that those dimensions entail, democracy always posits an open horizon. It looks toward a better future, expected and demanded by human beings who recognize themselves as carriers of inalienable rights that the political realm should respect and foster. This projection toward an unending and undefined, always risky yet promising future, runs counter to all kinds of authoritarian rule. It also runs counter to conservative or ethnocentric claims that we have reached some "end of history." [O'Donnell 2007b, 9]

For O'Donnell, democracy is necessarily an expansive project intimately intertwined with the struggle for "human dignity" and "inalienable rights." This vision of the permanently "open horizon" of political struggle grounded in both utopian hope and permanent critique, or "dissatisfaction," breaks with traditional political science approaches limited to creating the conditions for effective "governance." O'Donnell also makes a point to directly confront conservative approaches such as Francis Fukuyama's (1992), whose proclamation of the victory of "the West" after the Cold War he considers to be downright "ethnocentric."

Instead of corralling democracy behind the walls of the existing political institutions and economic orthodoxies of the Atlantic northwest, we should conceive of democratization as a transformative social process with profound roots in the global south.

For our author, the central purpose of democracy is not to generate a false consensus between political actors for the purpose of maintaining political stability, but to stimulate the peaceful conflict necessary to bring about social change.

> As intellectuals, I believe it is our duty to make a persistent, serious, and well-grounded democratic critique of these socially skewed democracies. This does not mean calling for the "wide consensus" that some voices invoke today. Rather, it is a matter of not being afraid of the conflicts that will arise from struggling to extend the civil and social aspects of these democracies. It also means helping these conflicts develop within parameters of democratic legality, although these same parameters will have to be extended along and as a consequence of these struggles. [O'Donnell 2007a, 153]

The key problem with today's democracies is that they are "socially skewed" and that their central challenge is to "extend [their] civil and social aspects." And if conflicts arise during this process of democratic expansion with those who aggressively defend their privileges, we should not shrink from the task. Indeed, we should even "help these conflicts develop" and allow the process to transform the legal framework itself.

One of the things that makes O'Donnell's approach so special is the fact that instead of writing for the academic establishment he wrote to change the world: "Politics and its conflicts have provided our subject matter, not so much the wish—justifiable, perhaps, but alien to the conditions of production of Latin American social knowledge—to fill this or that hole in the existing theoretical literature" (O'Donnell 2007a, 141–42). This unabashed commitment to writing with a political purpose has accompanied him since the 1970s:

> I and others did not just sit down to write theory; we used theoretical concepts, some preexistent and others created along the way,

> to write texts of a profound and primarily political intention and, in our case, of a democratic intention as well. This gave rise to a new literature that, with respect to myself and other authors in a similar line, was significantly based on the work of ECLAC and the dependency literature even when it dealt with a new subject, the BAs. [O'Donnell 2007a, 148]

Throughout his illustrious career, the struggle for human dignity and the fulfillment of material, social, and cultural needs have always been at the center of O'Donnell's work. In the contemporary context of ever-increasing academic specialization, combined with the pressure to apply strictly "scientific" methods to the analysis of political phenomena, O'Donnell's rigorous but also freewheeling focus on making a difference in the world is refreshing and inspiring.

II. The Dynamics of the Capitalist State

O'Donnell's firm commitment to an expansive notion of social change and the embeddedness of political institutions was born during the 1970s while researching and writing the texts included in the present volume. For instance, our author understood bureaucratic-authoritarianism not as a choice of governing style, but as a way in which a particular socioeconomic configuration responded to specific domestic and international pressures. A passage in Chapter III of the present volume on "The 'Stabilization Programs' Negotiated with the International Monetary Fund and Their Domestic Impact" lays out well the central coordinates of his approach:

> The implementation of the BA occurs as a fearful response to what many see as a deep economic crisis. On the political side, it is seen as a great "disorder" and, consequently, as a decline in the state's ability to guarantee the current system of domination, that is, as a threat of societal collapse. This sense of threat unites the bourgeoisie around its fundamental interest in reproducing itself as a class and propels it to support a coup that, imbued with notions of

> "national security" that converge on the same result, is unleashed by the armed forces. [O'Donnell 2026, 155]

In general, as O'Donnell explains in his new introduction to Chapter I on "State and Alliances in Argentina, 1956–1976," the real motivation for BA was the desire to exercise a "social vendetta":

> In contrast to those who believed that it was only a question of "restoring order," I was convinced that there was also a fierce social vendetta at play. . . . It was nothing less than an attempt to wipe out, once and for all, the rebellious, popular, and politically active Argentina that had already thwarted previous attempts to "clean up" the economy and, therefore, society as a whole. [O'Donnell 2026, 55]

A BA regime is not a simple power grab implemented by ambitious military officers, but a much more complicated phenomenon. It responds simultaneously to specific class interests, the fear of the bourgeoisie of losing its capacity to "reproduce itself as a class," and the desire to bring an end to the long history of "rebellious, popular and politically active" social mobilization in Argentina. Just as European fascism was designed to annihilate the thriving communist movements in both Italy and Germany after the First World War, BA regimes looked to stabilizing the control over the economy by sectors of the national bourgeoisie linked to foreign capital by resorting to "social vendetta" and ideological "cleansing."

O'Donnell's analysis of the dynamics of BA regimes is generally well known and amply cited in the literature (O'Donnell 1973 and 1988; Collier 2001). But the general theory of the capitalist state, which both grounded and arose out of this analysis, has until today been underappreciated. Chapter VI, "Notes for a Theory of the State," is a tour de force, previously unpublished in English, where we witness O'Donnell expounding on a solid political economy approach to the state. Although at first it appears to be radically different from his later work, I would argue that this framework accompanied him throughout his entire career and is the original source for much of his creative rethinking of contemporary political dynamics.

O'Donnell posits that under capitalism the state undergoes the same process of reification or "fetishization" as do commodities under capitalism:

> The reification (or objectification) of the capitalist state in its institutions is the typical modality of its appearance, which is why the critique of that state must begin by uncovering it as an aspect of domination in society. Like money and goods, state institutions are a fetish. Both an emanation and at the same time a concealment of the underlying contradictory relationship, the fetish does not appear solely as an external power. It is also a determinant of ordinary consciousness: its modality of externalization tends to govern a perception of the social world that is itself a concealment of the underlying reality. [O'Donnell 2026, 265]

Although O'Donnell does not cite Marx directly, this is clearly a reference to the arguments contained in the first chapter of the first volume of *Das Kapital* on the "fetishization" of commodities (Marx 2004 [1867]). For our author, the state is not an "autonomous" entity that stands above society, but something that arises out of and is configured through society. As O'Donnell explains in the initial paragraphs of Chapter II, "As such, the state must be understood within and from civil society, even though its institutional objectivations appear, and are often proclaimed, as being above it".[2]

When we pretend that the state exists independently from society we fall into a condition of false consciousness in which we confuse cause and effect, sickness and symptom, thereby generating a confusion that inhibits our capacity to transform political and economic domination,

---

2 In the first English version of Chapter II published in *Counterpoints* (O'Donnell 1999a), O'Donnell excluded the first three paragraphs of the first section of the original essay in Spanish. But when he decided to republish the original essay in Spanish in *Catacumbas* (O'Donnell 2024), O'Donnell included these three important paragraphs, which are now published in English for the first time in this volume. Significantly, the accompanying footnote to this chapter in *Catacumbas*, and the present volume, invites the reader to consult Chapter VI "For a more complete development" of his conception of the state.

which are in the end two sides of the same coin. As he writes in Chapter VI, "the split that thus occurs between society and the state, and the mutual externality to which it condemns them, is the main basis for the concealment of the state as the guarantor of domination in society and for the opacity of that domination" (O'Donnell 2026, 260).

Let us be clear. O'Donnell does not present an instrumentalist view of the state. The state, he explains, is only "an aspect of social domination" that is crisscrossed by a multiplicity of contradictory forces and interests. For him, the state is not a simple plaything in the hands of the capitalist class, as it appears in vulgar Marxist approaches. Indeed, O'Donnell's purpose is not to attack capitalism as such, but specifically to confront the Argentine generals' claims that they represent the universal principles of society by "bringing order" to the country. For our author, it is crucial to unveil the fact that the generals advance specific economic and social interests so as to open a space for productive political conflict and democratic transformation.

O'Donnell's historical critique of the BA state thereby parallels his contemporary critique of what we could call "neoliberal democracy" (Ackerman 2015 and 2025). In similar fashion to the BA regimes of the 1970s, many contemporary electoral democracies also present themselves as universal representatives of the people, while they in fact exclude the vast majority of their populations from authentic political participation, legal redress, and economic opportunity. Just as O'Donnell unmasked authoritarian dictatorship during the 1970s, he continued to unmask the hypocrisy of "delegative democracies" that function as if they were elected short-term autocracies (O'Donnell 1994).

In Chapter VI, O'Donnell also draws a direct parallel between the false liberty and equality that exists between abstract consumers in the capitalist market and the liberty and equality that supposedly exists between anonymous voters in the ballot box:

> Those who must appear abstractly equal in order to enter into contracts tend to appear abstractly equal in order to constitute political power; the free subject in the market mediated by capital-money is the exact counterpart of the voter. This has made the capitalist state the first that must tend to appear founded on some plane of equality among all subjects. [O'Donnell 2026, 284]

Our author is saying something quite profound here, and, I believe, it is an approach that remained central to his work throughout his entire career. Elections are not only not enough for democracy, but, in the wrong hands, they can also play a role in the mystification of power. When we are satisfied with only abstract equality, through the anonymous, individual participation of each citizen at the ballot box, we give up on the struggle for substantive equality through the transformation of the social structure. This is why it is so important to perform a permanent "democratic critique of democracy," as O'Donnell insisted time and again in his writings.

In his introduction to Chapter VI, O'Donnell writes that he first "hesitated" to include it in the compilation since in it he "paid little attention to . . . potential connections [of the state] with other issues, especially that of democracy" (O´Donnell 2026, 245). But this is not a fair evaluation of the essay since his firm commitment to social power and democratic process is in fact abundantly clear throughout. For instance, he writes that "this [abstract] equality represents immense progress compared to the non-belonging of slaves, metics, and serfs to the political community, as well as contemporary regressions in the validity of citizenship (O´Donnell 2026, 284). Later on in the same chapter, he explains that "despite the mediations of citizenship and nation, society can impose its own systems of solidarity" (O´Donnell 2026, 290) and concludes that "despite the imposing weight of the fetishized state, the decisive locus for the reproduction and potential transcendence of domination is society" (O´Donnell 2026, 296). He by no means disqualifies democracy and citizen participation as a bourgeoisie farce. To the contrary, although he criticizes the limits of abstract equality embedded in electoralist visions of democracy, he simultaneously recognizes that this equality is a step in the right direction toward social empowerment.

O'Donnell develops these themes more explicitly in Chapter II on "Tensions in the Bureaucratic-Authoritarian State and the Question of Democracy." He writes that "if political democracy were to be restored, at the very least the mediation of citizenship would reappear. As a result, many members of society would once again be treated as, and would see themselves as, participants in a form of abstract but not insignificant equality" (O´Donnell 2026, 112). In other words, instead of taking a maximalist position and casting aspersions on imperfect elections, such as those that take place in the context of "competitive authoritarian" regimes (Levitsky and Way 2010), we should try to leverage the hypocrisy of such voting exercises to achieve greater political and social change.

A transition to electoral politics can open the door to broader transformations. O'Donnell writes that, even in the depths of an authoritarian system, one of the key tasks is to give content to democratic forms. For instance, in the case of BA regimes, our efforts should be directed toward "the struggle for the appropriation and redefinition of the meaning of democracy, oriented toward impregnating itself with the meanings carried by those who are excluded by the BA and constituting, together with them, the basis for an alternative kind of state" (O'Donnell 2026, 116). For O'Donnell, long-term inclusion and social transformation are much more important than short-term governance and political stability. Democratization implies the expansion of the sphere of citizenship to include society as a whole, avoiding the exclusion of the popular and working classes typical of BA regimes, or contemporary neoliberal or competitive authoritarian regimes. As we saw in the previous section, this "struggle for the appropriation and redefinition" of democracy was precisely the backbone of O'Donnell's entire career.

In addition to his discussion of the state in general, O'Donnell also takes aim at the capitalist vision of the "rule of law" or "Estado de derecho" in particular:

> Rational-formal law emerged and expanded alongside capitalism. This is the expression of a profound relationship: this law is the formalized codification of domination in capitalist society through the creation of the legal subject implied by the appearance of free and formally equal relations in the buying and selling of labor power and, in general, in the circulation of goods. [O'Donnell 2026, 263]

Once again it would be a mistake to imagine that O'Donnell is taking an instrumentalist approach to law as always and everywhere a simple tool of the ruling class. He developed this analysis in the context of his critique of the false pretenses of the Argentine junta that claimed its only, and supposedly neutral and technocratic, purpose was to establish "law and order." Parallel to his critique of the capitalist state, O'Donnell argues that law is not a single immutable object that floats above society and can be imposed objectively and unilaterally on society. On the contrary, law is an integral part of society itself and responds to the powers that be in which the legal system is embedded.

His later writings on legality and the rule of law take a similar approach. For instance, his discussion of "brown areas," in which the lack of protection by the state deepens inequality by exposing vulnerable populations to the (un)rule of law, has been so influential precisely because it takes a bottom-up view on legality as something not only embedded in state institutions but also in society (O'Donnell 1998 and 2004). And his broader work on legality and inequality speaks directly to the relationship between judicial and social structures (O'Donnell, Méndez, and Pinheiro 1999). In general, O'Donnell saw legal reform to be a process of social and political liberation. This perspective breaks with both typical technocratic top-down approaches to "judicial reform" and ethnocentric approaches that blame rule-of-law problems in Latin America on the supposedly backward "culture of legality" in the region.

For O'Donnell, the experience of the Argentine dictatorship was the central motivating force for his entire career. "This memory, which should be unerasable, of the fear that we suffered, suggests a political agenda aimed, at the very least, at making Latin America cease to be a place where persons are subjected to the hard yoke of fear and humiliation" (O'Donnell 2007a, 152). It should therefore not be a surprise that the theoretical frameworks developed during the 1970s continued to hold their grip over our author throughout his life.

In the introduction to Chapter VI, O'Donnell states that the central contribution of this essay is that it serves as an antidote to those "views that either deny the very existence of the state and reify it as merely a set of bureaucracies, demonize it as the source of all evil, or see it as a neutral entity that only needs technical or bureaucratic refinement." (O′Donnell 2026, 245). The commitment to understanding the social bases of the state and the struggle to expand democracy and the rule of law as a means to achieve human welfare and dignity underpinned his work throughout his career.

III. "Elitist" Transitology

The profound engagement with the social bases of democracy and the state summarized in the previous section reveal why O'Donnell could never be considered an "elitist." He always rejected this characterization of the theories he developed in the context of the volumes of *Transitions from Authoritarian Rule*, edited with Philippe Schmitter and Laurence Whitehead (O'Donnell, Schmitter, and Whitehead 1986). Chapter V of the present volume, titled "Notes for the Study of Processes of Political Democratization in the Wake of the Bureaucratic-Authoritarian State," reproduces the original draft he wrote on his own for the project *Transitions from Authoritarian Rule*, ultimately published in altered form as a coauthored piece with Schmitter as the fourth volume of the series "Tentative Conclusions About Uncertain Democracies" (O'Donnell and Schmitter 1986). In the updated introduction to the chapter included in this volume, O'Donnell clarifies that:

> This framework (or, as some have called it, though I dislike the term, "model") . . . has given rise to numerous discussions, which have accumulated as other transitions have occurred. . . . I am surprised (and, I confess, displeased) when I read that this framework is "elitist," given that in it I placed so much emphasis on political reactivation and the "resurrection of civil society," both of which, along with victory in the field of democratic opposition, are necessary to achieve democracy. [O'Donnell 2026, 215]

Indeed, as we have seen in the previous section, for O'Donnell society rules supreme: "the decisive locus for the reproduction and potential transcendence of domination is society." And, in Chapter V, he writes explicitly that it is the "resurrection of civil society that sustains the opposition; in the absence of such a resurrection, or were the support that it affords not embraced by the opposition, the latter would be too weak to withstand the pressures and threats mounted by the various forces within the BA alliance" (O′Donnell 2026, 238).

There is no question that Chapter V gives much importance to inter-elite negotiation. O'Donnell understandably puts great emphasis on how to strategically achieve the key moment of rupture in the univocal power of an authoritarian regime. But this analysis is not intended to be understood as a "model" of "transitions to democracy," as is often thought, but as a study of the concrete dynamics of "transitions from authoritarian rule." O'Donnell has clarified that "we made a point of explicitly stating in the title of these volumes that they deal with transitions *from* authoritarian regimes—the inauguration of a democratic regime is only one of the possible outcomes of these transitions" (O'Donnell 2007a, 150).

In the new introduction to Chapter II, O'Donnell shares his distaste for the role that some elitists in the democratic opposition tend to play during the process of regime rupture:

> Typically, in these cases there is no shortage of opportunistic politicians and enthusiastic intellectuals (or worse) who turn to "the liberals" (as the military leaders came to be called) to offer their support in exchange for a privileged and protected place under a sun that only they would continue to ensure. [O'Donnell 2026, 99]

Later, he openly criticizes opportunists who forget about the mobilized society to which they owe their political influence and the possible success of the democratic movement:

> There will always be an opportunistic opposition (or pseudo-opposition) ready to accept practically any proposal made by the soft-liners. Objectively, this part of the opposition is an obstacle to democratization; to the degree that it succeeds in becoming the dominant voice within the opposition, the transition process will grind to a halt at a stage that closely reflects the initial proposals of the soft-liners—which is to say, short of political democracy. [O'Donnell 2026, 229]

According to O'Donnell, transitions from authoritarian rule are successful only when the opposition remains firmly rooted in its democratic demands and successfully unifies society against the authoritarian regime.

It is true that O'Donnell is explicit about the role "moderation" needs to play in the process:

> For the most part, what certain cases demonstrate positively, while others do so negatively, is that the fundamental issue for a viable democratization (that is, a democratization that is neither mortally wounded from the beginning nor merely the cosmetic liberalization of an authoritarian state) is the extent to which the moderates control the opposition camp. [O'Donnell 2026, 242]

But "moderation" is different from "elitism." O'Donnell's concerns about the radical faction dominating the opposition does not stem from a belief that elites are the only ones that matter, quite the contrary. Consistent with his understanding that one of the central undergirding reasons for the emergence of BA regimes is the intense fear that the elites have of the historical mobilization of the Argentine working class and their desire for "social vendetta" against this class; the problem is their excessive influence not their lack of importance. Indeed, following the logic of O'Donnell's argument, if mobilized society were not as strong as it was at the time in Argentina, then it wouldn't be necessary to bet on the moderates.

IV. Tentative Conclusions About O'Donnell's Early Writings

According to O'Donnell, the key contribution of his 1970s writings was not the BA model in itself, but the attempt to deal with underlying structural problems:

> Nowadays the subject of BAs is the only one, out of those I have looked over until now, that seems to have lost currency. There are still severe inequalities in international exchange, a strong dependency, voracious internal colonialisms, and increasing exclusion and marginality. But there are not BAs in the strict sense, although there exist authoritarian regimes of a different kind and weak democracies that thinly hide their authoritarian sides. [O'Donnell 2007a, 149]

I believe that he grossly underestimated the contemporary relevance of the BA model. Many aspects of today's "electoral authoritarian" regimes are similar to those diagnosed by O'Donnell as pertaining to the BA regimes during the 1970s. But the important point to glean from this statement is the way in which O'Donnell continued to insist late in his career on the importance of taking a broad approach to the social, economic, and international structures of oppression and exclusion.

The value of the texts included in the present volume is precisely that they show us the path for conducting the sort of profound structural "democratic critique of democracy" that O'Donnell considered to be his mission throughout his illustrious career. Indeed, without these initial writings it is difficult to fully understand O'Donnell's later work or comprehend his expansive influence on the field of political science.

O'Donnell's always open and dynamic approach to democratic politics comes from his emphasis on social power and structural inequalities. As he stated at the IPSA award ceremony:

> Many democracies are in crisis, though the crises vary as to depth and specific characteristics. Still, there is in these crises something that belongs to what is best and most distinctive about democracy. For the crises underline democracy's intrinsic mix of hope and dissatisfaction, its highlighting of a lack that will never be filled. [O'Donnell 2007b, 9]

This surprising embrace of crisis and dissatisfaction goes against the grain of much standard Anglo-American political science literature that tends to emphasize stability, governance, and agreement as the keys to maintaining a democratic regime. He then insists on the need to always understand the embeddedness of political dynamics in the broader social context:

> Democracy is more than a valuable kind of political arrangement. [. . .] It is the perpetual absence of something more, of an always pending agenda that calls for the redress of social ills and further advances in the manifold matters which, at a certain time and for a certain people, most concern human welfare and dignity. (O'Donnell 2007b, 10)

The struggle for democracy necessarily reaches beyond itself and toward social transformation. This is the key lesson of the seminal essays contained in the present volume. Structural injustice cannot be dislodged by an empty, formalistic defense of electoral institutions tout court, but can only be achieved by advancing simultaneously on a broad diversity of terrains toward a more full, transformative democracy.

O'Donnell was a rebel who always took pleasure in going against the current orthodoxy. His Kalman Silvert address concluded with these words:

> We intellectuals are annoying. We are also privileged persons who have the possibility of teaching, researching, and writing. I am convinced that this privilege generates a special duty in a region characterized by so much inequality and poverty: directing our knowledge to help achieve decent societies, ones in which everyone has at least their material, social, and cultural needs fulfilled, and where no one is humiliated or discriminated against. [O'Donnell 2007a, 154]

The publication in English of O'Donnell's early writings is a fitting way for our author to once again make himself present in contemporary discussions with surprising and, for some readers, "annoying" or bothersome essential points of view that force us to seriously rethink the state of democracy today and what we need to do in order to save its core values and practices.

Sources

Ackerman, John. 2015. *El mito de la transición democrática*. Mexico City: Editorial Planeta.

Ackerman, John, ed. 2025. *Más allá de la democracia (neo)liberal: los retos del segundo piso*. Mexico City: Programa Universitario de Estudios sobre Democracia, Justicia y Sociedad, UNAM.

Collier, David. 2001. "Bureaucratic Authoritarianism." In *The Oxford Companion to Politics of the World*, edited by Joel Krieger, 2nd ed. Oxford: Oxford University Press.

Eiff, Leonardo. 2022. *Revista Argentina de Ciencia Política* 1, no. 29: 192–216.

Fukuyama, Francis. 1992. *The End of History and the Last Man*. New York: The Free Press.

Huntington, Samuel. 1991. *The Third Wave: Democratization in the Late 20th Century*. Norman, OK: University of Oklahoma Press.

Levitsky, Stephen, and Lucan Way. 2010. *Competitive Authoritarianism: Hybrid Regimes after the Cold War*. Cambridge: Cambridge University Press.

Linz Juan, and Al Stepan. 1996. *Problems of Democratic Transition and Consolidation: Southern Europe, South America and Post-Communist Europe*. Baltimore: Johns Hopkins University Press.

Marx, Karl. 2004 [1867]. *Capital, Vol.1*. New York: Penguin Classics.

O'Donnell, Guillermo. 1973. *Modernization and Bureaucratic Authoritarianism: Studies in South American Politics*. Berkeley, CA: Institute of International Studies, University of California.

O'Donnell, Guillermo. 1988. *Bureaucratic Authoritarianism: Argentina 1966–1973 in Comparative Perspective*, University of California Press.

O'Donnell, Guillermo. 1998. "Polyarchies and the Unrule of Law in Latin America," Working Paper 254. The Helen Kellog Institute for International Studies, University of Notre Dame, Indiana.

O'Donnell, Guillermo. 1994. "Delegative Democracy." *Journal of Democracy* 5, no. 1 (January 1994).

O'Donnell, Guillermo. 1999. *Counterpoints: Selected Essays on Authoritarianism and Democracy*. South Bend, IN: University of Notre Dame Press.

O'Donnell, Guillermo. 2004. "The Quality of Democracy: Why the Rule of Law Matters." *Journal of Democracy* 15, no. 4 (October 2004).

O'Donnell, Guillermo. 2007a. *Dissonances: Democratic Critiques of Democracy*. South Bend, IN: University of Notre Dame Press.

O'Donnell, Guillermo. 2007b. "The Perpetual Crisis of Democracy." *Journal of Democracy* 18, no. 1 (January 2007).

O'Donnell, Guillermo. 2024. *Catacumbas*. Buenos Aires: Prometeo.

O'Donnell, Guillermo. 2026. *Catacombs*. Pittsburgh: LASA Press.

O'Donnell, Guillermo, Juan Méndez, and Paulo Sérgio Pinheiro, eds. 1999. *The (Un)Rule of Law and the Underprivileged In Latin America*. South Bend, IN: University of Notre Dame Press.

O'Donnell, Guillermo, Philippe C. Schmitter, and Laurence Whitehead, eds. 1986. *Transitions from Authoritarian Rule: Prospects for Democracy*. Baltimore: Johns Hopkins University Press.

O'Donnell, Guillermo, and Philippe C. Schmitter. 1986. "Tentative Conclusions About Uncertain Democracies." In Vol. 4 of *Transitions from Authoritarian Rule: Prospects for Democracy*, edited by Guillermo O'Donnell, Philippe C. Schmitter, and Laurence Whitehead. Baltimore: Johns Hopkins University Press.

Przeworski, Adam. 1999. "Minimalist Conception of Democracy: A Defense." In *Democracy's Value*, edited by Ian Shapiro and Casiano Hacker-Cordon. Cambridge: Cambridge University Press.

Review by Special Contributor

Practicing Political Science in the Catacombs: Argentina, 1975–1979

Oscar Oszlak

Introduction

Catacombs, sites of worship, burial, and, in times of persecution, protection and concealment. *Catacombs*, an apt title for a book written during a period of fear, repression, and physical disappearance. Historically, catacombs were sites of protection, with laws that barred persecutors from entering. Paradoxically, however, the military regime that governed Argentina during the years in which the essays in *Catacombs* were written offered no right of asylum or concessions to its victims, a point of no small importance.

This is not a book originally conceived as such, but rather a collection of essays. Nor is it an arbitrary compilation of documents, but rather the result of systematic reflection on a shared theme, progressively developed over a short period of time. It is, if you will, a series of preliminary sketches prepared before embarking on a larger work, which ultimately became *Bureaucratic Authoritarianism*.

There are at least three reasons to consider this book as a unified whole. First, all of the essays refer to certain aspects of political life

---

Also published in *La Ciencia Política de Guillermo O'Donnell,* Martín D'Alessandro and Gabriela Ippolito-O'Donnell, eds. (Buenos Aires: Prometeo, 2026).

in Argentina during one of the most dramatic periods in its history. Second, they were all written within just a four-year period, driven by a desire to understand the country's changing and conflictive reality. Third, they all identify classes, actors, and institutions whose complex interaction would go on to define the course of the social processes examined. Taken together, these essays provide a lucid diagnosis of the "laws of motion" of a society whose turbulent historical trajectory has never lent itself to straightforward academic interpretations.

Political and Theoretical Context

During the 1970s, most Latin American countries were governed by dictatorships. Following the 1964 military coup in Brazil, one by one, existing democratic regimes began to fall under the domination of the armed forces and their civilian allies, who embarked on a self-proclaimed mission to rebuild their respective societies. Argentina, Chile, and Uruguay saw their democratically elected governments successively overthrown, while Peru experienced a left-wing military coup. These regimes, which O'Donnell referred to as "BA" (bureaucratic authoritarian regimes), coexisted with "neopatrimonialist" regimes led by charismatic caudillos such as Stroessner in Paraguay, Duvalier in Haiti, Somoza in Nicaragua, Balaguer in the Dominican Republic, and Torrijos in Panama. They were all typical models of a traditional form of domination, according to Weber's characterization, based on populism, demagoguery, and ascriptive political exchange.

Even certain formally existing democracies were under the tutelage of the armed forces, as was the case in several Central American countries that experienced brief periods of apparent democracy, followed by military coups. Only Costa Rica, Colombia, Venezuela, and Mexico survived as democratic islands within a region that had practically eliminated elections as a normal mechanism for gaining access to government.[1]

---

1 The reality of democracy in Mexico under the Institutional Revolutionary Party (PRI) has been interpreted by some as a special case of BA.

The development of the social sciences in Argentina was not impervious to the impact of these political processes. The alternation between civilian and military rule following Perón's overthrow in 1955 had created conditions that were not conducive to the scientific development of the social sciences, which did not emerge as new academic disciplines until the 1960s. During the military government established in 1966, scientific activities were almost exclusively carried out in private research centers. The main center of influence was the Instituto Torcuato Di Tella, which paradoxically flourished under the dictatorship.

The Di Tella housed several centers specializing in economics; sociology; education; politics and public administration; and urban and regional studies. During the 1960s and early 1970s, almost all of these centers incorporated recent graduates of master's and doctoral programs at prestigious European and American universities into their staff. This pioneering group, of which O'Donnell was a prominent member, in a certain sense constituted the founding nucleus of the social sciences in Argentina.

The decade of the 1970s, which began with the assassination of General Aramburu by the Montoneros, was one of the most turbulent and eventful periods in Argentine political history. The final years of the so-called Argentine Revolution unfolded at an unprecedented speed: the clashes in Ezeiza upon Perón's return; the assassination of union leader José Ignacio Rucci; the Cámpora interregnum; Perón's death; the Rodrigazo; Isabelita, José López Rega, and the Triple A; the new military coup; and the disappeared. Under these circumstances, universities and the state apparatus closed their doors to any expression of critical thought, which is why academic activity ended up being virtually confined to the new private research centers.

Fortunately, many foreign foundations decided to finance this group of young researchers who were embarking on an intense and creative endeavor. This allowed several centers to become independent, establishing themselves as nonprofit organizations. It was in this context that, in 1975, Guillermo O'Donnell and several colleagues with whom he had been working at the Di Tella for a number of years created the Center for the Study of State and Society (CEDES, for its acronym in Spanish). Less than a year later, another military coup once again ended a short-lived democratic interval.

Given this climate, it is hard to believe that the social sciences flourished in Argentina, despite exile, censorship, economic and institutional crises, and the contempt for science displayed by those holding power. Just as the Di Tella institute had developed as an intellectual and artistic stronghold during the Onganía years, its successors, CEDES and other social science centers, expanded and were consolidated under the most brutal military regime in Argentina's history.[2]

Perhaps the most significant feature of CEDES's early years was the centripetal force created by authoritarianism, which helped position academic life as a refuge in the social science centers of the time. In 1966, La Noche de los Bastones Largos (Night of the Long Batons) had provoked the expulsion of many Argentine intellectuals from university life. The hope sparked in 1973 for their reintegration into the university was dashed just one year later, following Perón's death and the government's violent shift to the right. The Universidad del Salvador allowed professors to continue their activities for a little longer, but that too would end with the dictatorship. With the help of students from that university, O'Donnell created the database for his book *Bureaucratic Authoritarianism* during that brief democratic spring.

Political science in the early 1970s was also entering a period of upheaval. The paradigms constructed through the seminal work of prestigious authors such as Talcott Parsons, Robert K. Merton, Robert A. Dahl, and others, which had served to shape the academic profile of young Argentine researchers, proved insufficient or inappropriate for interpreting the complex reality they began exploring upon returning from their studies abroad. The Marxist tradition, from which they had also drawn inspiration along with behaviorism and structural functionalism, had exposed them to a veritable intellectual schizophrenia that José Nun reflected on in a widely read article at the time.[3] Structural functionalism and Marxism would have to find a more advanced synthesis, based on a Latin American political science still in its infancy

---

2 CEDES's founders: Guillermo O'Donnell, Oscar Oszlak, Eduardo Boneo, Elizabeth Jelín and Marcelo Cavarozzi.

3 In that work, Nun (1966) develops a typology that reflects the contradictory evolution of political science and the clash of paradigms.

that to make matters worse was deeply influenced by the rhetorical formalism of the legal and social sciences. It was in this context that the approach that O'Donnell and others characterized as "historical-structural" emerged.

Main Concepts and Arguments

As he does throughout his work, O'Donnell begins each piece by linking it to previous texts. The opening chapter of *Catacombs* is presented as an extension of the historical perspective used in his recently completed book *Bureaucratic Authoritarianism.*[4] Why does *Catacombs* begin with "State and Alliances in Argentina" and not, for example, "Notes for a Theory of the State," undoubtedly the most theoretical and abstract of this series of essays? In my opinion, this volume was organized with the intention of following a sequence of inferential theoretical construction, in which successive empirical analyses would add data, actors, conflicts, and confrontations, culminating in an excellent essay of theoretical interpretation with a broader level of generalization, that aims to uncover certain universal patterns, characteristic of the relations between the capitalist state and society, that underlie the situations analyzed in the previous texts.

In "State and Alliances," O'Donnell enters into the debate that was taking place in Argentina around two closely related issues: 1) the search for analytical frameworks that would allow for a better understanding of the relationship between economics and politics; and 2) the search for explanations for the repeated succession of authoritarian and democratic regimes, which the current literature interpreted in terms of a pendulum or "stalemate" (as O'Donnell himself termed it). He chose to engage in this debate without openly arguing with the political scientists and economists who had addressed the issue, but rather by subtly constructing a plausible argument about how the two issues are linked,

4 The first draft of the book was already finished, but it would not be published until 1982, during the transition to democracy following the Malvinas War.

while respectfully acknowledging his colleagues' contributions. To set the stage on which he would place his actors, he provides some historical background, alludes to certain unique features of the Argentine economy, analyzes economic cycles and trends, and carefully breaks down the social structure, differentiating between fractions of what had previously been characterized as "the bourgeoisie" or "the ruling class." This allows him to observe how the correlations of forces between political actors change according to the way the interests defended by each fraction or sector are affected by particular economic conjunctures and, in turn, how state policies generate shifts in the political alliances that are formed in order to gain control of the state and adopt policies that promote their interests.

The distinction between "offensive alliances" and "defensive alliances" and the analysis of their changing dynamics, with which he culminates his argument, constitutes, in my opinion, the most significant contribution and the most accurate interpretation of the long period of alternation between authoritarianism and democracy in Argentina. It is interesting that in this work O'Donnell only refers to the "state" at the end, when he highlights its inability to distance itself from the demands and interests of each ruling alliance, effectively putting an end to the controversy regarding the "weakness" or "strength" of the state. In O'Donnell's view, a state that is fragmented, colonized, and excessively subjected to the immediate demands of these contradictory alliances can only be a weak state, incapable even of seeking a way out of the cycles by moving toward state capitalism.

"Tensions," the second of the essays included in this volume, was written in 1978, when the most sinister characteristics of the BA regime, established two years earlier, had already become apparent. In the unique dialogue he always established between his works, O'Donnell begins by introducing a series of concepts already developed in "Notes," written in 1977. In particular, and for the purposes of this essay, he emphasizes that the organization of consensus is the inverse of the state's own legitimization as an agent of the general interest of a community.

But to the extent that the state and society appear divided, consensus (and the resulting legitimization of domination) depends on mediations, such as nation, citizenship, and the people, where members of society can identify with one another in terms of an "us" and as bearers of political and social rights. Drawing on his notes on the country's historical development and recalling the basic features that define his BA model, O'Donnell demonstrates the impossibility for this regime to achieve legitimacy, given that, by its very nature and due to its contradictory "regenerative" task, it is incapable of representing a shattered nation, a citizenry whose political rights it denies, and a people it represses. It must therefore appeal to what O'Donnell calls a "tacit consensus," a foundation he considers "too shaky to sustain the state." He therefore concludes that the BA is the negation of the usual mediations that legitimize a state.

A fundamental problem with the BA, however, is that one of its central actors, the armed forces, tends to be the most national and least capitalist of state institutions. As members of an ("offensive") alliance with the big bourgeoisie, they soon discover that many of their members reject the latter's internationalizing and chrematistic leadership, and this leads to discord and tension. In this way, O'Donnell ties the BA and the role of the armed forces to the dynamics of the formation and dissolution of political alliances discussed in his previous essay. He thus composes another section of his conceptual tapestry, rendering the fabric woven up to this point even denser and more complex. He also provides some explanations as to why Brazil is different and why the Mexican, PRI-style solution is excluded, once again demonstrating his status as an eminent comparativist.[5] The question of democracy appears in a final section as a "nostalgia for mediations" that the BA fails to establish as the basis for its legitimacy, as it is unwilling to renounce the exclusion of the popular sector.

---

5 O'Donnell constantly emphasizes the need to produce work based on comparative analysis. It is important to note that area studies as a branch of political science was still in its infancy. McGraw-Hill's Comparative Politics book series was only a few years old, and the influential Comparative Administration Group was at its peak. The discovery of the developing world following the Second World War had given a huge boost to comparative politics. One of the characteristic traits of this stage in the development of political science was the unusual creation of terms and analytical categories that researchers used to name the phenomena observed in these new scenarios.

In his essay with Roberto Frenkel, O'Donnell's concern with linking the ambiguous and reciprocal determining factors between economics and politics reappears. In "Stabilization Programs," he analyzes the stand-by agreements reached with the International Monetary Fund (IMF) shortly after the coups d'état that interrupted democratic institutions and that some sectors, especially the internal ruling classes and their external supporters, experienced as profound political and economic crises. Thus, new actors appear on the scene (international banking and international financial organizations associated with the most concentrated and transnationalized sectors of capital) that, in addition to those already analyzed in previous essays, play a crucial role in the outcome of the economic and political processes of the period studied.

Frenkel and O'Donnell clearly observe how state policies aimed at implementing the stabilization programs agreed on with the IMF generate biased impacts that benefit a narrow group of economic actors related, above all, to the export of raw materials and financial capital.

This is not a denunciatory work, as was common at the time in literature on imperialism and dependency, but instead a clarifying analysis of the subtle and complex connections between the centers of global capitalism and multilateral lending institutions. The authors express their surprise at how little was known, at least in Latin America, about the role that institutions played in designing national policies for the "stabilization" and "normalization" of economies and societies in crisis. In this sense, the contribution of Frenkel and O'Donnell was important in characterizing the power structure underlying global economic relations at the time. And their awareness of this lack of knowledge is so acute that they consider their work an incomplete and partial reflection on a subject they deem to be crucial. In it, they have already begun to outline the "normalizing" character of the policies inspired by the IMF, which other works—such as that by Adolfo Canitrot (1980)—would soon help reveal in full by positioning social discipline as the objective of the BA's economic policy.

Continuing to weave his conceptual tapestry, in 1978 O'Donnell revisited the theme of the bourgeoisie, which played a leading role in *State and Alliances*. In "Notes for the Study of the Local Bourgeoisie," he fine-tuned this theoretical category, which in his previous work had, somewhat ambiguously, been given different names. In this new text, he resolutely opts to refer to the "local industrial bourgeoisie" as a category to distinguish a particular segment of the bourgeoisie. His eagerness to avoid confusing it with the "national bourgeoisie," which, due to the specific adjective employed, can lead to ambiguous interpretations, is particularly noteworthy. Or with the "domestic bourgeoisie," used by other actors, or with the "internal bourgeoisie," as Nicos Poulantzas terms it. With a subtle scalpel, O'Donnell peels away layers of "bourgeoisies" (agrarian, financial, and, to a large extent, commercial) to carve out a specific social actor that he defines as urban and, primarily, industrial. He does so in order to avoid inappropriate generalizations, as his research material does not allow him to make analytical propositions about a broader social subject.[6] He is mainly interested in reflecting on the role that this actor plays in the process of a growing transnationalization of capital.

O'Donnell is surprised (once again, as mentions of this sort are almost constant in his works from that period) by the scarcity of studies on the topic, although he attributes this to the widespread acceptance of interpretations that saw this industrial bourgeoisie as a strategic actor in the process of modernization, which would contribute to the dual outcome of generating economic development and political stability.

Casually, with a certain degree of sarcasm, he reiterates his criticism of the dominant thinking of the time, according to which development would emerge out of a transition from "traditionalism" to "modernity," in which the actors analyzed could play a key role according to their tendency toward one extreme or the other.

However, after peeling away with his scalpel the layers that are irrelevant to his analytical interest, he continues to differentiate sectors and fractions according to their relationship with the productive system, technological development, the size of their industries, and their

---

6 It should be noted that, at that time, studies on the Argentine "ruling class" were not only scarce but also very superficial and heavily ideologized. For more on this topic, see Oscar Oszlak, *La Formación del Estado Argentino* (Buenos Aires: Ediciones de la Universidad de Belgrano, 1982).

insertion within the corporate institutional framework of the business community. All these distinctions serve to identify the interests of this local bourgeoisie, its conflicts, and its role in the game of political alliances in the face of the vicissitudes of the country's economic situation.

The merit of this work is its insistence on the need to analyze the issue of the local bourgeoisie from the broader and more dynamic perspective of the transnationalization of capital. Its authors demonstrate that, in their contradictory relationship, the local bourgeoisie and the state end up jointly promoting transnationalization. But this outcome is neither inevitable nor generalizable; it varies from case to case and can be explained, specifically, by more general characteristics in the productive structure of each society, the corporate organization of the bourgeoisie, political alliances, and, above all, the links between this bourgeoisie and the subordinate sectors of society.

In mid-1979, O'Donnell wrote the fifth essay in this volume, "Notes for the Study of Processes of Political Democratization," a text that anticipated what years later would become the project *Transitions from Authoritarian Rule*, developed at the Woodrow Wilson Center with Philippe Schmitter and Lawrence Whitehead. Although such transitions were taking place at that time in Spain, Portugal, and Greece, and a process of liberalization was underway in Brazil, Argentina was still several years away from its return to democracy. However, the "tensions" of the BA, which O'Donnell had analyzed in another essay, had become, in his view, real "fissures" in the regime.

This work makes a groundbreaking contribution to the definition and conceptualization of what would soon become a fruitful field of inquiry: the study of transitions from one type of state or regime to another. In this regard, it is important to remember that the social sciences did not (and do not) have concepts that make it possible to register, with indisputable analytical categories, the many shades of gray that reality paints within the black and white that distinguish a democracy from an authoritarian regime. We refer to one or the other as regimes or modes of social formation that, institutionally, may or may not coincide with the existence of governments elected through the ballot box. We tend to describe these democracies and authoritarianisms with labels that allow us to highlight certain distinctive features, as David

Collier and Steven Levitsky (1996) have already shown. However, we lack the precision of the entomologist, who is able to clearly differentiate between a caterpillar, a chrysalis, and a butterfly, even though they are the same creature at different stages of its life cycle.

In fact, we create "ideal types" that tend to exaggerate certain features of a phenomenon in order to highlight its differences from others. But when is a BA state, strictly speaking, a BA state? At the time of the military coup? When it manages to articulate its project of domination and expresses it through certain types of state policies? Or, to use Juan Linz's categories, do we solve the problem by referring to some of the gray areas as *dictablandas* ("soft dictatorships") or *democraduras* ("hard or limited democracies")? And above all, when does a BA state cease to be a BA state?

This concern can be noted in this essay when O'Donnell asks himself where a transition "comes from" and where it "goes." For this, he draws on the experience of the transition of the BA he is most familiar with, particularly the period of 1971–73, since strictly speaking, in 1979 the "transition" back to democracy in Argentina had not yet begun.[7] O'Donnell also draws on the experiences of Spain, Portugal, and Greece at that time, with full awareness and a knowledge of the very different conditions that existed in Argentina in these various contexts.

Once again, with methodological rigor, O'Donnell analyzes the transitions by focusing on two simultaneous processes that unfold in an almost mirror-like fashion: the emergence of what he terms a "liberalizing coalition" that breaks with the typical alignments of the BA; and what he dubs the "resurrection of civil society." To this end, he deploys a veritable arsenal of terminology to point out the rifts that are developing within the alliances he has already analyzed, observing one by one the factors that appear to explain the shifts occurring in the political coalitions within each of the camps. "Soft" and "hard," which are in turn not homogeneous and can switch sides; "moderate opposition," "opportunistic opposition," "maximalist opposition," participating in a complex play of positions, with uncertain outcomes. Here, O'Donnell

7 "The ballot boxes are well guarded," said dictator Leopoldo Galtieri, in 1980.

once again proves to be the game theorist he had revealed himself to be years earlier in "Un juego imposible" ("An Impossible Game").[8]

For its part, the description of the process of the "resurrection of civil society" and the way in which it is connected to the ruptures in the offensive alliance that supports the BA is a true work of literature, without sacrificing any of its analytical rigor. Designating a work of this caliber "Notes" is an unquestionable demonstration of academic modesty.

"Notes for a Theory of the State," the essay that closes this volume, holds a deep emotional significance for me. I received the first typewritten draft from Guillermo for comments and spent a sleepless night "savoring"—one might say—every idea, every paragraph, every turn of phrase. The next morning, still under the spell of that reading, I presented him with a lengthy memo containing my impressions. Some time later, I included this essay in a book on state bureaucracy (Oszlak 1985), and since then, it has become required reading for my courses.

O'Donnell confesses, in the introduction to this edition of the article, that he hesitated over its inclusion but ultimately decided that the text has "some value, at least as a counterpoint to views that either deny the very existence of the state and reify it as merely a set of bureaucracies, demonize it as the source of all evil, or see it as a neutral entity that only needs technical or bureaucratic refinement."

Indeed, several previous essays had anticipated various aspects of the argument developed in this one, but it is only here that, in my opinion, O'Donnell achieves a remarkable theoretical integration, despite considering it "notes." It would take more space than I have in this review to examine the conceptual richness of this work in terms of the analytical categories that retain their relevance and have had a notable influence on state theory. I will attempt a quick overview, beginning with the keen observation that the most problematic aspect of the state-society relationship is neither the state nor society, but the conjunction "and" that unites them in an ambiguous and misleading way.

---

8 Guillermo O'Donnell, *Modernization and Bureaucratic-Authoritarianism* (Berkeley, CA: Institute of International Studies, University of California, Berkley, 1973).

Some may see in this essay a strange collection of academic mentors, combined in a truly unique way. O'Donnell begins by adding a definition to the academic lexicon of the field that bears a certain Weberian hallmark, considering the state as a specifically political component of domination. Yet he immediately takes a decidedly more Marxist turn, highlighting the unequal quality of access to the resources of political domination, whose "great differentiator" is social class. In this dialogue between Weber and Marx, O'Donnell interjects, in passing, a notion and classification of the "resources of power," along the lines of those proposed years earlier by political scientists of "northwestern developmentalism," such as David Apter (1970) and Warren Ilchman and Norman Uphoff (1971). He then returns to the analysis of the capitalist relations of production, a classic of Marxist tradition, to show how the state acts as a guarantor of the economic coercion of the capitalist relationship and, in this capacity, ensures the existence and reproduction of the bourgeoisie and wage earners.

In this regard, he reinterprets the question of the "relative autonomy of the state," which Marx explores in *The Eighteenth Brumaire of Louis Bonaparte*, in terms of the imposition of negative limits on the socially destructive consequences of capitalist society. And rather than considering the state as the "executive committee of the ruling class" (like the Marx in *Dogma socialista* [Socialist Dogma]), he develops an interpretation that highlights state interventions as an apparent expression of a rationality superior to that of individual capitalists, whereby the state is "experienced as external." In this way, he explores the consideration of the state as an institutional apparatus in charge of safeguarding the "superior rationality" of capitalism and what he refers to as "the conditioning of the context," a topic that we alluded to in a previous work as "taking positions on socially problematic issues" (Oszlak and O'Donnell 1976). And, on analyzing the state in institutional terms, he considers law as the codification of the domination and the formalized crystallization of the state's contribution to capitalist society.

He later reiterates a question posed by Margaret Wirth as to how the state can know what conditions make capitalist social reproduction possible. He responds that, given its "bounded rationality" (a concept he borrows from Herbert Simon), it does so through trial and error, adopting suboptimal or merely "satisfactory" decisions, thus discrediting both the Hegelian self-image of the omniscient bureaucrat and the instrumental nature of the state serving the interests of a bourgeois fraction that controls it. However, he adopts Claus Offe's concept of "structural complicity" to assert that capitalist society, and the state as an aspect of it, is systematically biased toward its own reproduction as such.

In the second part of this work, O'Donnell develops in a more systematic way the question of mediations between state and society (nation, the people, and citizenship), which he had already anticipated in "Tensions." Through these mediations, the state attempts to legitimize its power in the face of a society whose subjects are in an unequal relationship, leading to the need to cover up its domination through these points of reference in order to present society with an image of an impartial arbiter and guardian. He thus reiterates the impossibility for the authoritarian state to legitimize its domination, as it has to resort to outright coercion and, in doing so, weakens its role as an organizer of consensus.

Influence on Political Science

The impact of the work of a scientist on their field of study can be evaluated using various indicators: the number of editions or copies of their books that have been sold, the number of bibliographic citations of their works by colleagues, and the extent to which their work is used in academic courses, among others.

However, *Catacombs* is a collection of essays written at an early stage in O'Donnell's academic career and also had limited circulation for the reasons outlined above. Therefore, rather than referring to the influence of these texts on political science, I will explore other aspects that, based on these essays, will allow me to reveal other forms of influence on our field.

One thing that strikes me as exceptional is the style that O'Donnell uses to establish a personal dialogue with his readers, seeking to ensure that the logic of his argument flows naturally until his reasoning is fully developed. His concepts and analytical categories appear time and again expressed as part of a complex theoretical puzzle where each piece finds its place. And if any doubts remain, he concludes his assertions with summaries that serve as a basis for further reflection, sparing the reader the arduous task of retrospectively reconstructing the theoretical argument he has just constructed. Furthermore, he constantly strives to persuade the reader of the plausibility of his assertions, adding a variety of comments and caveats about the place of each variable or concept within a broader theoretical framework.

Another characteristic of his "style," which not many authors practice, is the extreme care with which he weaves together ideas and analytical categories, imagining, paragraph after paragraph, how to convey to the reader, in the most didactic way possible, the contents of each piece of the conceptual puzzle he is assembling. To make the reader's task even easier, he warns them of difficulties that may arise in the analysis and reminds them of concepts developed earlier that may be useful in linking them to other topics. His prose is at times persuasive and intimate, as if he were engaging in an exclusive dialogue with that imagined reader. This personal and elegant way of relating to his readers represents an important stylistic innovation in itself.

O'Donnell also made a considerable contribution to the development of comparative politics as an approach to the study of political science. As mentioned above, in the 1960s, the volumes published by McGraw-Hill in its Comparative Politics series were widely read, while the Comparative Administration Group dominated studies on state bureaucracy in the Third World, endeavoring to explain the determining factors of development and modernization. At the same time, Thomas Kuhn revolutionized the thinking of the time with his paradigmatic vision of scientific progress, generating both support and rejection, as expressed by Albert Hirschman and David Apter, two of O'Donnell's academic mentors, in their respective publications.[9] Apter was brilliant at constructing highly abstract theoretical frameworks. Hirschman, on the other hand,

---

9 A final anecdote may serve to reflect the prevailing climate of the times. In 1968, I invited both scholars to participate in a conference on "Social Science Research and Political Development in Latin America," which a group of students from the University of California, Berkeley, and I organized in Pacific Grove, California. As a title for his paper, Hirschman proposed "The Use of Paradigms as a Hindrance to Understanding." When I subsequently invited Apter, after asking me about the title of Hirschman's paper, he chose

was a lucid empiricist who, through induction, was able to discover fascinating theoretical patterns in his data. The comparative style of O'Donnell's work reveals the combined influence of both authors.

When referring to his legacy in comparative politics in Latin America, Cintia Pinillos (2012) highlights that, unlike much of the work in this subfield, O'Donnell used comparison to show the limits of available generalizations based on evidence observed in historical processes. In doing so, he demonstrated his concern about the excessive stretching of concepts and stylized postulates, which, while they can be useful for including a wide and diverse number of cases, do not serve to explain the profound nature of the phenomena supposedly explained.

I would also like to comment on the way in which O'Donnell constructed his explanations. I agree with Ariel Colombo, who, in his prologue to *Catacombs*, states that in his essays O'Donnell "never concludes the action with inexorable fatality, but leaves the ending or outcome open to the protagonists' imagination." This is a singular feature and a trademark of all his work.

When explaining a social phenomenon, O'Donnell never adhered to deterministic, voluntarist explanations or those based on a random confluence of circumstances, although all of these were present in some way. Without resorting to syncretism, he combined perspectives, demonstrating an unusual ability to untangle complex social processes and discover interpretative elements that allowed him to weave together variables in order to create a dense conceptual fabric. I am sure that this approach to formulating propositions has had a profound, demonstrative effect on political scientists.

In the essays, there are few references to characters and events beyond those necessary to situate the action described. His pages are populated by actors and processes. And here, once again, we can see O'Donnell's extreme care and mastery in breaking down analytical categories. He does not attribute behaviors or strategies to overly generic actors, but rather attempts at all times to "embody" and break down

---

to call his "The Use of Paradigms as a Help to Understanding." Both papers were published several years later (Apter 1971; Hirschman 1970).

these actors, recognizing their fractions and the subtle networks that, on other levels, connect them to other classes.

O'Donnell never writes essays that are disconnected from one another. One of the merits of his writing is precisely the constant references he makes to previous texts, those in progress, or those to be undertaken in the future, as if each were part of a carefully planned, larger body of work. The very fact that he uses terms such as "notes for" or "notes on" in his titles highlights both the provisional nature of his reflections and his intention to create theoretical building blocks that will lead to a conceptual edifice that, at some point, will acquire greater consistency and interpretive power.

In conclusion, the footnotes in this volume are extremely revealing of the state of knowledge on the topics covered in the various essays, as well as the scant support that O'Donnell finds in northwestern literature, with very few exceptions. In general, there are relatively few footnotes, the vast majority of which are clarifications or brief extensions of the text, rather than citations of works by colleagues. This fact reveals two things: first, that despite his explicit acknowledgment of the sources he drew on during his doctoral training, he finds almost no body of "northwestern" literature with which to even polemicize; second, that even in the Latin American context, he finds no firm foundations or research tradition on which to base his theoretical construction. Indeed, O'Donnell is laying the foundations for a new field of scientific inquiry.

Sources

Apter, David E. 1970. "Sistemas políticos y cambio para el desarrollo." In *Estudio de la modernización*. Buenos Aires: Amorrortu.

Apter, David E. 1971. *Choice and the Politics of Allocation: A Developmental Theory*. London: Yale University Press.

Canitrot, Adolfo. 1980. "La disciplina como objetivo de la política económica: Un ensayo sobre el programa económico del gobierno argentino desde 1976." *Desarrollo Económico* 19, no. 76, January–March, 1980: 453–75.

Collier, David, and Steven Levitsky. 1996. Democracy "With Adjectives": *Conceptual Innovation in Comparative Research*. Notre Dame: Helen Kellogg Institute for International Studies.

Hirschman, Albert O. 1970. "La búsqueda de paradigmas como un impedimento de la comprensión." *Revista desarrollo económico* 10, no. 37: 3–20.

Ilchman, Warren. 1984. "Administración pública comparativa y el sentido común académico." In *Teoría de la Burocracia Estatal: Enfoques Críticos*, edited by Oscar Oszlak. Buenos Aires: Paidós.

Nun, José. 1966. "Los paradigmas de la ciencia política." *Revista Latinoamericana de Sociología* I, no. 2.

Oszlak, Oscar. 1982. *La formación del Estado argentino*. Buenos Aires: Ediciones de la Universidad de Belgrano.

Oszlak, Oscar. 1985. *Teoría de la burocracia estatal: Enfoques críticos*. Buenos Aires: Paidós.

Oszlak, Oscar, and Guillermo O'Donnell. 1976. "Estado y políticas estatales en América Latina: Hacia una estrategia de investigación." *Centro de Estudios de Estado y Sociedad (CEDES)*, Documento GE-CLACSO, vol. 4.

Pinillos, Cintia. 2012. "El legado de Guillermo O'Donnell a la política comparada latinoamericana." *Temas y debates*, no. 24: 67–73.

Foreword to the First Spanish Edition (2008)

Ariel Colombo

It would be impossible for me to do justice to the work and personality of Guillermo O'Donnell. His prolific industriousness, bold foresight, intellectual and personal generosity, his lucidity as a passionate witness, his drive to institutionalize the social sciences, his pioneering of new fields of inquiry, his rigorous and systematic approach, and the admiration his research has inspired around the world are worthy of an entire book and will one day be the subject of well-deserved study and recognition. *Catacombs* refers to the situation in which these notes were written, not to their content. Those were dark years of unspeakable death and suffering that will mark us forever. Many of us today are still surprised that we survived an infinitely destructive dictatorship whose purpose, among others, was to mercilessly seek the "final solution" to the pendulum-like cycles described by O'Donnell in one of the best working documents in this collection. Economic oscillation and political instability were the essence of the 1950s to 1970s, with extremes ranging from an extensive bourgeoisie in the Pampas that benefited from free transfers (without any productive counterpart) caused by the devaluations that followed recurring balance-of-payments crises, on the one hand, and on the other, an urban alliance between wage earners and protected industrialists, whose import dynamics led to that external deficit.

O'Donnell—who in his essays never concludes the action with inexorable fatality but leaves the ending or outcome open to the protagonists' imagination—had anticipated that a return to the bureaucratic-authoritarianism of 1966–73 was likely, and that it could acquire even more repressive characteristics. And this means only one thing: the outcome could have been avoided if political arrogance had prudently yielded to this anticipation and not forced the deactivation of popular support—the opportunity the coup plotters were waiting for.

However, when O'Donnell wrote these texts, it was already too late. The damage had been done. And so now, we can reflect on this in many different ways. The problem, for O'Donnell, is no longer how bureaucratic-authoritarianism emerges and functions. What matters now for him is which mechanisms of domination will be consolidated, what new conflicts will arise in society, what will become of traditional corporations, what internal tensions within the regime will enable liberalization, what will become of citizens and everyday life, and how the anti-authoritarian opposition will reorganize itself in the wake of the brutal inequality generated by income redistribution and speculative valuation processes. But above all, to use O'Donnell's characteristic language, if some form of democracy was still possible with a barely dynamic capitalism, with obsolete state apparatuses, and with speculative and transnationalized bourgeoisies of the worst kind, that is, as appendages of the financial system and not as competitors in the international market based on local production, what guarantees would the big bourgeoisie demand in order to be loyal to the rule of law? Where will capital come from in an economy in which it vanished, remaining abroad or converted into foreign debt? Given the speculative metamorphosis of capital, why would it reenter the country and what would the discount rate be that would make it rational to transform it into investments? And if there were a "price" to pay, could a democracy of unequal and impoverished citizens with disbanded political parties afford it? In contexts where little or nothing can be expected from dismantled, demoralized, and corruption-ridden state apparatuses, how can they be reformed in parallel with the government at a conjuncture that is always so urgent and difficult?

These concerns are already hinted at in the texts now published by Prometeo Libros. The fact that these documents contain a few inaccuracies or repetitions is of no importance. None at all. The author warns against them and perhaps would have preferred not to republish them. What matters in these "incunabula" is their profound intentionality, which reaches us as it would an image in a rearview mirror. For it is in relation to them that later bibliography, including O'Donnell's own work, can be evaluated in order to gauge how far we have come and the extent of that progress. Given their level of generality and abstraction and, at the same time, the fact that they capture the state of affairs at the time thanks to their broad bibliographic perspective, they undoubtedly offer a frame of reference for the (self)evaluation of political research and its revival. Especially since, even back then, O'Donnell began to offer the outlines of a political theory of the capitalist state that avoided the class reductionism, economic instrumentalism, and logical derivation that characterized other approaches of the time.

If this were the moment to devise a scientific agenda that is itself a dialectical promoter of a (constantly postponed) democratic reform to be undertaken by the state and society, and if social scientists were to give up a few of their legitimate obsessions in order to contribute to a common purpose such as rethinking the transition from capitalism to another type of society, these documents, which never reduce social practices to a mere consequence of structures or to an inexplicable force based on the structure on which they operate, represent a perspective of analysis that is both critical and compelling.

Finally, may these words serve as a warm welcome to Guillermo, the teacher who is once again, definitively, among us.

Introduction

Guillermo O´Donnell

I am grateful to my good friend and colleague Ariel Colombo and to the remarkable editor Raúl Carioli for coming up with an idea that initially surprised me almost as much as it concerned me, but that later ended up interesting me and, I confess, flattering me: to unearth some of the texts I wrote during my time as director and researcher at CEDES [Centro de Estudios de Estado y Sociedad, or Center for the Study of State and Society].[10] That period extends from June 1975, when CEDES was founded, to late 1979, when I left for Brazil with the intention of staying for only a short time. In other words, this period almost entirely coincides with the Proceso de Reorganización Nacional (Process of National Reorganization, or PRN) that began with the coup d'état in March 1976.

I have already recounted the history of the founding and operation of CEDES during those years,[11] so I will avoid repeating it here. I will only mention that it was founded by a small group of colleagues (Horacio Boneo, Marcelo Cavarozzi, Elizabeth Jelin, and Oscar Oszlak) who, as early as 1975, feared that our country, through a paroxysm of violence and authoritarian discourse that sought to legitimize it from virtually all sides, was rushing toward a more violent and, in many

---

10 I am also grateful to Gervasio Espinosa for his careful work in preparing these texts.

11 See, in particular, "Introduction," in *Counterpoints: Selected Essays on Authoritarianism and Democratization* (South Bend, IN: University of Notre Dame Press, 1999).

ways, more radical repetition of the experience of 1966–73, which I had characterized as a bureaucratic-authoritarian (BA) state (or, sometimes in my work, as a regime).

Our goal was to stay in Argentina as long as possible, creating a space, however limited, for freedom and criticism in the face of the dark times that lay ahead. Then, in March 1976, came the coup that marked the beginning of that period and monopolized violence in the worst possible way through clandestine state agents who did little to conceal their status as such.

So began the life that we, and others who inhabited similar spaces, soon came to characterize with the word from which this volume takes its title: the catacombs. Those were curious circumstances, difficult to faithfully re-create in memory: horror at the savage repression that was unleashed; real and imagined fears of falling prey to that violence; daily encounters with many who denied, ignored, or justified that repression… and efforts to write social science texts motivated by what was happening and referring to it, driven by the hope that, for better or worse, could be glimpsed at the time. And in the midst of it all, the daily news—almost all of it whispered—of new horrors, of friends or acquaintances disappearing or leaving the country, even the departure of some of those who had joined CEDES—among them our beloved and never-forgotten Oscar Landi—and of encounters in which, just in case, except among family or trusted friends, one kept one's feelings and opinions to oneself.

We were surrounded by solitude, cold, and fear, but CEDES provided a space where, even though we were no longer citizens and could not claim any rights against the powers that be, we could at least exercise our identity as critical social scientists. During those days of serious and sometimes overly harsh discussions of our work, close friendships were also forged, not only with colleagues but also with CEDES's secretary general, María de las Mercedes (Merchy) Puga, who was a true bastion of serenity and cheerfulness, and had an admirable work ethic.

Of course, there were vague limits to the practice of our critical work. With all of us expelled from universities, we risked believing that it was possible to publish certain texts as CEDES Working Papers. These were mimeographed texts that circulated among people we did not always know, but it was the only way, because we could not dream of publishing books that, in any case, no one would have dared to print and distribute at that time. These texts were veritable samizdat, and several of them were published abroad shortly after being released by CEDES, not only to satisfy our academic vanity but also because, in doing so, and accompanying them with our participation in various international institutions and meetings, we felt that they gave us some degree of protection against internal dangers.

For my part, I published several texts as working documents at the time, listed in the appendix following this introduction, a few of which are included in this volume. All of them are explicitly guided by the hope that, in the midst of and despite the turmoil, we could achieve a socially just, republican democracy in which the inevitable conflicts would unfold, so to speak, with respect for the humanity of all. In reality, these texts were part of—or exercises toward—the "book in preparation" or "forthcoming publication" to which I make several references: *El estado burocrático-autoritario: 1966–1973. Triunfos, derrotas y crisis* (*The Bureaucratic-Authoritarian State: 1966–1973. Triumphs, Defeats, and Crises*), published by Editorial de Belgrano in late 1982. I began researching the case in 1974, shortly after my first book, *Modernización y autoritarismo* (*Modernization and Authoritarianism*), was published by Editorial Paidós in late 1972. As the story behind these books is part of the surreal climate in which we lived, it is worth briefly recounting. First, no doubt mindful of the "surveillance" that the Triple A (Alianza Anticomunista Argentina, or Argentine Anti-Communist Alliance) and other hired assassins exercised over the distribution of "subversive books," Paidós withdrew it from circulation in early 1974, as its title and content could well be considered as such. The copies of *Modernización* remaining in bookstores were returned to the publisher (where a couple of times I was told with an air of resignation: "That's just the way things are") or, as in the case of the excellent poet and owner of Librería Norte, Héctor Yánover, they were hidden away to be offered to discreet buyers. Second, regarding my "book in preparation," I had undertaken it not only because I was interested in analyzing the bureaucratic-authoritarian period of 1966–73, but also because, as I mentioned earlier, I feared that the crises and multiple acts of violence that had been unleashed during that period and intensified toward its end heralded a more repressive and radical repetition of that type of state. But I knew full well, especially since March 1976, that the book was not publishable, so I kept it at my parents' house and limited myself to making a few references to it in the aforementioned Working Papers. Finally, in late 1982, it was published, not coincidentally when the Proceso was in clear decline and the repression, although certainly not exhausted, had diminished. But the surrealism continued, because publishing it had been a personal decision made by the excellent and, in this context, courageous director of Editorial de Belgrano, another leading poet, Luis Tedesco. Although it was already late 1982, the climate was still volatile, so much so that I fear that publishing this book cost Tedesco his job. As he stated years later, the publication earned him his "resignation from the Universidad de Belgrano, because some friends of the rector, Porto, told him that I was publishing subversive literature."[12] Of course, the few copies that had been distributed disappeared from bookstores, and I was never able to find out what happened to the rest, although I imagine that, since the book was sizable, it must have had some value when sold as scrap paper. Thus, in one of those twists and turns of life, my first two books almost instantly became incunabula…

In keeping with the surrealism, my second, a "non-book" for some time, met another fate. During that period, I held the position of independent researcher at Consejo Nacional de Investigaciones Científicas y Técnicas (National Council for Scientific and Technical Research, CONICET, for its acronym in Spanish) and, as such, had to submit annual reports summarizing my work accompanied by the papers that I had written, whether they had been published or not. I suppose that those reports did not please the CONICET authorities at the time, who were staunchly loyal to the extreme right wing of the BA. They adopted a procedure that, although its consequences were minimal compared to the much more horrific ones that were being perpetrated on lives and bodies at the time, reflected the same style as that of the leaders of the Proceso: my records at CONICET disappeared and I was erased as a researcher, as if I had never belonged to the Council. As a result, by

12 L. Longhi interviews Luis Tedesco, "Reportaje a Luis Tedesco," *La Idea Fija* 3, no. 5 (2002–3), http://www.laideafija.com.ar/larevista/numero05/TEDESCO_reportaje.html.

mid-1978, the Council stopped acknowledging my reports and requests for responses, and of course, stopped paying my salary. In the 1980s, I made several inquiries that were rejected by officials who, after consulting extensive files in which I did not appear anywhere, concluded that I must be a madman who, for some unknown reason, claimed to be a CONICET researcher. It was only in 2007, after further efforts, that the board of directors of this institution finally gave me the moral satisfaction of issuing a resolution formally recognizing the unusual procedure (and arbitrary exclusion) I described above.

Toward the end of 1979, tired of the fear and the threats that were repeated every so often, of the suffocating restrictions on the freedom of expression outside CEDES and a few other similar circles, and in the midst of a family crisis, I left for Brazil. I did so thinking it would be for a short period during which I would be a visiting researcher at the Instituto Universitário de Rio de Janeiro (IUPERJ) and also—accepting the invitation of Cándido Mendes, then president of the International Political Science Association (IPSA-AISP)—would serve as committee chair of the Program of the World Congress of Political Science to be held in Rio de Janeiro in 1981. However, like that of so many others, my absence was prolonged, beginning another chapter in a personal story that is not relevant here, among other things, because, fortunately, it extends beyond the period of the catacombs in which the now republished texts originated.

Regarding these texts, I can assure young readers that rereading something written roughly thirty years ago adds to the surrealism I mentioned above, albeit now in retrospect. Of course, today I would not write these essays as I did then—for better and perhaps also for worse. But here they are, for what they are still worth and as a small testimony to and from a time that, with its many harsh and few admirable lessons, should not be forgotten.

At the beginning of each chapter, I include a brief introduction to situate them more specifically. What they share, and what I believe marks the continuity of my intellectual work, is the effort to find paths toward a fuller democracy and a more just society in Latin America and—above all, why not—in Argentina, amid the stormy journey caused by deep inequalities, a disjointed economic structure, the strongholds of authoritarian power that shape it, and the delegative and personalistic ways in which many still engage in politics. This journey is certainly not over, although it has taken us out of the horrors of the Proceso and the violence that initially preceded it and grew particularly severe during that period. Perhaps this justifies Colombo and Carioli's generous initiative to unearth texts that belong, along with the turbulent period that preceded it, to the most tragic part of our contemporary history. We must firmly understand that the desire for democracy that was expressed toward the end of that period also included—and had to include—the unconditional condemnation of all violence.

Series of CEDES Documents

O'Donnell, Guillermo. "Reflexiones sobre las tendencias generales de cambio en el estado burocrático-autoritario." Centro de Estudios de Estado y Sociedad (CEDES), *Documento*, no. 1 (1975).

O'Donnell, Guillermo. "Acerca del 'corporativismo' y la cuestión del estado." Centro de Estudios de Estado y Sociedad (CEDES), *Documento*, no. 2 (1975).

O'Donnell, Guillermo. "Estado y Alianzas en la Argentina, 1956–1976," Centro de Estudios de Estado y Sociedad (CEDES), *Documento*, no. 5 (1976).

O'Donnell, Guillermo. "Apuntes para una teoría del estado," Centro de Estudios de Estado y Sociedad (CEDES), *Documento*, no. 9 (1977).

O'Donnell, Guillermo "Tensiones en el estado burocrático-autoritario y la cuestión de la democracia," Centro de Estudios de Estado y Sociedad (CEDES), *Documento*, no. 11 (1978).

Oszlak, Oscar, and Guillermo O'Donnell. "Estado y políticas estatales en América Latina: Hacia una estrategia de investigación," Centro de Estudios de Estado y Sociedad CEDES/GE-CLACSO., *Documento*, no. 4 (1976).

Social Studies Series

O'Donnell, Guillermo. "Notas para el estudio de la burguesía local, con especial referencia a sus vinculaciones con el capital transnacional y el aparato estatal," Centro de Estudios de Estado y Sociedad (CEDES), *Estudios Sociales*, no. 12 (1978).

Series of CEDES Studies

Frenkel, Roberto, and Guillermo O'Donnell. "Los programas de estabilización convenidos con el FMI y sus impactos internos." Centro de Estudios de Estado y Sociedad (CEDES), *Estudios Sociales* 1, no. 1 (1978).

O'Donnell, Guillermo. "Notas para el estudio de procesos de democratización política a partir del estado burocrático autoritario (Documento de trabajo)." Centro de Estudios de Estado y Sociedad (CEDES), *Estudios Sociales* 2, no. 5 (1979).

CHAPTER I

State and Alliances in Argentina, 1956–1976

Introduction

This is one of the two texts in this volume with which I feel the strongest emotional connection. I vividly remember the period in which I wrote it. It was in the old offices of CEDES on Córdoba Avenue in the winter of 1976, just as the full fury of the terrorist state established in March of that year was being unleashed, amid the news circulating, almost all of it in whispers, of the horrors being perpetrated, of the deaths and exiles of so many, and of the resulting fears for all of us who were known not to support what was happening.

It was at that time that I received an invitation from Professor David Lehmann at the University of Cambridge to participate in a conference on politics and development in Latin America. I was convinced that, in addition to the political and military repression, other fundamental issues had also come into play since the coup in March. That invitation was a good opportunity—and, legitimized in part by Cambridge, a pretext in the face of local powers—to express my opinions as explicitly as I felt I could.

In contrast to those who believed that it was only a question of "restoring order," I was convinced that there was also a fierce social vendetta at play. This was not only reflected in the economic policies that were immediately implemented, but also in the personalities of Martínez de Hoz and his team. It was nothing less than an attempt to wipe out, once and for all, the rebellious, popular, and politically active Argentina that had already thwarted previous attempts to "clean up" the economy and, therefore, society as a whole. The surgical image of a "cleanup" was not only used by those who murdered, but also by the dapper oligarchs of the much longed-for agricultural and financial Argentina that the "*negros*," "dirty Peronists," and businessmen with "strange surnames" had taken away from them.

This social revenge involved reducing and geographically dispersing the working class, stripping workers of many of the rights they had won, assassinating union activists, and many other things in which physical and economic repression were inextricably linked. Essentially, it was about putting an end to the fluctuations and alliances that I describe in this text. For this reason, economic policy—though disguised in sterile and technocratic language (even though, as demonstrated and argued in the text I co-authored with Roberto Frenkel in Chapter III, they were very bad technocrats)—was also, and just as importantly, social policy and the policy at the heart of the state as a whole.

Although considered by many at the time to be a renegade of my class, I knew from my origins and relationships (even remembering "Joe" Martínez de Hoz as a mediocre member of the polo team at the school I attended) how much hatred and frustration had accumulated over decades and how eagerly people had awaited a type of state that would put an end to that Argentina once and for all. Unfortunately, the events leading up to the coup in March 1976 presented a golden opportunity for this, which Martínez de Hoz and others were not going to let pass them by.

I remember and can relive the anger with which I wrote that text, as well as the many times I rewrote its last paragraph. In it, without being dangerously explicit, I wanted to make clear that the perverse combination of these two major forms of violence—physical violence and social revenge—were aimed at putting an end to an entire era in our country's history, leaving behind the legacy—explicitly desired by the economic "technocrats"—of an Argentina that was much more unequal, socially fractured, and deindustrialized than the one I explore in these pages. The changes also ended up affecting the agricultural sector as a whole, not just the Pampas region that I discuss in this text. This occurred first as a consequence of the policies of the Proceso itself and then in line with the crises and hyperinflation of the subsequent period. It was also the result of a major development with regard to the issues and problems I examine here; the recent and extensive expansion of an agricultural product that is not a wage good, namely soy. But this extends beyond that period which, as I mention below, the representatives of the 1976–83 BA had the perverse success of bringing to a close.

Obviously, the fact that I had already thought this out in the winter of 1976 and written it down did not change the course of events in the slightest. But I believe that these reflections serve to offer a more complex, and even more perverse, picture of those terrible years than the one that results from focusing exclusively on the repression that was carried out. It was not then, nor is it now, a question of in any way diminishing the importance of those horrors, but rather of framing them within a project of social revenge in which both sides of the repression supported and needed each other.

State and Alliances in Argentina, 1956–1976

I. Introduction

This paper pursues the historical perspective which I have employed in a recently completed book.[13] In that book I study the attempt, begun in 1966, to implant and consolidate in Argentina what I have called a "bureaucratic-authoritarian" (BA) state.[14] I have compared the modalities of its alliance with the large bourgeoisie and with international capital, its social impact and, finally, its collapse, with those of Brazil since 1964 and Chile after 1973. Rather than pointing out similarities between the Argentine case and the others, I shall stress here some differences, for these offer a basis for understanding why, in recent

13 This work was first presented at the Symposium on the State and Development in Latin America, held at the University of Cambridge, December 12–16, 1976. It was later published in English in the *Journal of Development Studies* 15, no. 1 (1979). O'Donnell refers to *Bureaucratic Authoritarianism: Argentina, 1966–1973, in Comparative Perspective* (Berkeley: University of California Press, 1988), a book that was completed shortly before this article but was not published until much later, for reasons that the author presents in the preface to this book.—Editor's note to O'Donnell, *Counterpoints*

14 For an already published characterization of this type of state see Guillermo O'Donnell, *Modernization and Bureaucratic-Authoritarianism* (Berkeley: University of California Press, 1972); and Guillermo O'Donnell, "Reflections on the Patterns of Change in the Bureaucratic-Authoritarian State," *Latin American Research Review* 13, no. 1 (1978).

decades, attempts to establish any type of political domination have failed in Argentina.[15]

The following pages contain no analysis of specific conjunctures. This work places itself at the level of the long-term tendencies which link the said conjunctures with the historical process in which they have emerged and dissolved. In the book already mentioned I indicate some specific differences between the 1966–73 Argentine case of "bureaucratic-authoritarianism" and other Latin American cases. Briefly, the principal differences were: (1) the smaller threat level before the implantation of the BA state;[16] (2) the less severe repression imposed on the popular sector and its political allies; (3) the greater autonomy of the popular sector (and, within it, of the working class) and of the trade unions, with respect to the state and the dominant classes; (4) the moderate fall of industrial wages and the more pronounced decline in the incomes of a sizable proportion of the employed middle sectors; (5) the rapid formation of an alliance of the popular sector and the unions

---

15 For a conception which considers any kind of political domination preferable to "political instability," this cannot but seem the consequence of an acute pathology. Listing the dysfunctional psychological traits of Argentine "masses and elites" has been one of the favorite occupations of influential currents in the social sciences (see among others, Jean Kirkpatrick, *Leader and Vanguard in Mass Society* [Cambridge, MA.: MIT Press, 1971]) and of the apocalyptic elements of the Argentine right. Reflections on the "stalemate," or mutual blockings of political and social forces in Argentina, have been more fruitful, above all those which have connected it with the Gramscian view of hegemonic crisis (see Juan Carlos Portantiero, "Clases dominantes y crisis política en la Argentina," in Oscar Braun, ed., *El capitalismo argentina en crisis* [Buenos Aires: Siglo XXI, 1973]). But beyond describing the stalemate and outlining some of its consequences, the question still remains: What are the power relationships which have produced this stalemate?

16 The "threat" concept refers to the degree to which internal and external dominant classes and sectors considered that the breach of the capitalist parameters and of the society's international alignments was imminent and willingly sought by the leadership of the popular sector (Guillermo O'Donnell, "Reflections").

with the domestic bourgeoisie,[17] against the new state and, particularly, against its "efficientist" and internationalizing policies; (6) the conflict between the government—and, with it, the large bourgeoisie—and the pampa bourgeoisie; and (7) the decisive role of Peronism as the expression and mobilization channel of a heterogeneous constellation of forces in opposition to the BA state. These elements are fundamental in an explanation of the unusual conflicts which arose within the state's institutions and, also, of the social explosions which provoked a collapse unparalleled so far in the other Latin American BA states.[18] These factors account for the short-term differences between the fate of the BA state in Argentina in the period 1966–73 and other comparable experiences. But these, in turn, call for an explanation, which requires a longer historical perspective.

---

17 I define "domestic bourgeoisie" as the fractions of the urban bourgeoisie which control enterprises mostly or totally owned by nationals. The definition excludes, therefore, the local subsidiaries of transnational firms and the agrarian bourgeoisie. Within the latter, the "pampa bourgeoisie" is that which controls the grain and beef exporting region of the Argentine Pampas. The domestic bourgeoisie must in turn be disaggregated, since it ranges from the urban bourgeoisie's fully national and weakest layers to oligopolistic corporations intimately connected—by diverse mechanisms—with international capital. Making a different distinction, I shall also further speak on the "large (urban) bourgeoisie," when referring to the set formed by the branches of transnational corporations and by the domestic bourgeoisie's oligopolistic action. "Below" the large bourgeoisie, what I shall call the "local"—or simply "weak"—bourgeoisie is left, made up of capitalists controlling nonoligopolistic firms, smaller and usually less capital intensive than the large bourgeoisie's. I shall also refer to the General Economic Confederation (CGE), an organization which throughout invoked the representation of the local bourgeoisie. The "popular sector" means the working class and the employed and unionized middle sectors; the General Confederation of Labor (CGT) is the national organization of the working class and middle sector unions and federations of unions.

18 Such a collapse happened in Greece, a case which has significant similarities with the one we shall examine here, especially the combination of a low threat level, a fairly autonomous popular sector, and a relatively moderate earlier economic crisis.

II. Historical Background

In this section I shall point out certain features of Argentina's incorporation into the world capitalist system which gave rise to the country's peculiarity in comparison with the rest of Latin America.[19] These differences continue to bear upon certain characteristics of Argentine capitalism and class structure and also—centrally for our subject—on the power resources and on the political alliances available to the popular sectors.

The following are the most crucial features for our analysis:

1. As in the rest of Latin America, the pace and characteristics of Argentine capitalist expansion were fundamentally determined by the incorporation of some of its regions as exporters of primary products. This allows us to make an initial distinction between those vast regions of Latin America with no direct linkage to the world market[20] (such as the Andean *hacienda*) and those which were directly linked to such a market as exporters of primary products. Among these the *estancia* of the Argentine Pampas and Uruguay differed substantially from the enclaves and plantations, which were the principal form of incorporation elsewhere in the continent. The *estancia* was less labor intensive than the plantation and the *hacienda*, and it was also less capital and technology intensive than the plantation and the enclave. Largely because of the latter, the control of the principal productive resource (land) was left, in the Argentine Pampas and in Uruguay, in the hands of an early domestic agrarian bourgeoisie, while the enclave and the plantation were usually directly owned by international capital, and the *hacienda* was left in the hands of an oligarchy with hardly any capitalist traits.

---

19 And of Uruguay, to which I shall briefly return.

20 When I speak of direct incorporation or linkage I refer to the role which some regions had as (an exporting) part of the world capitalist system. This of course does not imply that regions not linked to the world capitalist system were not importers of products from the center, nor subject to the effects of world capitalist expansion, often through directly incorporated regions.

This pattern, combined with a high differential rent, endowed the pampean and the Uruguayan bourgeoisie with an important capital accumulation base of their own. This bourgeoisie did not escape dependence on European capital via the transport, finance, and international marketing of its products, but its base of capital accumulation did foment a significantly wealthier and more diversified urban, commercial, and incipient industrial sector than was to be found in those economies which revolved around the *hacienda*, the enclave, and the plantation. These characteristics are well known,[21] but others, to which less attention has been given, stem from them.

2. The cereal, wool, and later also beef exporting economy covered a relatively larger portion of the national territory than the exporting sectors of other countries. Above all, in Argentina the areas not directly incorporated with the world market carried much less economic and demographic weight than in the rest of Latin America. Furthermore, in Argentina and Uruguay there was only a very small peasantry subject to precapitalist relations of production compared with much of the continent. The insertion of a much larger proportion of the population into the export economy meant that, from the end of the nineteenth century, Argentina exhibited a

---

21 Above all since Fernando H. Cardoso's and Enzo Faletto's book, *Dependency and Development in Latin America* (Berkeley: University of California Press, 1979), where we find the characterization of the types of exporting economy I have mentioned; an important recent contribution is that of Albert Hirschman, who adapts elements of staple theory to his concept of "linkages," widened to include not strictly economic relationships, and from there explores the consequences of the type of export product through which incorporation into the international market took place; unfortunately, this author does not deal with pampean and Uruguayan products. See Albert Hirschman, *A Generalized Linkage Approach to Development, with Special Reference to Staples* (Princeton: Institute of Advanced Study, 1976).

significantly greater homogeneity than the rest of Latin America,[22] which, in spite of later mishaps, continues to be noticeable.[23]

3. Besides the sizable base of local accumulation due to direct control of land, the high productivity of land in international terms until approximately 1930[24] and the low labor requirements of "extensive" farming contributed decisively to the greater diversification and prosperity of the pampa region and its urban centers—compared to the regions dominated by the enclave, the plantations, and the *hacienda*. Suffice it to say that wages in the pampa region and the

---

22 With the exception of Uruguay, a case of even greater intranational homogeneity, since practically all its territory and its population were incorporated in the world market in conditions similar to those of the Argentine pampean region. Another exception, though partial and more complicated, is that of Chile; here, in the last third of the nineteenth century, the highly homogeneous agrarian economy of the central valley, partly oriented towards the export of foodstuffs, underwent (in contrast with Argentina and Uruguay) a decline, and the mining enclaves of the north emerged. But in contrast with other cases, those enclaves were inserted in a national market and a national state already constituted around the central agrarian region. Uruguay's greater intranational homogeneity allowed the earlier and fuller development of a "liberal" and "welfare" state. But for this very reason the problems concealed by the initial bonanza exploded earlier than in Argentina. Besides, the smaller absolute size of the Uruguayan internal market was decisive in interrupting its industrialization much earlier and thus, in recent decades, the relative weight of its working class has been significantly less than in Argentina.

23 For data and references on Argentina's greater intranational homogeneity with respect to most of Latin America, see O'Donnell, *Modernization*, chapter 1. For an analysis of the differences in the distribution of income and of its political correlates in Latin America, see Jorge Graciarena, "Estructura del poder y distribución del ingreso en América Latina," *Revista Latinoamericana de Ciencia Política* 2, no. 2 (August 1971).

24 Since then, the increasingly capital intensive modalities of the production of wool, cereals, and beef in the world market implied that agrarian productivity in Uruguay and Argentina rapidly fell behind in comparison with other exporters; see Carlos Díaz Alejandro, *Essays on the Economic History of the Argentine Republic* (New Haven: Yale University Press, 1970).

Argentine urban centers, until approximately the Second World War, were higher than in many European countries,[25] whilst those of the rest of Latin America—if and when wage relationships were established—were much lower. Thus, not only was intranational homogeneity higher, but also the region of Argentina, which was directly incorporated into the world economy, was more diversified and generated a significantly higher income for its popular sector than in the other Latin American countries. This, in turn, had other consequences: in Argentina, both industrialization and the formation of a working class occurred prior to the world crisis of 1930 and proceeded faster than in the rest of Latin America.[26] Around the beginning of the twentieth century, the existence of a fully capitalist and relatively wealthy urban (and, largely, also pampean) consumer market in Argentina induced an industrialization which received further stimulus from the import restrictions resulting from the First World War. An early working class therefore also emerged, which developed organizational patterns autonomous both of the state and of the incipient industrial bourgeoisie, although it entered the political arena only later.[27] In the absence of a large peasantry providing cheap labor, the strong demand for labor could only favor

---

25 Lucio Geller, "El crecimiento industrial argentino hasta 1914 y la teoría del bien primario exportador," in Marcos Giménez Zapiola, ed., *El régimen oligárquico: Materiales para el estudio de la realidad argentina (hasta 1930)* (Buenos Aires: Amorrortu, 1975).

26 The exception to this generalization is São Paulo. Brazil's industrialization, based on the dynamizing stimulus of the coffee economy, does not correspond to any of the generic types I have employed (see Hirschman, "A Generalized Linkage Approach"). But its original use of slave labor, its labor intensive character compared with the pampa economy and—most important for our argument—its location in a national context in which the slave system weighed overwhelmingly, contributed to the lower degree of autonomous organization and political weight of the Brazilian working class compared with Argentina's.

27 This is related to the Spanish and Italian immigration which nourished that class and the anarchist ideology that prevailed in it until approximately 1920. The main source on this point continues to be Gino Germani,

> such an outcome. Because of the specific characteristics of Argentina's insertion in the world capitalist system, its economic growth was powered fundamentally by its civil society and its relationships with the international market. The dynamizing impulse did not depend on the state, as generally tended to happen—with many difficulties—in the other Latin American economies. This point must be developed in greater detail.

In the period between roughly 1870 and 1930,[28] the Argentine state had certain features in common with the liberal states of the great world centers: although a more ostensibly fraudulent political democracy, the level of electoral participation was not lower,[29] and the state machine did not go beyond providing crucial, though limited, general conditions for the functioning of the economy.[30] But this state was the creation of the pampa bourgeoisie and its financial and commercial appendages, by means of a process which also entailed the making of the bourgeoisie, and of the system it dominated, in a marginal yet integral comer of the world capitalist market. To clarify this statement we must resort to some comparisons.

---

especially *Política y sociedad en una época de transición* (Buenos Aires: Editorial Paidós, 1962).

28 That is, between the strong exogenous impulse of the incorporation of the pampa region in the international market and the world crisis which altered the main basis of the system.

29 See Atilio Borón, "El estudio de la movilización electoral en América Latina: Movilización electoral en Argentina y Chile," *Desarrollo Económico* 12, no. 48 (1972).

30 Above all the transport and warehouse network necessary for shipping the pampa's production, the capture of which by international capital was generously subsidized by the state. If the small technology requirements of direct exploitation of the pampean region permitted domestic control of the land, the much greater requirements of such a network (and later on, of the meatpacking industry) determined a high and early inflow of international capital.

The pampa bourgeoisie and its urban branches directly constituted a national state, not the regional state,[31] which was the main political power base of the dominant classes in so many Latin American countries. The Argentine national state also eliminated—earlier, and with greater ease and completeness—the autonomy of the regions not directly linked to the world market, largely because those regions carried much less weight in the country as a whole than in most other Latin American cases.[32] This implied that the state was an expression of changing power relationships between regions directly incorporated in the world market and others marginal to it to a much smaller extent than in the rest of Latin America.

Thus the pampa bourgeoisie and its urban tentacles held both a central economic position and, through the national state, a central political position as an internally dominant class burdened by other regions. Furthermore, the shifts in the relative importance of export products took place within the pampean zone and its bourgeoisie[33] and not, as in most other cases, by means of the incorporation of new products from new regions

---

31 I am not concerned here with the details of the respective historical processes. In particular the imposition of the nationalization of Buenos Aires by a coalition of provinces of the interior against the opposition of a sizable part of the pampa interests was no obstacle, once the vigorous exogenous impulses of the European demand for foodstuffs were felt, to the processes alluded to in the text.

32 Even in a case such as Brazil, characterized by relatively early industrialization and by the great weight of the state bureaucratic apparatus inherited from the imperial period, the subordination of the dominant classes of the Northeast and the elimination of the barriers interposed by the regional states to the effective functioning of a national market were only completed after 1930; see CEBRAP, *Estado y sociedad en el Brasil: La planificación regional en la época de SUDENE* (São Paulo: 1976). It should be borne in mind that I am excluding Chile and Uruguay from these generalizations.

33 Of course, economic factors were not the only ones operating in this. Its greater weight, condensed in the national state, with respect to the oligarchies of other regions, allowed the pampean bourgeoisie to "discourage" the emergence of other dynamic exporting industries by means of diverse economic and political mechanisms.

leading to shifting alliances with existing locally dominant classes and established segments of the international capital.

Nevertheless, the pampa bourgeoisie and the national state became the principal channels of the internationalization of both society and economy, because of the nature of their insertion in the world market. The "liberal" characteristics of the Argentine state and the strong relative weight of its civil society can only be understood as consequences of the position of the state at the intersection of the pampa bourgeoisie with international capital—which had deeply penetrated the economy through its control of the financing, transportation, and external marketing of pampa production. Paradoxically therefore, this original internationalization of an economically dynamic and internally homogeneous region, including a decisive part of the country with barely any peasants, through the local retention of capital accumulation shares, enabled a highly internationalized state to become devastatingly national with respect to the regions marginalized from the pampean system. In contrast, the Andean oligarchy or that of Brazil's Northeast could directly and diaphanously control "their" regional state apparatus, while international capital, based on enclaves and plantations, controlled a state which was less an emanation from than a graft imposed upon a society which lacked a local bourgeoisie endowed with its own accumulation base. Instead, in Argentina, the existence of such a bourgeoisie arising from the very process of incorporation into the international market generated a situation in which the regional states were of little weight; furthermore, the national state was one of the crucial channels of the rapid and early internationalization, which, due to the weight of the pampa economy, covered much more of the country than in other Latin America cases. That is why—not in spite of, but as a very condition of, its centrality—the relationship between the pampa bourgeoisie and the state did not exhibit the transparency and immediacy which the regional oligarchies and international capital imposed in a large portion of Latin America's regional and (for a long time, mostly nominal) national states.[34]

---

34 Of course, if instead of making these comparisons with other Latin American cases we had made them with Australia and New Zealand, the dimensions Argentina and Uruguay had in common with the other Latin

Although the liberal Argentine state did not survive the crisis of the thirties, the factors summarized above allowed it to recover from the economic impact of the world crisis more quickly and easily than most other Latin American countries. The crisis induced a new wave of industrialization through import substitution (helped by a comparatively broad internal market)[35] and the absorption of a large part of the still available workforce from the nonpampa regions, thus reducing their relative weight even further. However, this is not the place to analyze how this affected the emergence of Peronism; instead, we turn to the central theme of the paper.

III. Dilemmas

I have already mentioned the emergence in Argentina of a popular sector, which included a politically significant working class, with larger economic and organizational resources than those of the rest of Latin America.[36] This in turn resulted from the combination of large available economic surpluses and the negligible pressure exerted on the urban labor market by an almost nonexistent peasantry. If this was an advantage for Argentina's capitalist development, it also strengthened its popular sector. When the bonanza disappeared and the economic conditions approached zero sum, there was no sizable peasantry to bear a substantial part of the costs of agreements negotiated between the classes located within the fully capitalist region.

American countries would be more noticeable. For some comparisons in that direction, see Geller, "El crecimiento industrial," and Héctor Diéguez, "Argentina y Australia: Algunos aspectos de su desarrollo económico comparado," *Desarrollo Económico* 8, no. 32 (1969).

35 The effective market is a function not so much of the total population as of that part of the population subject to capitalist relationships and with a monetary income sufficient for the purchase of mass consumption industrial goods; see O'Donnell, *Modernization*, chapter 1.

36 As always with the exception of Uruguay and partly—and too complicated to be dealt with here—of Chile.

The second point to be singled out arises from another peculiarity of this economy: its main export products—cereals and beef—are wage goods, foodstuffs which constitute the main consumption item of the popular sector. Let us initially note some general consequences of this peculiarity. Other Latin American primary export products have less influence on the consumption of the popular sector and therefore, on the relative prices of their consumption baskets. Furthermore, the way in which their price changes influence popular consumption is, in most cases, indirect, generated by mechanisms which are difficult to apprehend; in this situation in contrast, a change in the relative prices of foodstuffs is immediately perceivable. In addition, this perception arises in a popular sector with a significantly higher level of income (and, presumably, of expectations) and organizational autonomy (and therefore greater capacity for resistance) than in the other Latin American cases. We are now in a position to analyze more concrete processes.

The world crisis of the 1930s depressed the prices of pampean goods. Subsequently the Peronist government (1946–55) offered a foretaste of the problems which would explode later. First (1946–50) the state appropriated a substantial part of the proceeds of pampean exports, kept internal foodstuff prices depressed, and thus increased the income of the popular sector and provoked an expanding demand for other goods, especially industrial ones. But this was to generate a balance-of-payments squeeze, due to the "discouragement" effect of low prices on pampa production and to increasing internal consumption of exportable foodstuffs. Subsequently (1952–55) agricultural prices improved, whereupon—because of the operation of the inverse joint effect—the balance-of-payments situation improved. But this in turn generated political troubles, due to the regressive redistribution of income it entailed and to the reduction of the domestic demand on which the urban bourgeoisie depended.

Following this, around 1960, a wave of direct foreign investment in industry and services provoked a rapid internationalization of the urban productive structure[37] (by means of capital and activities different from

---

37 It is impossible to quote here all the pertinent references. The data and main sources can be found in Pablo Gerchunoff and Juan Llach, "Capitalismo

those involved in export activities). Contrary to the "developmentalist" hopes, this new stage resulted in a marked increase in demand for imports, which outran the growth rate of GNP, exports, and pampa production.[38] Faced with this situation the only economically "evident" solution—repeatedly expounded—lay in a large increase of exports, which would have provided the urban productive structure with the imports necessary for "self-sustained development." Assuming the capitalist parameters of the situation, this solution entailed, fundamentally, an increase in pampean production (and productivity) and/or a reduction in real wages, so as to "free" exportable surpluses of food. But the Cartesian simplicity of these solutions—which were indeed attempted—ran into political complications which we must now analyze.

IV. Cycles

Several consequences arose from the fact that wage goods were also the main export products. In the first place, it offered an objective basis, which was also subjectively acknowledged,[39] for repeated alliances between a sizable part of the weaker fractions of the urban bourgeoisie and the popular sector. These alliances were forged around the defense of the internal market against the recessive effects (via the increase of domestic food prices) of every significant rise in the price of pampa products. In the second place, the mobilizations of the popular sector in defense of its consumption levels reinforced its capacity for organizational and political action through partial but repeated victories. A

---

industrial, desarrollo asociado y distribución del ingreso entre los gobiernos peronistas," *Desarrollo Económico* 15, no. 57 (1975); and Juan Sourrouille, "El impacto de las empresas transnacionales sobre el empleo y los ingresos: El caso de Argentina" (Geneva: International Labor Office, 1976).

38 See, above all, Juan Ayza, Gerard Fischet, and Norberto González, *América Latina: Integración económica y sustitución de importaciones* (Mexico: CEPAL and Fondo de Cultura Económica, 1976).

39 This was one of the constant themes of the CGE and the CGT after 1955.

third consequence was that the above-mentioned alliance again and again provoked and revivified a deep horizontal cleavage within the urban bourgeoisie, between its oligopolistic fractions and those weaker ones which found a welcome ally in the popular sectors. Fourth, these same processes determined the appearance of another fundamental intrabourgeois cleavage, by separating the economic interests and political goals of the urban bourgeoisie (including its oligopolistic fractions) from those of the pampean bourgeoisie. These changing alliances lie at the basis of the economic and political cycles on which students of Argentina have fastened their attention.[40]

The solution of Argentina's balance-of-payments bottlenecks requires a substantial increase of pampean exports. However, when, around 1960, the demand for imports rose rapidly, the exports themselves rose much less. This was partly the consequence of an increase

---

40 The subject of the stop-go cycle has elicited important contributions from various theoretical perspectives. See, above all, Carlos Díaz Alejandro, *Devaluación en la tasa de cambio en un país semi-industrializado: La experiencia argentina, 1955–1966* (Buenos Aires: Editorial del Instituto, 1966); Carlos Díaz Alejandro, *Essays on the Economic History*; Marcelo Diamand, *Doctrinas económicas, desarrollo e independencia* (Buenos Aires: Editorial Paidós, 1973); Mario Brodersohn, "Política económica de corto plazo, crecimiento e inflación en la Argentina, 1950–1972," in Consejo Profesional de Ciencias Económicas, *Problemas económicos argentinos, diagnóstico y política* (Buenos Aires: Macchi, 1974); Juan Sourrouille and Richard Mallon, *Economic Policy-Making in a Conflict Society* (Cambridge, MA: Harvard University Press, 1974); Aldo Ferrer et al., *Los planes de estabilización en la Argentina* (Buenos Aires: Editorial Paidós, 1969); and Javier Villanueva, "Una interpretación de la inflación argentina," *Revista de Ciencias Económicas* (April–September, 1972). Adolfo Canitrot, "La experiencia populista en la redistribución de ingresos," *Desarrollo Económico* 15, no. 59 (1975), has a different viewpoint, but is nevertheless an important contribution. For attempts to connect this type of analysis with a more specifically political level, see Oscar Braun, "Desarrollo del capital monopolista en la Argentina," in Oscar Braun, ed., *El capitalismo argentino*, and Guillermo O'Donnell, *Modernization*. From another angle, the literature already mentioned on the political "stalemate" in Argentina is relevant to this subject. However, not much has been done so far to capture the formation and shifts of political alliances which have stimulated those cycles.

in the internal consumption of exportables and, also, of slow improvements in the pampean region's production and productivity.[41] Neither the space available nor my knowledge allow for a satisfactory explanation of this failure, but it seems obvious that, assuming the capitalist parameters of the context, a necessary (but not sufficient) condition for rising production of pampean goods lies in "satisfactory" prices for the pampean bourgeoisie. The meaning of "satisfactory" is complex, but it includes at least two further necessary conditions: one is that prices should make feasible the investments necessary to increase the capital density of the pampean region and its productivity. The second condition—less obvious but more important—is that those prices should be stable and that they should be perceived as such at the microeconomic level. I do not know of any studies which establish this, but there is no reason to suppose that, in the 1956–76 period, the profit rates of the pampa bourgeoisie were lower than that of the urban bourgeoisie. However, Figure 1 clearly shows the enormous instability of the main pampean wholesale prices (cereals, linseed, and beef), measured in relation to wholesale urban prices.

A substantial increase in pampean production (and exports) cannot take place without converting the *estancias* into a much more capital intensive agribusiness. Discarding explanations based on the economic "irrationality" of the pampa bourgeoisie—which are an implicit avowal of their authors' ignorance—it seems clear that the answer must be found at the level of the parameters which govern microeconomic decisions. These parameters do not spring from some economic "necessity" but from political struggles and from the swings of the state, which in turn result from the specificities of a class structure whose origins I have summarized in the previous sections. This is what we must analyze.

41 On this subject the principal source is Díaz Alejandro's important book, *Essays on the Economic History*, where the slow growth of the physical quantity of these exports and the spectacular lag of pampean productivity with respect to its principal competitors in the world market are shown. Also see Sourrouille and Mallon, *Economic Policy-Making*.

FIGURE 1

Relative Prices in Argentina, 1956–1976 (wholesale cattle and cereal prices against wholesale non-agricultural prices)

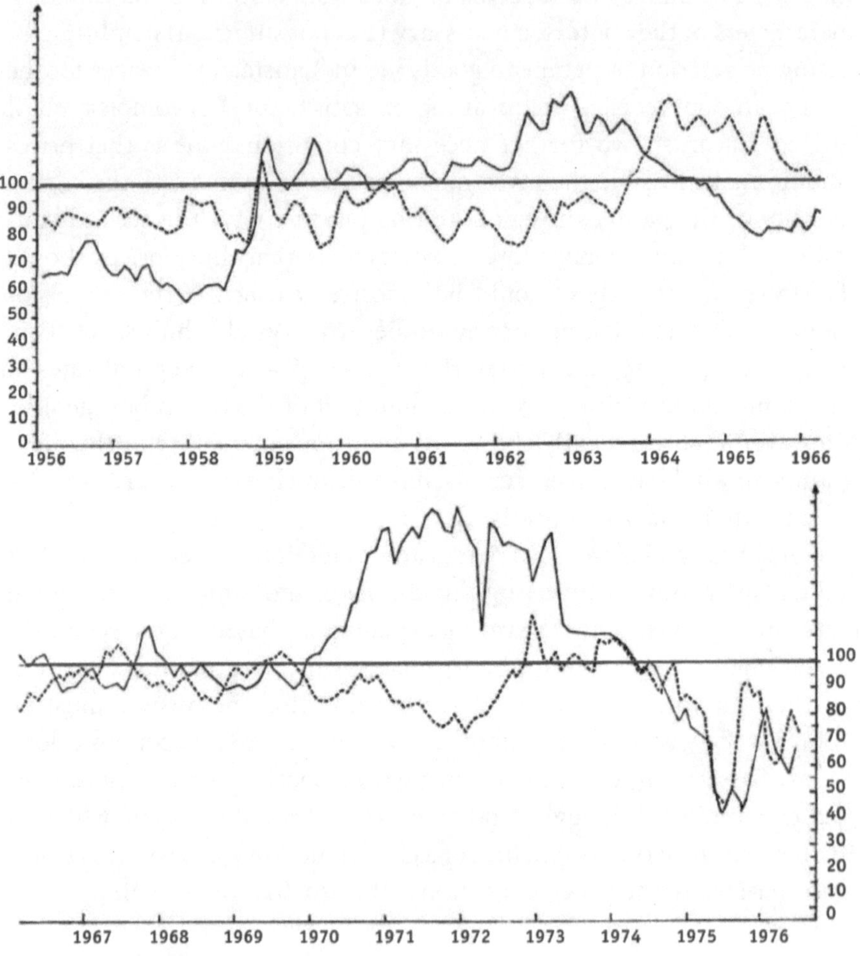

——— Wholesale cattle prices as a percentage of wholesale non-agricultural prices

--------- Wholesale cereal and flax prices as a percentage of wholesale non-agricultural prices

Source: Ministerio de Economía: Boletín Trimestral de Estadísticas and Boletín Mensual Precios Mayoristas

The conversion of the pampean *estancia* into a capital and technology intensive agribusiness[42] entails making rather long-term investment decisions. The instability of pampean relative prices, the historical awareness of this, and, above all, the difficulty of forecasting future price instability[43] have prevented those decisions. Thus, the pampa bourgeoisie, once dynamic (even in international terms, during the period before 1930), has become less and less so in recent times. The basic reason is that relative prices made it microeconomically rational to maintain the "extensive" exploitation of the land.[44]

---

42 I hope it is clear that I am speaking at the class level. That is, the change towards an agribusiness would surely displace more than a few individuals who at present constitute the pampa bourgeoisie.

43 The pampa bourgeoisie's demands and declarations, at least of the last twenty years, constitute a repeated complaint that it does not receive profitable or stable prices.

44 See the microeconomic studies quoted in the works I mention below. The issue is, however, more complicated, as appears from the controversy which took place in *Desarrollo Económico* between Flischman, Braun, and Martínez (see Guillermo Flichman, "Modelo de asignación de recursos en el sector agropecuario," *Desarrollo Económico* 10, nos. 39–40 [1970]; Guillermo Flichman, "Nuevamente en tomo de la eficiencia en el uso de la tierra y la caracterización de los grandes terratenientes," *Desarrollo Económico* 14, no. 54 [1974]; Oscar Braun, "Comentario al trabajo de Guillermo Flichman," *Desarrollo Económico* 10, nos. 39–40 [1970]; Oscar Braun, "La renta absoluta y el uso ineficiente de la tierra en la Argentina," *Desarrollo Económico* 14, no. 54 [1974]; and Carlos Martínez et al., "Nuevamente en tomo al problema de asignación de recursos en el sector agropecuario pampeano," *Desarrollo Económico* 16, no. 51 [1976]). The central point of these for our analysis is that the differential rent which the pampean region still enjoys and, especially, the great fluctuations of the whole economy and the high (and erratic) inflation rate, made the purchase of pampa land an excellent speculative investment—and a defense against the effects of inflation—for the urban and agrarian capital surpluses. This combines to reinforce the microeconomic rationality of maintaining the region's extensive exploitation. But, from the perspective of this analysis, the subject which these authors discuss seems to be a consequence (although in time it nourishes them in turn) of the economic and political factors I analyze here.

In the short term, the rise in relative internal prices of pampean production entails an almost equivalent net loss for the whole of the urban sector. The income redistribution, and the recessive effect on the urban economy which (*ceteris paribus*) this entails, increases the export surpluses (via their immediate effect on the internal consumption of exportables) and might induce a medium-term increase of pampa production by satisfying the necessary condition of "satisfactory" prices.[45] This would not be too onerous for the oligopolistic fractions of the urban bourgeoisie. They have an objective interest in increasing the balance-of-payments surplus because of their high import coefficient.[46] The recessions and redistributions of income which usually accompany increases in food prices are less harmful for these oligopolistic fractions than for the weaker ones. In effect, the former have economic resources and preferential access to internal credit[47] which enable them to shoulder the burden of the recession and, indeed, to promote capital concentration to their advantage at the same time.[48] Besides, the urban bourgeoisie's oligopolistic fractions aim much of their production and supply of services at the relatively high income strata, whose income is less affected, absolutely and proportionately, by rises in food prices.

Although this generalization would require qualification in a more refined analysis, it provides the objective basis for a long-term alliance between the large urban bourgeoisie and the pampa bourgeoisie, which could guide the "modernization" of Argentine capitalism simultaneously

---

45 Further on I shall complicate this matter by introducing other factors.

46 Not only is the coefficient high but it grows with an elasticity greater than 1.0 with increases in its production level; see Ayza et al., *América Latina: Integración económica.*

47 For data on this point see especially FIEL, *La financiación de las empresas industriales en la Argentina* (Buenos Aires: 1971), and Mario Brodersohn, *Financiamiento de empresas privados y mercados de capital* (Buenos Aires: Programa Latinoamericano para el Desarrollo de Mercados de Capital, 1972).

48 On this point and others closely connected with it, see Guillermo O'Donnell and Delfina Linck, *Dependencia y autonomía* (Buenos Aires: Amorrortu, 1973).

through capital concentration in the urban sector and the development of capital intensive agribusiness in the countryside. However, at least until 1976, this alliance lasted only for short periods, dissolving rapidly in situations which repeatedly put these two dominant fractions of the Argentine bourgeoisie in different political camps.

Why this deviation from economic "logic"? Fundamentally because this alliance has been confronted again and again by another—basically made up of the popular sectors and the weak fractions of the urban bourgeoisie—which, in spite of its economic subordination, has been able to prevent it from holding together beyond the short term. In the Latin American context this has been one of Argentina's (and, with its own characteristics, Uruguay's) peculiarities, which can only be understood in terms of the historical perspectives summarized in the previous sections. But we still have new elements to introduce into our analysis.

Which processes posed these dilemmas and conflicts? The periods of low internal prices of foodstuffs and stable foreign exchange rates have, not by chance, been those of the highest growth rates and—until the approach of the end of the cycle—lowest inflation rates.[49] But they have also led to balance-of-payments crises, which brought about the introduction of controls, especially on internal prices and the foreign exchange movements, although these were not enough to stave off the crises. Once a balance-of-payments crisis was unleashed, it was dealt with by means of devaluations which (with the exception of the 1967–69 period) implied a correlative increase in the internal prices of exportables. These devaluations formed part of stabilization programs which accentuated the recessive and redistributionary effects of the devaluation by means of a restriction of money supply, reduction of the budgetary deficit, wage freezes, and increases in the real interest rate, tending, on the one hand, to consolidate the transfer of income to the exporting sector and, on the other, to adjust the internal level of economic activity to meet the balance-of-payments restrictions.

The effects were not only recessive and redistributive but also inflationary ("stagflation" is no novelty in Argentina), through the rise in domestic food prices caused by the growth of their export value, and

49 See the pertinent data in Brodersohn, "Política económica de corto plazo."

the rising cost of imported goods and credit—at times when, on the other hand, wages and salaries were kept frozen or systematically lagging and recession increased unemployment. In the short term (and, as we shall see, in these processes there was never more than a short term), the transfer of income towards the exporting sector did not induce an increase in pampean production,[50] but the stabilization programs were instrumental in easing the balance-of-payments squeeze.

True, such successes were due to factors very different from those proclaimed in official speeches, in the "recommendations" of the International Monetary Fund, and in the exultant statements of the organizations of the pampa bourgeoisie. They were achieved not by an increase of exportable production but by recession, which diminished the demand for imports and increased the exportable surplus, especially of foodstuffs. But this generated resistance among the many penalized by these policies, while the resulting easing of the balance-of-payments made possible economic reactivation policies. Consequently, the liquidity increase, the relaxing of controls on the fiscal deficit, the availability of foreign exchange, the growth in employment, and the salary increases ended the downward phase of the cycle and inaugurated the upward phase. But the latter led into a new balance-of-payments crisis,[51] after

---

50 Actually, the price elasticity of pampean production is nil or slightly negative in the short term. This is because for cattle "an increase in relative prices reduces supply and increases the stocks. Besides, an increase in the cattle stock implies a greater use of land due to the rigidity in the supply of land. Therefore, an increase in the relative prices of beef also negatively affects the production of cereals since to the lesser supply of beef is to be added the smaller area for cultivation" (Brodersohn, "Política económica de corto plazo," 28).

51 In contrast with what I noted above concerning exports, the income elasticity of imports is extremely high. It was estimated at around 2.6 for the 1947–67 period (Díaz Alejandro, *Devaluación en la tasa de cambio*, 356); for the period after 1966, Ayza et al., *América Latina: Integración económica*, 13), with a different methodology, estimate an elasticity of 1.8. One piece of information which indicates how internal consumption causes this pincer movement to close on the balance-of-payments in the upward phase of the cycle is that the wage earners' marginal propensity to consume exportable

which further devaluation, and the consequent stabilization program, opened up another downward phase.[52]

V. Pendulums

In each phase of the cycle, the large bourgeoisie has played on the winner's side. I have already pointed out that the recessions provoked by stabilization programs have, at the very least, not damaged that fraction. At the same time, as a direct appendage of (or intimately linked to) international capital, it is the large bourgeoisie which best perceives—and most fears—the costs of international insolvency.[53] It has the most

---

goods (foodstuffs, drinks, and tobacco) is 0.36 and that of nonwage earners is 0.16.

52 This is the briefest of summaries of the principal theme of the works quoted in note 40, to which I must refer. A useful presentation of the economic mechanisms operating in the upward and downward phases of the cycles—which unfortunately came to my attention only when this work was substantially finished—is Marcelo Diamand, "El péndulo argentino: Empate político o fracasos económicos?" (ms., 1976).

53 As the upward phase approached the balance-of-payments crisis, state controls were imposed on prices and foreign exchange, thus particularly troubling this fraction. I cannot deal with these points at greater length; suffice it to point out that, as far as price controls, which are typical of the final moments of the upward phase, are concerned, they could only really be attempted with the "leading firms." In other respects, when the balance-of-payments crisis occurred, the imposition of foreign exchange controls and of restrictions on capital transfers abroad became serious hindrances, particularly to firms more closely connected with the centers of world capitalism. Admittedly, none of these controls achieved their goals, nor did they prevent massive flights of capital, but many of the high-ranking staff of large firms (national and transnational), whom I interviewed in 1971 and 1972, said that for that reason they "had" to act "excessively" beyond the pale of Argentine legislation, with consequent uneasiness at times when, during the upward phase of the cycles, "demagogues" and "nationalists" with access to state institutions were not lacking.

direct interest in an improvement of the balance-of-payments.[54] Furthermore, the free international movement of capital enhances the privileged position, in an ever narrower domestic credit market, of this most internationalized (and therefore internally dominant) fraction, while at the same time reopening the "normal" channels for the transfer of capital accumulation towards the center of the system,[55] of which it is the most intrinsic part. In the final stretch of the upward phase of the cycle, these factors turn the large bourgeoisie into an ally of the pampa bourgeoisie (and of the whole of the exporting sector) in the clamor for the devaluation and deflationary policies which launch the downward phase. Thus, faced with the onset of the balance-of-payments crisis, the large bourgeoisie swings towards the objective interests of the pampa bourgeoisie, favoring and supporting stabilization programs which transfer a mass of resources toward the latter, mostly at the expense of the urban sector.

But the regressive and recessionary impact of these measures generated a reaction among the weaker fractions of the urban bourgeoisie and of the popular sector[56] at the same time as the improvement in the foreign exchange position made feasible the economic and reactivation measures for which they were clamoring. Faced with this, the large bourgeoisie did repeatedly what all bourgeoisies do in the absence of a tutelary

---

54 In terms of their high import coefficient and demand for foreign exchange, and in spite of their better access to international finance, which allows them to make excellent deals in pre- and post-devaluation periods of acute scarcity of foreign exchange.

55 Even within private capital's oligopolistic fraction, the more fully and directly internationalized firms—the subsidiaries of the transnational corporations—are usually the largest (in capital and sales), the fastest growing, and the most capital intensive; see especially Sourrouille, "El impacto de las empresas." Of course this is not peculiar to Argentina; on Mexico see Fernando Fajnzylber and Trinidad Tarragó, *Las empresas transnacionales: Expansión a nivel mundial y proyección en la industria mexicana* (Mexico: Fondo de Cultura Económica, 1976), and Carlos Von Doellinger and Leonardo Cavalcanti, *Empresas multinacionais na industria brasileira* (Rio de Janeiro: IPEA/INPES, 1975).

56 These in turn carried with them a large part of the nonpampean regions, which also had to "contribute" to these income transfers.

state to induce them to adopt longer-term strategies: they looked to their short-term economic interests, supported the economic reactivation policies, and thus rode the crest of the wave of economic recovery—from which, we may safely assume, they were able to profit in a privileged manner.[57] In this it covered a full swing of the pendulum, joining the rest of the urban sector and abandoning the pampa bourgeoisie to a solitary lament for the deterioration of its relative prices;[58] all of which produced the great fluctuations of relative prices observable in Figure 1.

Although this describes the recurrent pendulation of the large bourgeoisie, I have still to explain it. However, it must be added that, apart from their economic consequences, these displacements had political implications of the greatest importance: they repeatedly broke up that intrabourgeois cohesion essential for its stable political domination. More precisely, they broke the cohesion of its two superior fractions (the urban oligopolistic and the pampa bourgeoisie), whose respective capital accumulation base made them potentially capable of "modernizing" Argentine capitalism. Another aspect, no less important and to which I shall shortly turn, is that such swings not only generated the political space for, but also were to a large extent the consequence of, an alternative alliance which encompassed the weaker fractions of the bourgeoisie and the popular sector.

Let me insist on a crucial point. The alliance of the dominant fractions of the bourgeoisie could have borne fruit if it had lasted long enough to bring about significant productivity increases in the pampa region. This was prevented by the large fluctuations in relative prices. But in their political demands the pampean bourgeoisie concentrated on the level and not the stability of their prices, thus contributing to the pendulations I have already mentioned. The productivity increases could have taken place with relatively depressed but stable pampean prices (thus meeting the necessary condition of stability stated above), combined

---

57 At least, the more concentrated and internationalized industrial branches usually responded with greater dynamism to the reactivation.

58 Maintaining a fixed exchange rate—or systematically allowing it to lag behind domestic prices—was the main mechanism which turned relative prices in favor of the urban sector (including wages and salaries).

with public policies which would have forced them through by more structural measures. This was the motivation behind the various projects designed to tax the difference between the potential and the actual productivity of pampa land.

Such an alternative, obviously conflicting with the short-term interests of the pampa bourgeoisie in its present composition, is not against those of the urban sector as a whole (since it does not presuppose a fall in their relative prices), and in the medium term it could have achieved the sought-after increase in pampa production and productivity. However, the attempts to impose such a tax on the "potential rent of the land" repeatedly failed. This must be contrasted with what has happened in many other Latin American countries, where the state—impelled by and allied with the large bourgeoisie—has usually been able to force through the "modernization" of agrarian regions and their dominant classes.[59] But those agrarian classes were fundamentally regional ones[60] and, although their production might temporarily fall, their contribution to total exports was not comparable to that of the pampa bourgeoisie. That is why other Latin American states have been able to subordinate those classes, and the regional states which they controlled, without simultaneously worsening their balance-of-payments problems.

The case of the pampa bourgeoisie has been very different. I have pointed out its early position as a national class, even with respect to its

---

59 This of course did not prevent these processes from being acutely conflictive. The point is that the capacity of these classes to resist was less than that of the pampa bourgeoisie and that, besides, the cost of such policies—in terms of their short-term impact on the level of internal economic activity and exports—was lower.

60 In the case of the enclaves it obviously was not a matter of modernizing the economy's most capital—and technology—intensive sector, but of renegotiating with international capital the percentages which could be retained locally. In the cases in which "excessive" pressure was exerted (reaching or threatening nationalization, above all) and the enclave's product was as important as the pampa production for total exports (Bolivia and, more recently, Chile) the familiar falls in production, prices, or both—equivalent in this sphere to the pampa bourgeoisie's recurrent "discouragements"—unleashed the consequent balance-of-payments crisis.

linkage with a national state. This meant that intrabourgeois struggles usually occurred, in contrast with other Latin American cases, at the very heart of a national state which was continually fractured by them. Besides, the "discouragement" of the pampa bourgeoisie[61] caused by the fall in its prices and attempts to "restructure it" by means of tax mechanisms had strong immediate repercussions on the balance-of-payments—at the same time that, in the upward phase of the economic cycle, the increase in domestic consumption of exportables further diminished the potentially available exports, before pampean productivity had undergone any substantial improvement. Thus a balance-of-payments crisis ensued, and its alleviation by means of devaluations not only turned relative prices against the urban sector but also entailed the expulsion from the governing alliances of the sectors which had impelled the reactivation of the cycle.

As long as the stabilization programs lasted, the immediate interests of the pampa bourgeoisie weighed heavily in the institutional system of the state. Naturally enough, it opposed any prospect of its own "restructuring," centering the issue on a sharp increase in its prices and thus creating the conditions for a renewal of the cycle. In other words, although it has long lost its position as the dynamic vanguard of Argentine capitalism, the pampa bourgeoisie, compared with other Latin American agrarian classes, has retained an unusually central economic and political position. This position was sufficient both to block any attempt to "restructure" it and to use periodic balance-of-payments crises to bring about massive income transfers for its benefit. Meanwhile, and as a consequence, channels for capital accumulation in Argentina were repeatedly short circuited and the state danced to the pendular tune of civil society.

This accounts for some of the characteristics of the period beginning in 1966, especially the economic policies followed between March 1967 and May 1969. The Economics Minister, Krieger Vasena, transparently carried out the policies of the large bourgeoisie. This entailed, among

---

61 For the pampa bourgeoisie's insistence on its "discouragement" because of its internal prices and the attempts to "smother it" with taxes, it is enough to consult collections of documents of the Argentine Rural Society (SRA) and the Coordinator of Rural Associations of Buenos Aires and the Pampas (CARBAP).

other things, a large devaluation which for the first time did not benefit the pampa and exporting sector. On the contrary, the March 1967 devaluation (40%) was wholly appropriated by the state, which withheld a percentage of the value of pampa exports equivalent to the devaluation. This fiscal revenue was used in a substantial program of investment in physical infrastructure and communications. A fixed *peso* price of pampean production depressed the internal price of pampean foodstuffs, as can be seen in Figure l. It also allowed a rapid reduction of inflation and—in contrast with other cases of bureaucratic-authoritarianism—only a moderate fall in industrial wages (see Figures 2 and 3).

Even so, this situation could not be maintained and, as can be seen in Figure 1, after 1970 pampean prices (especially those of beef) rebounded until they reached a very high level in 1971–72. Krieger Vasena's was the only clear and sustained attempt by the large bourgeoisie unilaterally to subordinate the pampa bourgeoisie[62] to its own accumulation needs. But the result was an internal rupture in the cohesion of the BA state and a political and economic collapse impelled from outside by other social actors. While this attempt marked the limits of a unilateral enforcement of supremacy by the large bourgeoisie, the history of previous devaluations, by pushing the upper bourgeoisie into alliances with the urban sector, had shown that it was impossible to return to the good old times of pampean supremacy.[63]

62 Even by trying to introduce a tax on potential rent which, like so many other things, faded away with the social explosions of 1969.

63 Another exception—less clear, but also a telling one—can be found in the economic policy followed during 1964 and 1965. Then, as can be seen from Figures 1 and 2, high pampean prices coexisted with an improvement of real wages. But this attempt ran into its own limitations, since it entailed the reduction of profits for the urban bourgeoisie—which actively contributed to the 1966 coup—a large increase in the fiscal deficit, and severe restrictions on imports.

VI. The Defensive Alliance

If the political and economic centrality of the pampa bourgeoisie marks an important difference with respect to other Latin American countries and their agrarian classes, a no less important difference stems from the greater political vulnerability of the weaker (and genuinely national) fractions of the urban bourgeoisie in those countries when faced with the expansion of the large bourgeoisie. The growth of the dominant productive structure, oligopolistic and internationalized, has occurred at the expense of many fractions of national capital, weakening its position vis-à-vis international capital and the state. This has caused complaints and strains, but has not, so far, been translated into serious political challenges to such "development" patterns. No such development has taken place in Argentina. The reason for the local bourgeoisie's comparatively greater political capacity is to be found not so much in itself as in the characteristics of the popular sector and in the country's relative national homogeneity. Elsewhere, a weaker urban sector, less organized and autonomous, deprives the weaker fractions of the Latin American bourgeoisie of the extremely important ally they had in Argentina. This is a crucial point.

Not only is the Argentine popular sector endowed with greater autonomy and organizational capacity than in most other Latin American countries. It also so happens that the medium- and long-term alliance of the upper fractions of the bourgeoisie depends on the level and stability of the relative prices of the main internal foodstuffs. This gives the popular sector a precise target for its political action, which has interrupted the accumulation circuits of those upper bourgeoisie fractions. These are necessary but not sufficient conditions for the recurrent breakdown of the latter's alliances. To account for the specificity of the phenomena with which we are concerned we must also see how the popular sector associated itself with the objective interests and political action of the weaker fractions of the urban bourgeoisie.

These fractions are usually penalized by devaluations and stabilization programs. Given an alleviation of the balance-of-payments squeeze, their immediate interest lies in economic reactivation policies which increase employment, liquidity, and credit availability, and give the state an expansionary role once again. This is also a direct effect of wage and salary increases; thus, it is not surprising that the bourgeois fraction in control of the most labor intensive enterprises should support these increases, when the even greater costs to them of recession are taken into account. The concurrence with the unions in demanding wage increases is, besides, a token which it offers the popular sector to forge the alliance.[64] Such a bourgeoisie—more or less weak and more or less penalized by the expansion of oligopolistic and internationalized capital—exists in other Latin American countries, but only in Argentina has it found a popular ally whose immediate short-term interests are compatible with its own, and which possesses a significant capacity for political action.[65]

The main organizational supports of this alliance have been the CGE, the CGT, and the national leadership of the main unions. Its first, principal, and possibly last expression has been Peronism. It was not the only one, since—above all in the periods in which Peronism was proscribed—it was channeled through other parties and within state institutions by diverse "nationalist" military and civilian groups. Their banner has been the defense of the internal market, in the sense both of raising the level of its activity and of limiting the expansion of international capital in it.

---

64 Since these wage and salary increases encourage economic activity at the same time that other policies, made possible by the transitory easing of the balance-of-payments, raise the employment level, the orthodox warnings that all this feeds inflation matter little—particularly since inflation, with a fixed or systematically lagging exchange rate, accelerates the reversal of relative prices in favor of the urban sector.

65 In Uruguay the lower level of industrialization, fundamentally due to the smaller internal market, weakened both agents much more; the local bourgeoisie has in itself been weaker and in the popular sector the working class has had relatively less weight. In Chile the political expression of the working class in Marxist parties (and the absence of a direct target in the relative price of foodstuffs as in Argentina and Uruguay) made this alliance more ambiguous and discontinuous. In the remaining countries of the region the relative weakness of the popular sector—due to a greater intranational heterogeneity—deprived the local bourgeoisie of that fundamental ally.

FIGURE 2
Inflation in Argentina, 1956–1976

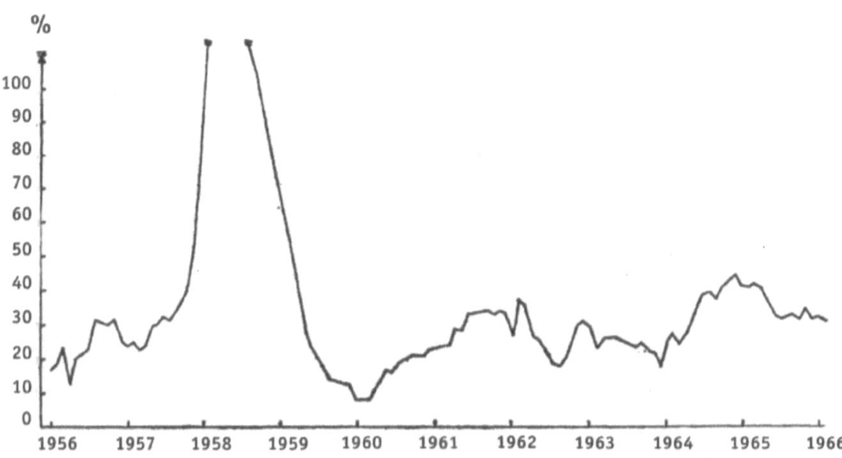

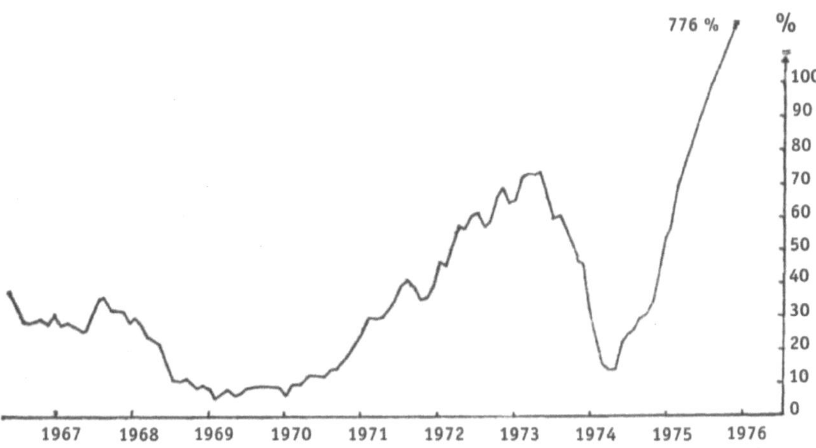

Monthly percentage increase in the cost-of-living index for the city of Buenos Aires. The high points where the curve is interrupted should reach 126.9 percent (1959) and 776 percent (1976).

Source: Ministry of Economics: *Boletín Estadístico*

FIGURE 3
Monthly Series of Selected Industrial Wages, 1956–1976
(at constant prices: 1966=100)

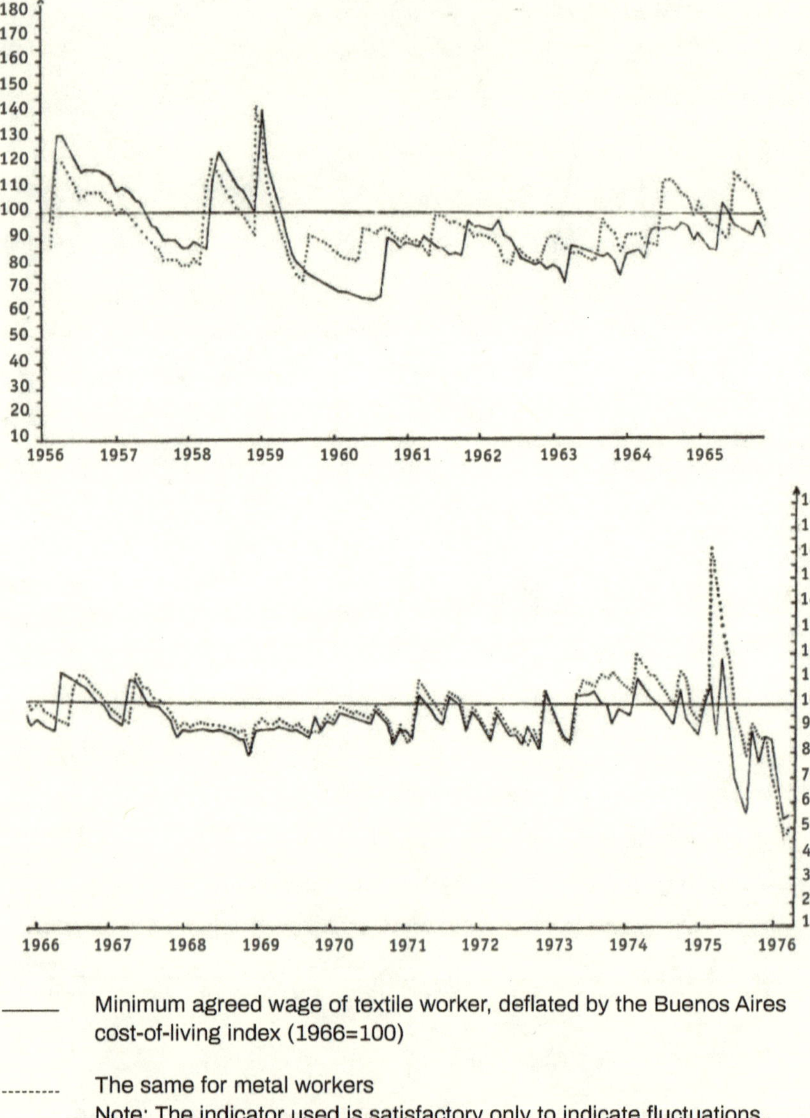

_____ Minimum agreed wage of textile worker, deflated by the Buenos Aires cost-of-living index (1966=100)

--------- The same for metal workers

Note: The indicator used is satisfactory only to indicate fluctuations, and not to show absolute levels of the wages charted.

Sources: Ministry of Labor: *Boletín de Estadísticas Sociales*, and Ministry of Economics: *Boletín Trimestral de Estadísticas and Boletín Mensual de Salarios de Convenio*

The characteristics of this popular sector and of this local bourgeoisie cannot be understood in isolation from each other. It has been their conjunction in the multiplying effect of their alliance which has made it possible to impose, again and again, the satisfaction of their immediate demands. We can now examine the characteristics and principal consequences of this alliance:

1. The alliance was sporadic but recurrent. It appeared only in the downward phases of the cycle, when demands for wage and salary increases and for diverse measures to relieve "the suffocation of the small and medium sized national enterprise"[66] concurred in the reactivation of the internal market at the expense of the pampean exporting sector. Once the cycle revived the alliance dissolved, partly due to the attempts of the local bourgeoisie and the unions to negotiate special agreements individually with the state and with the large bourgeoisie, partly because of the return of more "normal" class cleavages.
2. The alliance was defensive. It arose against the offensives of the upper fractions of the bourgeoisie. Its ideology of "nationalist" and "socially just" development overlooked what it was unable to problematize: the deeply oligopolistic and internationalized structure of the capitalism of which its members were the weakest components. It was defensive because in its victory it could not create an alternative capital accumulation system. All it achieved was the transition from the downward phase to the upward phase in conditions which were doomed to provoke the repetition of the cycle.
3. But despite its defensive nature, and although its victories signified the completion and not a way out of the cycle, this alliance was quite successful. It scored repeated victories in annulling the stabilization programs, limiting the domestic expansion of international capital, and launching economic reactivation policies and new "discouragements" for the pampa bourgeoisie. Thus, it is not surprising that the wage series of Figure 2 should also show erratic behavior; its

66 These are subjects and terms which recur in the CGE's demands and declarations; see, e.g., its *Memorias Anuales*.

peaks are the result of victorious struggles which soon led to marked reductions in wages. The upward movements of wages were accompanied by growth of the GNP and, in general, by higher profit rates for the industrial bourgeoisie as a whole—although, being also subject to the overall cycle, profits also seem to have undergone marked fluctuations.[67] The consequence of these processes may be seen in a phenomenon as intrinsically political as it is economic: the inflation which, as can be seen in Figure 3, is even more remarkable for its fluctuations than for its generally high level.

More basically, the defensive alliance was victorious because it managed to destroy the alliance between the two dominant fractions of the bourgeoisie. The large bourgeoisie, when the time came to weigh the immediate benefits from a revival of the economy against the political abyss entailed by aligning with the pampa bourgeoisie and the exporting sector when the remainder of civil society had joined forces against them, opted to support a new upward phase. Repeatedly the defensive alliance politically broke "from below" the cohesion of the dominant fractions and—economically—blocked the only alliance which could implant a new capital accumulation system and move the economy off its cyclical path.

4. The alliance was polyclassist, in the sense that it included the popular sector (with a strong working-class component) and various bourgeois fractions. Its repeated successes were based on this conjunction. But, on the other hand, this ensured that its orientations were nationalistic[68] and capitalist. Its polyclass character, based on the achievement of shared tactical goals, offered a popular base for the demands of the weak bourgeoisie. This fraction thus appeared as a "progressive" one which, contrasting with the large bourgeoisie's "efficientist" orientations and the "landholding oligarchy's"

---

67 At least using as a proxy the relationship between urban wholesale prices and wages.

68 Basically, it was prevented from uniting to defend the domestic market against the internationalized character of export-related activities and of the large bourgeoisie.

archaism, seemed to embody the possibility of a "development with social justice." On the other hand, the popular sector (especially the unions and the working class) gained, through the polyclassist nature of the alliance, access to resources and mass media which it could not otherwise have had.

In particular, the bourgeoisie respectability of the alliance made more difficult the harsh repression which has been directed at the popular sector elsewhere in Latin America when it has acted in isolation and/or in pursuit of more radical goals. The impact of this alliance stemmed from the multiplying effect of the concurrence of social actors who had their own resource base and who could cooperate in very concrete and short-term goals. In other Latin American countries, the absence of these joint conditions has meant that the local bourgeoisie has lacked popular support and that the popular sector (weaker, in any case, because of greater intranational heterogeneity) has not enjoyed the political protection of a bourgeois ally. This, in turn, has made it possible for the large bourgeoisie to advance unhindered, naturally encountering protests and conflicts, but not the limits and oscillations which this peculiar alliance imposed in Argentina.

5. Locked in capitalist parameters, the principal political channel of the defensive alliance, Peronism, did not transcend these limits. These limitations also arose from the experience of repeated victories and subsequent defeats. The political activation of the popular sector in pursuit of the goals of the defensive alliance, the protection granted by its bourgeois component, and the changes in public policies which it achieved, led, on the one hand, to a positive reinforcement of that activation and, on the other, to the solidifying of the organizational basis—above all the unions—which articulated the popular sector's action. Let us take a closer look at this.
6. In historical terms, the alliance stemmed from the fresh memory of previous mobilizations which had managed to reverse the downward trend of real wages and of economic activity. It was also a function of the low deterrent effect of a repression which tended to cease the moment the state, indicating a shift in the governing alliances, launched a new upward phase of the cycle. This increased the popular sector's capacity for and disposition to political activation,

but it also led to an equally repetitive experience of defeat: periods of low wages and salaries, and of mounting unemployment, during which the spokesmen of the defensive alliance were removed from the governing coalition.

However, in contrast with the transparent stimulus entailed by rising food prices and falling salaries and wages, the reversal of the cycle took place because of problems (such as balance-of-payments crises) and through mechanisms (such as devaluations and restrictions in the money supply) whose functioning and impact were harder to grasp. The benefits derived by the pampa bourgeoisie and the exporting sector, and the initial support lent by the large bourgeoisie to each downward reversal of the cycle, fostered the hostility of the popular sector against both fractions and against the internationalization and big business which they embodied. At the same time, the defensive alliance could not abandon its capitalist ideology and goals.

Thus, the interpretation of the sequences of such successes and defeats became a mythology of conspiracies of "powerful interests" which had a magical ability to defeat the "people" and hinder "development." Failure and tension generated in some cases a fascist ideological syndrome and in others a challenging of the capitalist parameters of the situation. But against these centrifugal tendencies a powerful centripetal force operated: as the CGT, the CGE, and Peronism tirelessly repeated, since 1955 they had been prevented from carrying out the kind of "socially just" capitalist development which, "placed on the people's side" and exercising wide control of the state's institutions, the local bourgeoisie and the unions seemed to offer.

The feasibility of uniting the "national and the popular" against the "landholding oligarchy" and the "intonational monopolies," which the short-term coincidences of the defensive alliance seemed to confirm, were expressed in Peronism's unusual appeal and were a decisive element in the great wave which in 1973 returned it to government. A further condition for this was that in the previous period the large bourgeoisie had ignored the limits of its supremacy and had tried to impose it unilaterally, even on the pampa bourgeoisie. The social explosions of 1969 and 1970 sealed the defeat of that attempt and, impelled by a great popular activation, forced the political withdrawal of the large bourgeoisie which, in 1973, lost its place in the governing alliance for the first time. Only then could the alternative which the main spokesmen of the defensive alliance claimed to embody be positively put to the test.

7. Rather than cycles we must now speak of spirals, inasmuch as—politically, above all—each swing of the pendulum, with its succession of temporary victories and defeats, sharpened the conflicts from which they derived. The actors were not classes, fractions, and organizations which retained their "structural" characteristics unchanged, beyond these struggles. Rather, they were the political, organizational, and ideological expression of classes and fractions created and transformed during and through this pattern of alliances and oppositions. In particular, the popular sector found in the unions and—politically in Peronism—an organizational, ideological, and political expression which corresponded closely to the limits of the situation. The mobilization behind the defensive alliance's demands, with its precise aims and polyclass framework, achieved frequent and spectacular victories. This explains the peculiar combination of impressive popular activation with economistic demands, which emphasized—as a token of its alliance with the local bourgeoisie—its rejection of any leap beyond capitalism. Precisely this militant economism, combined with the weaker fractions of the bourgeoisie, permitted repeated defensive victories and perpetuated the illusion of an alternative path of capitalist development.

   On the other hand, the moments of political victory and reversal—at any point in the economic cycle—were those when the temporary victors took the state apparatus by storm, seeking to strengthen institutional positions from which they would fight future battles when the situation was once again reversed—as experience taught them it would be. Of course, the unions were no exception to this: the history of the defensive alliance is also that of the extraction from the state of important institutional concessions. These, in turn, reinforced the possibility of renewing the mobilization of the popular sector. The conquest of institutional positions enabled the unions to cover the popular sector with a fine organizational net, from which they could direct it repeatedly towards a militant economism, towards the polyclass alliance, and towards the mirage of the "other" capitalist path which Peronism proclaimed.

8. These multiplying fusions of the defensive alliance forced the large bourgeoisie repeatedly to abandon the pampa bourgeoisie to a solitary lament at the falling prices of their products. Such fusions both impelled economic reactivation and opened up the political abyss of a wide and active "national and popular" mobilization which had somehow to be reabsorbed. By swinging from support of the pampean bourgeoisie to support of a new upward phase of the cycle, the large bourgeoisie closely followed its short-term economic interests and managed to remain the only stable member of the governing alliance. It did not lose its dominant position, but the peculiar conditions outlined meant that its domination had to shift continuously backwards and forwards. At the same time and for the same reasons, the channels of capital accumulation were repeatedly short circuited. These clues enable us to understand Argentine politics as a less surrealistic phenomenon than its "political instability" and erratic "development" might lead one to believe.

As I hope is clear, insofar as this discussion refers to the constitution of the classes, it also refers to the state. It is from this viewpoint—starting from and returning to civil society—that the problem of the state must be approached.

VII. The State

The state is not merely a set of institutions. It also includes—fundamentally—the network of relationships of "political" domination activated and supported by such institutions in a territorially defined society, which supports and contributes to the reproduction of a society's class organization. In the Argentine case the pendular movements of the large bourgeoisie and the difficulties it has faced in subordinating civil society as a whole are a tangible indication of a continued crisis of the state as a system of political domination. So are the defensive alliance's recurrent and partially victorious fusions. Out of this was born a democratization by default, which resulted from the difficulties in imposing the authoritarian "solution" that seemed to offer a chance of extracting Argentine capitalism from its political and economic spirals.

By "governing alliance" I mean an alliance which imposes, through the institutional system of the state, policies conforming to the orientations and demands of its components. The large bourgeoisie was the stable member of the governing alliance, but each phase was marked by a temporary change in its partners and by an alternation of scarcely consistent circuits of capital accumulation. That is why public policies were continually changing and hardly ever implemented, as the state danced to the tune of the dynamics of civil society.

The state was recurrently razed to the ground by civil society's changing coalitions. At the institutional level, the coalitions were like great tides which momentarily covered everything and which, when they ebbed, washed away entire segments of the state—segments which would later serve as bastions for the piecing together of a new offensive against the coalition which had just forced its opponents into retreat. The result was a state apparatus extensively colonized by civil society. The upper fractions of the bourgeoisie were not the only ones to hang on to it. Its weakest fractions and part of the subordinate classes did the same—another fundamental difference from other Latin American examples. Civil society's struggles were internalized in the state's institutional system in a way which expressed not only the weight of the bourgeoisie's upper fractions but also the peculiar characteristics of a defensive alliance endowed with a remarkable capacity for partial victory. As a consequence, this colonized state was extraordinarily fragmented, reproducing in its institutions the complex and rapidly changing relationships of dominant and subordinated classes—classes which could use these institutions to fuel the spiraling movements of civil society.

Such a state could not "keep at a distance" from the governing alliance's immediate demands and interests; it could only reinforce the cycles and swings. It was, quite clearly, a weak state; as a support of social domination, because of the recurrent (and increasing) weakening of such domination implied by the popular sector's mobilizations and the unions' bargaining power; as an institutional sphere, because it was deeply colonized and fractionalized. This meant that one possible way out of the cycles—a shift towards some sort of state capitalism—was blocked; the fairly stable and consolidated bureaucratic apparatus, with non-negligible degrees of freedom vis-à-vis civil society, which would have been a necessary condition for such a solution, was not available.

Another obstacle arose from the fact that at times when the large bourgeoisie was in alliance with the pampa bourgeoisie, the stabilization programs entailed an "antistatist" offensive aimed not only to slash the fiscal deficit but also to dismantle the advances which had taken place in a statist direction during the previous phase, when the defensive alliance had been part of the governing alliance. Those attempts blocked any trend towards state capitalism, by dismantling the institutions which could have encouraged it and by dismissing the "technicians" who could have carried it out, replacing them with others who would issue a string of "antistatist" pronouncements and decisions.

In addition, any movement towards state capitalism by the defensive alliance encountered the ambivalence (and, frequently, the opposition) of the governing alliance's permanent member—the large bourgeoisie. Feasible or not, this possibility was blocked *ab initio* by the dynamic of civil society.[69] It can be said, then, that at all levels the Argentine state of the 1956–76 period was an example of extremely limited autonomy. Its peculiarity was not only that it basically moved in time with the upper fractions of the bourgeoisie, but also that it reflected the fluctuating political strength of the subordinate classes in their alliance with the weaker fractions of the dominant classes. The limit of the alliance—which shows that it must not be mistaken for an equilibrium of forces—arose from the fact that, on the one hand, it had to cooperate in the

---

69 Even ignoring possibilities which would presuppose a change in the capitalist parameters of the situation, tax policies might have cushioned the cycles to an extent which would have modified many of the political aspects we have analyzed. But the ability to extract and reallocate resources by means of fiscal instruments (not only taxes on pampean land) also presupposes the medium-term stability of those instruments and their implementation and a fairly consolidated bureaucracy which can "ignore" immediate pressures from the interests involved. These conditions could hardly be met in the midst of the pendular motions and the consequent colonization and fractionalization of the state's institutional system.

governing alliance with the large bourgeoisie and, on the other hand, that it could only be a defensive alliance.

Could this defensive alliance constitute an independent governing alliance, excluding the large bourgeoisie (and, of course, the pampa bourgeoisie)? Only a crude mechanism could lead us to believe this to be impossible on the grounds that the defensive alliance contained Argentine capitalism's weakest and least capitalist fractions. In fact, it did happen in 1973, when the defensive alliance achieved an extraordinary but pyrrhic victory.

VIII. Provisional Epilogue

The experiment initiated in 1966 sought, on the one hand, to rebuild capital accumulation mechanisms which subordinated the whole of society to the large bourgeoisie and, on the other hand, necessarily and correlatively, to introduce a system of political domination which, reversing the preceding situation, would aggressively impose itself on civil society. I have mentioned the collapse of that attempt and how this made possible, for the first time, the conquest of the state's institutional system by the defensive alliance, independent of the large bourgeoisie. Recent history cannot be written here. But it is necessary to point out that this alliance could only briefly ignore the economic supremacy of the large bourgeoisie and the pampa bourgeoisie; a glance at the data already presented demonstrates how, after a brief truce in 1974, the cyclical fluctuations were repeated much more violently. Even before Perón's death, the intrinsically defensive content and limitations of the alliance had been shown beyond question. The old crisis reproduced itself with unusual acuteness and the local bourgeoisie had to abandon ship without even rescuing its organization. On the other hand, the exacerbation of "union power" could not go beyond a repetition, with increased force after the retreat of the local bourgeoisie, of the practices which had made it what it was: an aggressive economism and a search for new institutional advantages—pursued now from the very heart of the state institutional system. This cumbersome heritage of past victories created ominous gaps between the union leaders and their own class. It also generated conservative reactions, which threatened the substantial autonomy which the unions and the popular sector had retained throughout this complex process.

Perón's death, a peculiar "palace" irrationality, and a violence which speedily fed on itself helped to shake the foundations of a society and accelerated the spirals of its crisis; this happened with a state that too obviously failed to guarantee the survival of this capitalism. But beneath those facts was the fact that, when the defensive alliance managed, at least, to become the governing alliance, it ran up against its own limitations; the very reasons which had brought about its extraordinary victory precipitated an unprecedented crisis. The promise of a "nationalist" and "socially just" path of capitalist development was subjected to a positive test and the alliance's centrifugal tensions fired off in their opposing directions.

The great victory of the defensive alliance led to the paroxysm of the political and economic crisis, to the ebbing away of the nationalist ideology, to the implantation of a new bureaucratic-authoritarian state, and to the dissolution or subjection to government control of the main organizations of the popular sector and the local bourgeoisie. As a result, for the first time, the defensive alliance's political, ideological, and organizational supports have been neutralized. This has enabled the dominant fractions of the bourgeoisie to explore the possibilities for a long-term reaccommodation on more egalitarian terms—between themselves—than those prevalent in 1967–69. The implication of and precondition for such a reaccommodation is the dispersal of the defensive alliance. This does not entirely preclude a return of that alliance or of the spirals we have studied. But for such a thing to happen, the local bourgeoisie would have to set itself on a hazardous road to Damascus towards a renewed alliance with the popular sector; and it is not certain that, by then, the popular sector will still be confined within the ideological and political parameters which cemented the defensive alliance before its greatest and most catastrophic victory.

CHAPTER II

Tensions in the Bureaucratic-Authoritarian State and the Question of Democracy

Introduction

This is another text with which I feel a strong emotional connection. In "Alliances" (Chapter I in this volume), I looked back at the past and ended up casting an angry initial glance at a troubling future. In the present text, I examine with no less anger the situation of a BA state that had by then been in power (and wreaking havoc) for nearly two years, and based on that assessment, I speculate about the future.

These were times of fear, of the privatization of lives, and of a difficulty in envisioning a better future. Those in power, both military and civilian, trumpeted their speeches of patriotism and rationality: they, and they alone, knew what had to be done, and we had to keep quiet and obey, at least until they finished—who knew when—their heroic task of "cleaning up" everything.

At the same time, there were signs that some sectors of the military wanted to promote some kind of "political opening." Of course, everything that happened in this area would have to be tightly controlled by them, without deviating in the slightest from the requirements of "national security" or hindering the numerous "cleanup" tasks that, in their view, were still pending. Typically, in these cases there is no shortage of opportunistic politicians and enthusiastic intellectuals (or worse) who turn to "the liberals" (as the military leaders came to be called) to offer their support in exchange for a privileged and protected place under a sun that only they would continue to ensure.

This text is based on my previous studies on the BA state,[70] which had taught me that behind its imposing facade and capacity for repression, there are fissures and tensions (hence the title of this essay) that, upon closer inspection, reveal it to be intrinsically incapable of stabilizing itself in any kind of moderately legitimate domination. I felt it was important to show this, not as a merely intellectual exercise but as an argument against the enthusiasts and opportunists who, with their eager offers of collaboration, threatened to prolong the existence of that state. And drawing on the opinions about democracy that I had already expressed in my first book, I also wanted to argue that the desirable and possible solution, although it seemed distant at the time, was democracy, democracy tout court, not the poor simulacrum of the "liberals," opportunists, and enthusiasts. In doing so, I also took sides against those who still believed that, after a future collapse of the BA, it would be possible to make the leap to some form of socialism that would render the democracy I was referring to unnecessary.

Later, it became clear how, through events that included the spectacular economic—but not social—failure of the policies of Martínez de Hoz and his successors (as I mention in the introduction to the previous chapter); the disaster of the Malvinas War; and the fact that political forces committed to achieving democracy finally prevailed among the opposition (quite a significant achievement by Alfonsín and his supporters that I think is fair to acknowledge, regardless of how one might judge his administration), we arrived at the democracy we have today, which should never allow us to forget the horrors that preceded it, despite all its imperfections.

---

70 I am referring to *Modernization and Bureaucratic-Authoritarianism: Studies in South American Politics* (University of California, Berkley, Institute of International Studies, 1973).

Tensions in the Bureaucratic-Authoritarian State and the Question of Democracy

To the memory of Kalman Silvert, whom I admired.

I. Introduction

Reality is compelling. In 1974 I wrote an essay in which I focused on the BA states that existed at the time—and was convinced of the imminent reappearance in Argentina of this type of state.[71] In this essay I discussed the conditions that contribute to the emergence of BA states, but my interests had already shifted toward the study of the dynamic generated by the internal tensions of this kind of state and by its impacts on society. Now, at the end of 1978, with Brazil making cautious yet significant advances toward political democracy, with Chile and Uruguay subjected to systems of domination that seemingly face no serious challenge, and with Argentina in the first stages of the implantation

---

71 First published in English in David Collier, ed., *The New Authoritarianism in Latin America* (Princeton: Princeton University Press, 1979).—Editor's note to O'Donnell, *Counterpoints*. Guillermo O'Donnell, "Reflections on the Patterns of Change of the Bureaucratic Authoritarian State," *Latin American Research Review* (Winter 1978): 3–38, presented first at the Conference on History and the Social Sciences, University of Campinas, Brazil, and published as *CEDES Documento*, GE-CLACSO, no. 1 (1975).

of a BA, I would like to reconsider the interrelationship between the internal tensions of the BA and its impacts on society.

In contrast to my earlier essay, I will examine here only the first stage in the evolution of the BA and, within it, the effects of factors which previously I insufficiently analyzed: i.e., strictly political factors and, in particular, the problem of democracy. On a superficial level, that the possibility of a return to democracy is being raised by leaders of the existing Latin American BAs might be attributable to their "false consciousness" or to external pressures. At a deeper level, however, I will argue that profound and abiding issues are involved regarding the nature of this kind of state. I will maintain that the fact that the issue of democracy has arisen at all (regardless of whether it is qualified as "organic" democracy, "responsible" democracy, or even "authoritarian" democracy) is an indication of fundamental tensions within the core of the BA, as well as with the social sectors that this kind of state excludes.

This topic is important because focusing on the superficial features of the BA can lead to erroneous conclusions. The institutions of the BA often appear as a monolithic and imposing force whose rhetoric celebrates the superior rationality which they impose upon the nation in order to save it from its deepest crisis. These institutions also give the appearance of change and adaptation on the basis of the "impartial" and "technical" evaluation of the progress they claim to be making. Yet behind this facade, the BA state is subject to tensions—contradictions, dilemmas, and perils[72]—which reflect the extraordinary difficulties of consolidating a system of domination that can conceal neither the fact that it is founded on coercion nor the fact that its most crucial supporters represent a spectrum of society far more narrow than that of the entire nation which the BA claims to serve. Its domination is particularly repressive because, by the nature of its emergence, the BA entails an anticipated abdication of its own legitimacy. The BA arises from an overwhelming political defeat of the popular sector and its allies, who came to be perceived as a serious threat to basic parameters of society. It

72 A similar argument is presented by Philippe C. Schmitter, "Liberation by *Golpe*: Retrospective Thoughts on the Demise of Authoritarian Rule in Portugal," *Armed Forces and Society* 2, no. 1 (November 1975): 5–33.

is from this perspective that one must consider a topic which, under the BA, might seem as surrealistic as that of democracy.

II. Concerning the State[73]

The principal mediation [between society and the state] is the nation. I mean by nation the collective identities that define a "we" that consists, on the one hand, of a network of solidarities superimposed upon the diversity and antagonisms of civil society and, on the other hand, of the recognition of a collectivity distinct from the "they" that constitutes other nations. The nation is expressed through dense symbolisms epitomized by the flag and the national anthem, as well as by an official history that mythologizes a shared, cohesive past and extols a collective "we" which should prevail over the cleavages of civil society.

There are two other fundamental political mediations. One is citizenship, in the double sense of (1) abstract equality, which—basically by means of universal suffrage and the corresponding regime of political democracy—is the foundation of the claim that the power exercised by the occupants of governmental roles is based on the consent of the citizens; and (2) the right to have recourse to legally regulated protection against arbitrary acts on the part of the state institutions.

The second mediation, particularly important in Latin America, is the *pueblo* or *lo popular*.[74] This mediation is based on a "we" that derives neither from the idea of shared citizenship, which involves abstractly equal rights, nor from the idea of nation, which involves concrete

---

73 At several points in this chapter (each marked with an ellipsis) one or more paragraphs have been deleted because they repeated points made in other chapters in this volume. The notes corresponding to deleted passages were also left out.—Editor's note to O'Donnell, *Counterpoints*

74 These two terms were not translated because the most nearly equivalent terms in English, "people" and "popular," have different meanings. The meaning intended by O'Donnell is indicated in the text.—Editor's note to O'Donnell, *Counterpoints*

rights which apply equally to all those who belong to the nation without respect to their position within society. Rather, *pueblo* or *lo popular* involves a "we" that is a carrier of demands for substantive justice which form the basis for the obligations of the state toward the less favored segments of the population.[75]

The effectiveness of this idea of the nation allows the state institutions to appear as agents which achieve and protect a general interest—that is, the general interest of a "we" that stands above the factionalism and antagonisms of civil society. Moreover, the effectiveness of the ideas of citizenship and *lo popular* provides another consensual basis for the exercise of power, and ultimately of coercion, by the state institutions. They do this because the state can only be legitimated by referents that are external to itself, and whose general interests the state institutions are supposed to serve. As noted, these referents are normally the nation, citizenship, and, at least in Latin America, also the *pueblo*. From these referents there usually emerge collective identities that stand above the class and other cleavages that potentially arise from civil society. Each of those referents mediates the relation between the state and society, playing a crucial role in achieving consensus and, correspondingly, in legitimating the power exercised by the state institutions.

On the other hand, these mediations are the means through which the social subject, as a member of society, rises above his/her private life. Identifying herself in the symbols of the nation, exercising the rights of citizenship, and eventually making demands for substantive justice as part of the *pueblo*, the social subject transcends daily life and recognizes herself as part of a "we" which is the same referent evoked by the state institutions. Hence, these institutions do not usually appear as organizers and guarantors of social domination, but rather as agents of general interests expressed through the mediations of nation, citizenship, and/or *pueblo*.

---

75 The remainder of this section is deleted because it refers to themes that are covered in greater detail in chapter 1 of this volume [O'Donnell, *Counterpoints*]. See also Guillermo O'Donnell, *Bureaucratic Authoritarianism: Argentina, 1966–1973, in Comparative Perspective* (Berkeley: University of California Press, 1988).—Editor's note to O'Donnell, *Counterpoint*

III. The Bureaucratic-Authoritarian State (BA)

The BA is a type of authoritarian state whose principal characteristics are:

1. It is, first and foremost, guarantor and organizer of the domination exercised through a class structure subordinated to the upper fractions of a highly oligopolized and transnationalized bourgeoisie. In other words, the principal social base of the BA state is this upper bourgeoisie.
2. In institutional terms, it comprises organizations in which specialists in coercion have decisive weight, as well as those whose aim it is to achieve "normalization" of the economy [by means of orthodox neoliberal policies].[76] The central role played by these two groups represents the institutional expression of the identification, by its own actors, of the two great tasks that the incumbents of the BA are committed to accomplish: the restoration of "order" in society by means of the political deactivation of the popular sector, on the one hand, and the normalization of the economy, on the other.
3. It is a system of political exclusion of a previously activated popular sector which is subjected to strict controls in an effort to eliminate its earlier active role in the national political arena. This political exclusion is achieved by destroying or capturing the resources (especially those embodied in class organizations and political movements) which supported this activation. In addition, this exclusion is guided by a determination to impose a repressive type of "order" on society and guarantee its future viability. This order is seen as a necessary condition for the consolidation of the social domination that the BA guarantees and, after achieving the normalization of the economy, for reinitiating a highly transnationalized pattern of economic growth characterized by a skewed distribution of resources.

---

76 I use this phrase to refer to the tasks undertaken by the civilian technocrats in charge of the economic apparatus of the BA, whose aim is to stabilize certain crucial variables (such as the rate of inflation and the balance-of-payments) in a manner that will gain the confidence of major capitalist interests—above all, in the first stage of the BA, of transnational finance capital.

4. This exclusion involves the suppression of citizenship, in the twofold sense defined above. In particular, this suppression includes the liquidation of the institutions of political democracy. It also involves a denial of *lo popular*: it prohibits (enforcing the prohibition with coercion) any appeals to the population as *pueblo* and, of course, as class. The suppression of the institutional roles and channels of access to the government characteristic of political democracy is in large measure oriented toward eliminating roles and organizations (political parties among them) that have served as a channel for appeals for substantive justice that under the BA are considered incompatible with the restoration of order and with the normalization of the economy. In addition, the BA appears as if placed before a sick nation whose general interest it invokes; yet, because of the depth of the crisis that preceded its installation, the BA cannot claim to be the representative of that nation, which is seen as contaminated by innumerable internal enemies. Thus, the BA is based on the suppression of two fundamental mediations—citizenship and *lo popular.* Furthermore, in an ambiguous way it evokes the other mediation—the nation—but only as a "project" (and not as a present reality) which it proposes to carry out through drastic surgical measures.
5. The BA is also a system of economic exclusion of the popular sector, inasmuch as it promotes a pattern of capital accumulation which is highly skewed toward benefiting the large oligopolistic units of private capital and some state institutions. The preexisting inequities in the distribution of societal resources are thus sharply increased.
6. It corresponds to, and promotes, an increasing transnationalization of the productive structure, resulting in a further denationalization of society, in terms of the degree to which it is contained within the territorial scope of the authority which the state exercises.
7. Through its institutions, the BA endeavors to "depoliticize" social issues by dealing with them in terms of the supposedly neutral and objective criteria of technical rationality. This depoliticization complements the prohibition against invoking issues of substantive justice as they relate to *lo popular,* which allegedly introduce "irrationalities" and "premature" demands that interfere with the restoration of order and the normalization of the economy.

8. In the first stage of the BA that we are considering here, its political regime—which, while usually not formalized, is clearly identifiable—involves closing the democratic channels of access to the government. More generally, it involves closing the channels of access for the representation of popular and class interests. Such access is limited to those who stand at the apex of large organizations (both public and private), especially the armed forces and large oligopolistic enterprises. . . .

IV. Ambiguities in the System of Domination

What goes on behind the imposing facade of power of the BA? In what way is the rhetoric of its institutions, directed at an ailing nation which the state is determined to save even against its will, a sign of uncertainties and weaknesses inherent in this state? The BA is a type of state which encompasses sharply contradictory tendencies. On the one hand, the BA involves the sharp denationalization of society that occurs first as a consequence of the urgent search for the transnational capital which is a requisite for the normalization of the economy, and later due to the need to maintain a "favorable investment climate" in order to sustain the inflow of such capital. At the same time, the BA entails a drastic contraction of the nation, the suppression of citizenship, and the prohibition of appeals to the *pueblo*. This contraction derives from the defeat of the popular sector and its allies; from the reaction triggered by the threat that the political activation of this sector seemed to pose for the survival of basic capitalist parameters of society; and, once the BA is implanted, from the aim of imposing a particular social "order" based on the political and economic exclusion of the popular sector.

Such exclusion appears as a necessary condition for healing the body of the nation, seen from the BA as an organism with infected parts upon which, for its own good, it is necessary to perform the surgery of excluding the popular sector and its "subversive" allies. This exclusion involves redefining the scope of the nation, to which neither the agents that promoted this illness nor the parts that have become infected can belong. They are the enemy within the body of the nation,[77] the "not-we" of the new, healthy nation that is to be constructed by the BA. When the rulers speak of the nation, the referent is restricted, by the very logic of their views, to a far less comprehensive "we" than in the past; only those can belong who fit into their design—socially harmonious and technocratic—of the future nation.

Yet, like all states, the BA claims to be a national state. Lacking the referent of the nation as a comprehensive idea that encompasses the entire population, the rhetoric of the institutions of BA must "statize" the meaning of the nation—at the same time that, in relation to the normalization of the economy, the same rhetoric defends an intense privatization. Such statizing of the idea of the nation implies that its general interest be identified with the success of the BA in its quest to establish a repressive order in society and to normalize the economy. As a result, the state institutions no longer appear to play the role through which they usually legitimate themselves, that of serving an interest superior and external to themselves. Rather, under the BA, when the state institutions redefine the nation in terms of exclusion and of national infirmity, the power they exercise no longer has an external basis of legitimation and cannot but appear as its own foundation. In other words, domination becomes naked and dilutes its consensual mediations; it manifests itself in the form of overt physical and economic coercion. In addition, the suppression of citizenship, together with the prohibition against invoking *lo popular*, radically eliminates other legitimating mediations between the state and society.

The institutions of the BA attempt to fill the void thus created through an intensive use of martial and patriotic symbols. But these symbols must be anchored in some of the aforementioned referents if they are not to be merely grandiloquent rhetoric. The BA leaders also attempt to re-create mediations with society by inviting "participation"; but the state's denial of its own role as representative of the nation and the elimination of *pueblo* and citizenship mean that such participation

---

77 This organic image is, of course, reinforced by the doctrines of "national security."

can only involve a passively approving observation of the tasks that the state institutions undertake.

Under these conditions, the best that the BA can hope for is what its incumbents often call "tacit consensus," i.e., depoliticization, apathy, and a retreat of the population into a highly privatized daily existence. And fear. Fear on the part of the losers and the opponents of the BA, which results from BA's conspicuous capacity for coercion. And fear on the part of the winners, who face the specter of a return to the situation that preceded the implantation of the BA. And there is also the fear, on the part of those who carry out the physical coercion, of any "political solution" that could possibly lead to such a return. This last fear at times appears to drive them down a path of coercion that knows no limits.

There cannot be consensus unless the connection between coercion and economic domination is veiled. Yet the opposite occurs in the BA. Moreover, in the BA the proximity of coercion and economic domination juxtaposes two social actors—the armed forces and the upper bourgeoisie—who usually are separated, on the political level, by the mediations mentioned above and, on the institutional level of the state, by various agencies of civilian bureaucracy and democratic representation. That is to say, the decisive support given to the BA by the upper bourgeoisie, and its "bridgehead" in the state apparatus in the form of the economic policymaking technocrats, intersect directly with the armed forces. The upper bourgeoisie and the technocrats have a strongly transnational orientation, both in their beliefs and in their economic behavior. For them, the political boundaries of the nation are basically a useless constraint on the movement of the factors of production, on the free circulation of capital, and on considerations of efficiency at the transnational level. These views clash with what is perceived by these same actors as the narrowness of the nation and of "nationalism." Furthermore, these actors are the most fully and dynamically capitalistic members of these societies: they are unabashedly motivated by profit, the driving force behind a highly concentrated accumulation of capital that they claim will, in due time, contribute to the general welfare.

But a great problem in the BA is that its other central actor—the armed forces—tends to be the most nationalistic and least capitalistic of the state institutions. With their sense of mission, the martial values with which they socialize their members, and their doctrines of national security which presuppose a nation characterized by a high degree of homogeneity, the armed forces are the state institution most predisposed to define appropriate political behavior as that which is inspired by an introverted and exclusivist vision of the nation. In addition, the profit motive appears to most members of the armed forces to be at most of secondary importance, and sordid in comparison with the larger concerns and ideals that derive from their own orientations. Profit may be necessary, but in any case it should not become "excessive" or work against the mission of homogenizing the totality of the nation.[78]

V. The Nostalgia for Mediations or the Question of Democracy[79]

The existence of a BA is comprehensible only as an alternative in the face of the abyss of a severe perceived threat—both in the past and potentially in the future—of elimination of the capitalist parameters of society. I have presented the reasons for this assertion, but it is appropriate

---

78 After closely examining the orientations of the armed forces in the countries in which the BA has emerged, I am convinced that this is a valid generalization. However, this assertion does not preclude the possibility that in some cases the upper echelon of the armed forces might be controlled by groups more favorably disposed toward the orientations of the upper bourgeoisie. This greater affinity would doubtless mitigate the problems which I analyze below—but it does not eliminate them, since it seems to mean that the control over the armed forces exercised by this military leadership will be more precarious. The most important case of such congruence between the attitudes of high level military leaders and the upper bourgeoisie and the officials in the economic team of the BA is that of Castelo Branco and his group in Brazil, from 1964 to 1967. Another case is that of the Lanusse presidency in Argentina, from 1971 to 1973. However, in this case it was not the consolidation of the BA that was being attempted, but rather the negotiation of its liquidation.

79 No discussion of this theme is complete that does not mention the fundamental contributions of Fernando Henrique Cardoso. See especially his *Autoritarismo e Democratização* (Rio de Janeiro: Paz e Terra, 1975).

to summarize here the principal ones: (1) the BA drastically curtails or suppresses mediations on the basis of which consensus is normally established; (2) it reveals starkly what is the underlying, but not normally the exclusive, reality of the state—coercion; (3) it likewise reveals the fact that the upper bourgeoisie is the principal—and, at least in the initial period of economic normalization, virtually the only—social base of this state; (4) as a result of the historical context in which these countries have evolved, this fraction of the bourgeoisie is conspicuously their least national element; and (5) the organizations specialized in coercion acquire enormous importance within the institutional system of the state, while the values and behavior of these organizations are not consonant with those of the principal social base of that state—i.e., the upper bourgeoisie.

The suboptimal character of this type of political domination manifests itself in the fragilities that derive from the shrinking of the legitimating referent of the nation, the suppression of the mediations of citizenship and *lo popular*, the political and economic exclusion of the popular sector, and the fear by its incumbents of the reactions that may be brewing beneath the silent surface of society, as a result of the heavy costs that derive from the imposition of order and normalization . . . .

Yet how can mediations be created that would resolve for the BA "the difficulties that derive from the solitude of power"?[80] One solution would be, of course, to reinvent the Mexican political system with its dominant party, the PRI, which provides these mediations and at the same time efficiently helps prevent popular challenges. However, the PRI can be only a nostalgic aspiration because its origin is precisely the opposite from what occurred in cases with which we are concerned here: a popular revolution, rather than the terrified reaction that implanted the BAs. Another possibility would be that of a corporative structuring of society. But for corporatism to truly take the place of the missing mediations, it would have to incorporate in a subordinate fashion the entire society rather than simply restricting itself to being a form of state control of workers. Yet this is precisely what the upper bourgeoisie

80 Phrase used by the Argentine president, Lt. General Videla, as quoted in *Cronista Comercial*, April 27, 1977, 1.

cannot accept. With good reason, it has no objection to the reimposition of strict controls over the popular sector, but why should the upper bourgeoisie, an indispensable supporter of the BA, accept to be incorporated into a state that subordinates it? For this reason corporatist ideology, in spite of its important influence on many actors in the BA, is a utopia as archaic as it is unachievable. Corporatism can serve—in the form of tight control over unions—to consolidate a class victory, but not as a means of replacing the mediations between state and society that the BA suppresses.[81]

If some version of the PRI is not possible, if corporatism cannot replace the mediations which are lacking, and if the state's exhortations for "participation" bounce off of the silence of society, then the only solution that remains is the aspiration for the very thing that the BA radically denies: democracy. The use of this term from the BA would be inexplicable if we did not recognize that it reflects the fundamental problem of a state without mediations and, hence, of a system of naked domination. If political democracy were to be restored, at the very least the mediation of citizenship would reappear. As a result, many members of society would once again be treated as, and would see themselves as, participants in a form of abstract but not insignificant equality—in addition to the implication of the restoration of some basic legal guarantees. In this way, the basis of state power could be attributed to this source exterior to the state—a condition which is not sufficient, but yet is necessary, for its legitimation. The restoration of political democracy would also permit the resolution of another problem that arises from the lack of mediations and from the militarization of the state: that of presidential succession. From the perspective of the upper bourgeoisie, solving this problem would have the advantage of reducing the institutional weight of the armed forces, of allowing it to cushion its ties with the armed forces through various civilian groups, and—ultimately—of reducing the visibility of the coercion through which the BA supports its social domination.

---

81 I have dealt with this topic in "Corporatism and the Question of the State," in James M. Malloy, ed., *Authoritarianism and Corporatism in Latin America* (Pittsburgh: University of Pittsburgh Press, 1977).

But what kind of democracy? From the perspective of the BA, it would have to be one that achieves the miracle of being all of this and that at the same time maintains the exclusion of the popular sector. In particular, it would have to be one that sustains the suppression of invocations in terms of *pueblo* and class. Such suppression presupposes that strict controls of the organizations and political movements of the popular sector are maintained, as well as controls over the permissible discourses on the part of those who occupy the institutional positions which democracy would reopen. The search for this philosopher's stone is expressed in the various qualifying adjectives that, in the rhetoric of the BA incumbents, customarily accompany the term "democracy."

How long can a kind of domination endure which is based in "tacit consensus" and which is so overt—and particularly so overtly coercive? How long can a state apparatus sustain itself in the face of the silence and opacity of civil society? How many Franco's Spains and Salazar's Portugals can there be nowadays? How can the leaders of this kind of state help but search for solutions that would permit the system of political domination that the BA embodies, and the social domination which it supports and organizes, to believe that it can be extended into the distant future, and become hegemonic? These questions point to the weaknesses of a state which proclaims itself to be, and for a time is widely perceived as being, an imposing power. The terror of the incumbents and supporters of this kind of state in the face of the silence of civil society, their aborted attempts at introducing corporatism, and their nostalgia for democracy are oblique yet crucial expressions of the difficulties faced by a type of power that lacks both mediations and legitimacy.

But, how to democratize? It seems clear to the rulers that any move in this direction can open the Pandora's box of popular political reactivation, along with invocations in terms of *pueblo* and eventually of class, which could lead to a renewal of the crisis that preceded the BA. And for the BA alliance this outcome would be worse than continuing to rule without mediations and legitimacy. Moreover, if the BA emerged in response to threatening political activation, and if the silence that it imposes on society does not hide the heavy costs of economic normalization and the imposition of "order," is it not reasonable to fear that this threat would reappear even more acutely as soon as the dike of exclusion that the BA has constructed is even partially opened? Because of this fear, the restoration of some of the mediations of democracy is both the hope and the dread of this system of domination.

The philosopher's stone would be a kind of democracy which is carefully limited, especially in the sense that invocations in terms of *pueblo* or class are prohibited, but which at the same time is not such a farce that it cannot provide the mediations and, ultimately, a legitimacy that could transform itself into hegemony. The question of how this kind of democracy could be achieved severely tests the ingenuity of the "political engineers" who offer their expertise to accomplish a task which amounts to squaring the circle. Yet the goal which the most enlightened actors in the BA seek to achieve is clearly this type of restricted democracy. In cases of a high level of prior threat and crisis, as in Chile, a democratic alternative was not proposed by the state apparatus and was introduced instead by members of the initial BA alliance who subsequently withdrew their support: the Catholic church and the Christian Democrats. In the case of a low degree of prior threat, Argentina in 1966, the issue of democracy was posed almost at the beginning of the BA, as an alternative to the corporatist leanings of the governing military group. In Argentina in 1976, as a result both of the "lesson" derived from this earlier experience and of the underlying tensions discussed in this text, no pro-corporatists have appeared and the goal of restoring democracy also has been mentioned from the start, although the obstacles that must be overcome in order to achieve this goal appear more difficult than they did in 1966. In Uruguay, the topic of democracy continues to be mentioned, accompanied by curious contortions intended to preserve an image of civilian government in the form of a figurehead president completely subordinated to the armed forces. In the case of lower previous threat, Brazil, there was even an attempt during the Castelo Branca period to retain some of the institutions of political democracy. The authoritarian dynamic of the situation took the process in a different direction, but some of the initial elements nonetheless remained: the parliament, two official parties, and periodic elections for some governmental positions. In this country the experience with elections, albeit tightly controlled, has made quite evident the potentially disruptive dynamic that is set into motion when the alternative of democracy is raised, regardless of how surrealistic this alternative may appear to be when it is done by, and under the aegis of, a BA.

The nakedness of BA domination and of the alliance that supports it, as well as the highly visible character of its negative social consequences, generate the great issues raised by those who oppose the BA: human rights, economic nationalism, and demands for substantive justice. The great dread of a system of domination which is simultaneously so imposing and so insecure is the fear that the opponents—who, despite their silence, quite clearly exist—will galvanize themselves around these issues into one great explosion that will destroy not only the BA but also the social domination that it has helped to reimpose. The [1969] "Cordobazo" and the events that followed it are the symbol of this possibility, and not just in Argentina. The unsuccessful attempts to reestablish a cohesive and harmoniously integrated nation, the prolongation of the ominous silence of society, and the notoriety of the domination which the BA supports are the basis of the insecurity of this system of domination, which often tends to make it more dangerous and coercive. This coercion further biases the institutional system of the BA toward a larger role for the armed forces and further deepens the silence of society, which is exactly the opposite of what should happen if the BA is to achieve some legitimacy. Nevertheless, democracy continues to be mentioned, at times eclipsed but then reemerging in the official rhetoric or as the proposal of one or another of the groups that struggle for power in the BA.

The issue of democracy is important not only because it indicates the Achilles heel of the BA, but also because it contains a dynamic that can be the unifying element in the long-term effort to establish a society that is more nearly in accord with certain fundamental human values. The proposal from the BA for a limited form of democracy, without *pueblo* and ultimately without nation, is not the gracious concession of a triumphant power, but the expression of its intrinsic weakness. The ambivalence with which democracy is mentioned from the institutional apex of the BA and by its principal allies, and the evident fear of transgressing limits beyond which it would be too risky to advance in a process of democratization, does not generate its own contrasting negation as do other policies and impacts of the BA. The antithesis of the distorted and limited democracy proposed by the BA's incumbents and supporters does not have to be the political and social authoritarianism which is, precisely, the true and evident reality of this state. As a result, the issue of democracy, even the mere mention of the term, remains suspended in political discourse, and thus liable to be expropriated by giving the term meanings that supersede the limitations and qualifications that the voices heard from the BA try to impose.

The possibility of democracy may simply represent an invitation to opportunism for those who wish to use it just to enter into a game to be played with rules predetermined by the BA's incumbents. This possibility may also invite the imbecility of rejecting democracy out of hand because it is initiated from above and because there is such a careful effort to impose limits upon it. But what democracy can also be, if indeed the powers-that-be are not the only ones who have learned something from the tragedy of the Southern Cone, is the discovery of a purpose and style of politics that would not be limited to a careful calculation of the limits up to which it can be expanded at each point in time. It would be, more fundamentally, a struggle for the appropriation and redefinition of the meaning of democracy, oriented toward impregnating itself with the meanings carried by those who are excluded by the BA and constituting, together with them, the basis for an alternative kind of state.

There are circumstances in which the discussion of certain topics can seem useless nostalgia. But the fact that nowadays certain words, such as democracy, are employed at all cannot simply be attributed to idiosyncrasies, to tactics of accommodation with the international situation, or to false consciousness. Under the BA, the evident contradiction between the mere mention of democracy and the reality of daily life is much more than this. This contradiction is a key to understanding the weaknesses and profound tensions of the present system of domination. It is also an indication of the immense importance of what remains behind the superficial appearance of these societies—the importance of those who are excluded and forced into silence, who, on one hand, are the focus of any hopes for achieving legitimacy for the BA and yet, on the other hand, as seen from this same BA, are a Pandora's box that must not be tampered with. This implicit presence of those who are excluded and silent is a source of the dynamic and tensions of the BA, to no less a degree than that which occurs in the grand scenarios of this state.

Later on, after the first period of BA—that of its installation, on which this essay has focused—its dikes of exclusion begin to crack, fear dilutes, and some of the voices which had been silenced are heard once again. Then, more or less obliquely, but with a meaning that no one can fail to understand, these voices resound, not only throughout society but also within the state apparatus. These changes do not just involve the end of the silence imposed on those who were defeated by the installation of the BA, nor the thousand ways of demonstrating that the "tacit consensus" in fact represented a suppressed opposition. Nor are these changes merely a search for mediations on the part of some incumbents in the BA who know, on the one hand, that without these mediations they cannot continue to rule for long and, on the other, that by attempting to restore the mediations they revive the ghosts which they attempted, at such high risk and cost, to destroy. At such point, the fissures of the BA which are opened by its absence of mediations pose a great opportunity. The response to this opportunity—in terms of the scope of the potential democratization that it involves—in large measure depends on those who in the phase of the implantation of the BA are so radically excluded. But for a whole series of reasons, this still unmapped future lies beyond the scope of the present analysis.

CHAPTER III

The "Stabilization Programs" Negotiated with the International Monetary Fund and Their Domestic Impact

Introduction

Given the period in which it was written and the topic explored, this text ties in with the previous ones. At CEDES, we began a project to critically examine the economic stabilization programs being implemented in Argentina, Chile (carried out by CIEPLAN), and Brazil (by CEBRAP). For a variety of reasons, this project was never completed, but several texts remain, including this one, co-authored by Roberto Frenkel and myself.

This essay explores three main themes. First, it enters into a critical examination of the "adjustment" policies promoted by the International Monetary Fund and strongly supported by the governments of core countries (particularly, but by no means exclusively, the United States) and by international and domestic financial capital. Second, an evaluation of the policies of Martínez de Hoz and his people in terms of their theoretical assumptions and, above all, their failures in economic policy and the harsh social consequences. The last theme is an attempt to answer a question: How is it possible that—despite so many obvious failures in the premises of this economic policy, and despite the fact that it seriously affected the interests of classes and sectors that had enthusiastically supported the implementation of that BA—instead of learning from the experience and correcting course, Martínez de Hoz and his team stubbornly continued to insist on the same policies, adding to failures and costs?

Although this is truly a co-authored text, since Frenkel was obviously primarily responsible for the first two themes in question, I feel free to comment on how much and to what extent what we say there also applies, in terms of content and consequences, to the "stabilization" programs that were subsequently attempted with the support of the IMF and financial capital. Likewise, I believe that examining why such obvious and harmful economic policies were insisted upon for so long also helps to explain subsequent situations, including the preservation of convertibility and the "one-to-one" exchange rate during two administrations as seemingly different as those of Carlos Menem and Fernando de la Rúa.

In any case, as in the preceding chapters, these are lessons that, having learned them the hard way, those who lived through them in their youth hope that they will be reclaimed by new generations.

The "Stabilization Programs" Negotiated with the International Monetary Fund and Their Domestic Impact[82]

Roberto Frenkel and Guillermo O'Donnell

I. Introduction

This paper is the result of a broader interest on the part of the authors in the interactions between politics and economics in the periods preceding and following the establishment of what we have termed BA states in contemporary Latin America. Here we address one of the themes involved in this issue: the stand-by arrangements reached with the International Monetary Fund (IMF) soon after the coups d'état that abruptly cut short processes that were experienced by numerous actors (including, most prominently, the domestic ruling classes and their foreign supporters) as a profound political and economic crisis.

With this in mind, we will begin with an overview of what we understand to be the purpose of IMF guidelines and interventions.[83] We will then show how these guidelines and interventions, regardless of the current political situation, have impacts that are inconsistent with such

82 CEDES/G. E. CLACSO, *Documento*, no. 1 (1978).

83 This review is complemented by a few notes on the foundations of these guidelines, presented in the appendix to this essay.

guidelines and differ from those that tend to occur in more homogeneous productive structures. This will enable us to see how the state policies established due to the agreements with the IMF have impacts that are highly biased in favor of a small group of economic actors, mainly the sectors linked to the export of primary products and financial capital. From there, we will introduce a few specificities resulting from the upheavals in the productive structure and the system of sociopolitical domination that the implementation of the BA state seeks to "solve," as well as the ensuing efforts to reinstate a peculiar order in society. These processes intersect with the policies accorded with the IMF, which in turn are the main instrument of the new state in undertaking another of the major tasks arising from the previous crisis: the achievement of a no less peculiar "normalization" of the economy. Given this dynamic interplay between politics and economics, some of the questions raised in sections II and III are worth revisiting, namely those concerning the factors that may account for the adoption and maintenance of certain economic policies and the impact that agreements with the IMF may have on them.

Unfortunately, our answers will have to be very tentative. There are several reasons for this. One is that they are based on only a single case within the research we are conducting on various aspects of the global problem mentioned above, namely that of Argentina. In addition to the difficulties of generalizing based on a single case, a proper understanding of this issue requires a comparison, over time and under different political situations, of various attempts at "normalization" carried out in Latin America over the last two decades; this research is still in its early stages.[84] There is also a considerable degree of ignorance on our part due to problems that are not easy to solve. These arise from the fact that we can only offer a view on this subject from one side of it. In other words, based on information from the "recipient country," which

---

84 This shared perspective will be addressed through a joint project by CIEPLAN (Chile), CEBRAP (Brazil), and CEDES (Argentina) to study the respective "economic normalization programs" based on the implementation by their current governments. The long-term study of these programs in Argentina under different political regimes is the subject of Roberto Frenkel's research.

receives the premises, guidelines, and interests of the IMF (and, in general, those of public and private transnational financial capital), already essentially defined, having been previously determined in the centers of global capitalism. We are continually surprised by how little we know, at least from here, about the IMF and other transnational public and private institutions. We are referring mainly to their internal power structures, their main criteria and decision-making processes, and their ties with other segments of financial capital and with the governments of member countries. In particular, there is a lack of studies that identify this institution as an important player in the global political economy and the network of social relations that would help us understand the direction and main impacts of its premises, actions, and omissions. Without a doubt, the veil of confidentiality with which financial capital covers its operations prevents any empirical work from being carried out, as has been done, for example, on the U.S. Congress.[85] But we suspect that this lack is also due to the fact that the place to carry out such studies is the center of global capitalism, and it is there that the impacts of this institution are the least visible.

That is why these pages can only be a reflection—and an incomplete one at that for the reasons noted above—on a "part" of the issue: certain impacts and interactions in a case on the periphery. Thus, our aim is to initiate a discussion that will help minimize the shortcomings identified and, in so doing, avert the risk of adopting the IMF's views and criteria as the sole expression of economic rationality or, alternatively, as the result of omniscient conspiracies.

---

85 An interesting exception is Cheryl Payer, *The Debt Trap: The International Monetary Fund and the Third World* (New York: MR Press, 1974).

II. The IMF's Vision

The IMF formalized its "tranche policy" in the mid-1950s in response to the new problems posed by the financing of peripheral countries.[86] As is well known, the essence of this policy is the distinction in how foreign currency requests are handled according to the proportion they represent of the quota of the requesting member country. Applications for the gold tranche are approved almost automatically, and this first tranche applications are usually approached with a "liberal" attitude; beyond that, applications require "substantial justification." The nature of "substantial justification" was clarified in 1958, when it was decided that applications beyond the first tranche would receive favorable treatment when the credit, or stand-by arrangement, was intended to "support an effective program to establish or maintain the stability of the member country's currency at a realistic exchange rate."[87] The conditioning of withdrawals on the presentation and approval of stabilization programs became the IMF's main activity, especially through stand-by arrangements. The importance of this type of agreement increased until it accounted for a high proportion of the credits granted. The stand-by arrangement is an instrument created by the IMF in an impromptu manner, with no reference to it in the founding documents. Technically, it consists of the member country having the possibility of acquiring foreign currency up to a certain limit during a defined period, without the need for its situation and policies to be globally rediscussed during that period. It originally took the form of an open credit line for a certain

---

86 In late 1951, changes were approved to the rates charged, emphasizing the short-term nature of the loans. In these same resolutions, the duration of these loans was reduced. Shortly thereafter, the so-called Rooth Plan was approved, with provisions that anticipated future stand-by arrangements and set a normal repurchase period of three years, with a maximum of five. They also anticipated the "tranche policy," distinguishing between requests for support corresponding to the gold tranche and others. Cf. J. Keith Horsefield and Gertrud Lovasy, "Evolution of the Fund's Policy on Drawings," in *The IMF 1945–1965: Volume II. Analysis* (Washington: 1966), chapter 18.

87 *IMF Annual Report 1959*, and cf. Horsefield and Lovasy, 404.

period, which members could draw on without restrictions beyond those set out in the IMF's general regulations. However, it subsequently became the main instrument for imposing conditions on resources, forcing the adoption of certain policies when the request exceeded the first tranche. Approval of the stand-by arrangement involves the signing of a "letter of intent," in which the member government formulates and commits to implementing its policies after discussing them with IMF representatives. The stand-by arrangement is an IMF resolution that sets the terms under which the country can purchase foreign currency, including the policy objectives and procedures that it must achieve and use, as well as the criteria it must observe so that the IMF does not interrupt the right granted. The letter of intent includes benchmarks for economic performance and economic policy, which the member country must maintain during the stand-by period, and clauses under which noncompliance can lead to the suspension of the agreement. The agreement generally contains clauses requiring consultation with the IMF on certain policy decisions or renegotiation in the event that any of the objectives are not met. Through stand-by arrangements, the IMF tended to define itself as an independent and interventionist body, especially with regard to countries with less economic power. There has been a constant fine-tuning of the clauses in stand-by arrangements to "protect the Fund's resources against misuse."[88] From the point of view of the legal status of the agreement, access to resources can be interrupted based on the IMF's contractual right to unilaterally decide that noncompliance with the program may imply a misuse of its resources. But of far greater importance to the IMF's ability to exert pressure is the fact that it appears to act as a "technical secretariat" for the financial capital of core economies. Indeed, the IMF's agreement to a stand-by arrangement is considered by other sources of international financing as a sign of approval of the stabilization program presented in the letter of intent. The clauses on the consultation and evaluation of economic performance included in the agreement allow the IMF to regularly determine its approval or disapproval of the performance of the

---

88 Joseph Gold, "Use of the Fund's Resources," in *The IMF 1945–1965. Volume II. Analysis*, chap. 23, 534.

economy in question, so that, once the stand-by arrangement has been approved, the IMF exerts a kind of audit over the national economy that is of interest both to itself and to financial capital. The unwritten rules of international finance have led these financiers, both private and public, to await the IMF's decision on a stand-by arrangement before negotiating their own agreements, often for amounts significantly higher than those agreed upon by the IMF. By behaving in this way, transnational financial capital acts as a massive monopolist toward countries in need of external resources, imposing conditions that are made explicit by the IMF. It would be hard to find a better indication of the correspondence between the interests of financial capital in the economic evolution of the debtor country and the IMF's policy and evaluation criteria. We will return to this point after examining these criteria.

The quantitative criteria and targets that must be met through economic policy during the stand-by period constitute a program, the content and objectives of which are determined by the guidelines used by the IMF to address the problems of external imbalance and inflation. These phenomena are addressed in many peripheral countries through programs that, while not identical, are based on a common set of ideas that make up what we might call the IMF's "vision," which includes not only a diagnosis but also guidelines on the most desirable state of the economy of the country in question and of international economic relations. These concepts are expressed in the form of "technical" criteria, apparently indisputable as an expression of rational economic axioms. The IMF thus confers attributes of universality and objectivity on one perspective of the functioning of the global economy and on what constitutes the "optimum" situation for national economies.

Based on the IMF's conduct in several Latin American countries, particularly Argentina and Chile over the last two decades, we will attempt to summarize this vision. The IMF views external imbalances and inflation in peripheral economies as problems caused by "distortions" in the process of economic development. As countries seek to expand public services and accelerate economic growth, there is often a tendency for expenditures to exceed available resources, resulting in pressure on the balance-of-payments and on prices. Excessive credit expansion to finance consumption or private investment is sometimes responsible for this pressure, but the most common cause is large fiscal deficits financed by bank credit. The IMF explains excessive public spending in terms of subsidies to producers or consumers (including an "excess" of public employees), operational deficits of public enterprises (largely determined by their pricing policy), and excessive public investment. Inflation and balance-of-payments deficits are signs of imbalances caused by excess demand relative to available supply, attributed to an overabundant money supply generated primarily by public deficits and excess credit. On the other hand, market imbalances distort the pricing system—both domestically and in relation to international prices—due to state-imposed barriers to free price determination in those markets. It is this distorting state action that prevents the self-correction of imbalances. Excess demand on available resources would largely stem from the desire of various sectors to increase their share of limited national income. As a result of poor economic management or political incapacity, distorted relative prices are maintained, partly in response to pressure from these social sectors.

In short, the IMF's vision can be summarized as follows: there is a system of prices—for goods, wages, exchange rates, interest rates—that balances markets and keeps the economy stable. If inflation and difficulties in relation to external payments arise, it is because the price system is distorted by an excess supply of money and by obstacles to the action of market forces. This ideal system of equilibrium is optimal in the sense that it makes full use of resources and provides the best indicators for their allocation. In particular, the better the international price system is reflected, the better it guides investment and production according to the country's advantages in international trade. This view provides the basis for stabilization programs whose content is relatively simple: it is a matter of bringing markets and prices to their conditions of equilibrium, allowing broad action by market forces and eliminating excess money supply. With regard to balance-of-payments difficulties, the main objective is to "adjust" the disparities between domestic and international prices, which generally involves a significant change in the exchange rate.[89]

---

89 If the devaluation required to achieve this is considered too high, the IMF contemplates the possibility of "gradualist" policies that would increase the

To eliminate the "excess" money supply, the IMF establishes programs that include overall limits on its expansion, as well as more specific limits on the expansion of private and public credit and fiscal financing. In the latter case, control clauses may include quantitative specifications regarding the fiscal deficit, spending limits, and public savings targets. In general, public sector financial objectives require sharp increases in the prices of services and goods produced by this sector. The exchange rate and financial measures that constitute the core of the program are usually complemented by direct actions on prices and wages. In this regard, stabilization programs demonstrate a striking asymmetry in the treatment of goods and labor markets. When price controls and regulations are in place, the program usually requires their elimination, but conversely, when the IMF considers that the state has sufficient power to set limits on wages, the program imposes them. This inconsistency extends beyond the criteria inspired by the theoretical "vision" and denotes a socially biased pragmatism whose political significance is most evident in authoritarian regimes.

We are unable to provide an exhaustive analysis of the vision we have outlined here, but we must mention two lines of criticism of this vision, both of which emerged largely as a result of the debate sparked by our countries' repeated experiences with these programs. The first refers to the supposed optimality, from a welfare and development perspective, of the situation pursued by the stabilization policy. We refer to the objectives that the program is expected to achieve, under the assumption that its measures would in practice tend to place the economy in the desired position of stable equilibrium. Criticism of this aspect of the IMF's vision began in Latin America with the first postwar

---

exchange rate in several stages. In cases of very high inflation, exchange rate policy provides for periodic adjustments of the exchange rate, depending on the evolution of domestic prices; in these cases, the stabilization program aims at a gradual reduction in the inflation rate, but as long as inflation persists, successive devaluations are required to achieve the initial target change in relative prices. In these cases, the control clauses include specifications designed to tie the evolution of the exchange rate to certain price indices, in addition to the usual controls on the budgetary situation and balance-of-payments.

writings on development and international trade.[90] From that moment on, it was repeatedly argued that trade and the pattern of capital accumulation generated by allowing the international market to operate without regulation led to a persistent deterioration in the relative position of peripheral economies. More recently, emphasis has been placed on the fundamental inequality between core and peripheral economies in international trade.[91] At the time, the ideas that gave rise to the IMF were suited to the task of rebuilding the world that had existed prior to the crisis of the 1930s. But in that world order, there was no place for peripheral economies other than as producers of raw materials and consumers of manufactured goods. The persistence of these concepts—and the corresponding promotion of the old international division of labor that they imply—in its regulatory substrate appears to reflect in the IMF the specifically financial and commercial interest of the centers of global capitalism. These centers are partially but decisively unified in this institutional crystallization for the imposition of certain economic orientations on the periphery.

The content of these guidelines is more evident when considering the second line of criticism of the IMF's vision. This criticism is aimed at the theory that the IMF uses to explain inflation and balance-of-payments deficits, which serves as the basis for the policies that shape the stabilization programs. This aspect has also been a focus of Latin American economic literature for some time. Beginning with the work of the "structuralists,"[92] a wealth of literature has been devoted to implicitly or explicitly refuting the IMF's view.

---

90 Cf. Raúl Prebisch, *The Economic Development of Latin America and Its Problems* (New York: UN, 1950).

91 Cf. Arghiri Emmanuel, *L'échange inégal* (Paris: 1969), and Samir Amin, *La acumulación a escala mundial* (Paris: Ed. Francesa, 1971).

92 Juan F. Loyola, "El desarrollo económico y la inflación en México y otros países latinoamericanos," *Investigaciones económicas* XVI, no. 1 (1956); Osvaldo Sunkel, "La inflación chilena, un enfoque heterodoxo," *Trimestre económico*, Mexico, XXV, no. 4 (October–December 1958); and Julio G. Olivera, "La inflación estructural y el estructuralismo latinoamericano," in Osvaldo Sunkel et al., *Inflación y estructura económica* (Buenos Aires: Paidós, 1967).

There is no need to repeat these arguments here. What is important to note is that, based on these works, it has been possible to begin to develop a theory of inflation and foreign trade that recognizes the structural specificity of Latin American economies. In contrast, the IMF's view is ahistorical and abstract, in the sense that its diagnosis and the policy it bases itself on are proposed as valid in almost any temporal or geographical circumstance. The IMF's ideas stem from the neoclassical and monetarist perspective that has exerted considerable influence in academic economic circles since the 1950s. These intellectual currents "guarantee" the scientific veracity of the IMF's vision, which thus appears to have a monopoly on technical rigor. But this is not merely an academic issue. The IMF's perspective has become the official doctrine of several Latin American governments and has long been the language of most international financial institutions. It thus fulfills the important function of providing a logical, elegant, and simple rationale for stabilization policies that have had a profound and painful social impact. This reference to the IMF's vision as an ideological body supporting certain policies leads us to consider the impact of the stabilization programs and the international interest that the IMF appears to embody.

The level of the medium- and long-term foreign debt of peripheral countries and the trend it reveals have given rise to a growing sense of crisis in financial centers. Foreign debt rose from $36 billion (in U.S. dollars) in 1967 to approximately $200 billion by the end of 1976. Even more significant than the rapid growth of the debt is the fact that, during this period, international private banks replaced multilateral financial institutions and the governments of core economies as the main source of financing. A calculation based on World Bank figures estimates that of the $200 billion in external debt owed by peripheral countries by late 1976, some $120 billion (60 percent) corresponded to commitments to private financial sources.[93] It seems logical that the zeal of financial centers has been exacerbated by these processes, as the balance-of-payments

93 Miguel S. Wionzek, "La deuda externa de los países de menor desarrollo y los euromercados: Un pasado impresionante, un futuro incierto," *Comercio Exterior* 27, no. 11 (November 1977).

crisis in some peripheral countries may endanger not only their direct creditors but also the stability of the entire global financial system. It also seems logical that, under these conditions, international creditors would more strongly promote economic policies in peripheral countries that, through "healthy" balances of payments, would ensure the payment capacity of these economies. The Latin American experience shows that IMF stabilization programs are well suited to this requirement, promoting policies aimed at achieving balance-of-payments equilibrium, although their internal impact imposes a high cost in terms of growth and income distribution. Hence, the intensification of the influence of IMF concepts is not unrelated to the processes experienced by the global financial system in recent times. The IMF's vision and growing influence seem to correspond to the renewed weight and interest of private financial capital in its relationship with peripheral economies. In a context of greater demands generated by the spectacular increase in external debt, stabilization programs are primarily aimed at guaranteeing the external financial capacity of debtor countries. The IMF, acting as the "technical secretariat" of transnational financial capital, provides these programs with a rationale that lends them coherence and an "audit" designed to ensure the debtor country's fidelity to the agreed program.

III. Impacts of the Stabilization Programs

The objective of this section is to show, through the analysis of a case study, the recessionary and redistributive impacts caused by stabilization programs based on the IMF's vision. To this end, we will examine a few aspects of Argentina's recent experience.

Clearly, Argentina's economic and social structure, as well as the characteristics of its current situation, are not immediately generalizable. On the other hand, the economic policy that has recently been implemented in Argentina covers aspects and problems that we cannot address here, especially those related to the long term. However, our purpose in these pages is not to provide a comprehensive analysis of this economic policy, but rather to show, through an examination of a few of its aspects, the marked inconsistency between its short-term impacts and the vision that justifies and frames it. This vision largely coincides with the one that guides the IMF's stabilization policies, which we have summarized above.[94] For the purposes outlined above, we first present a simplified model of the Argentine economy, and based on this we describe, in terms of comparative statics, some of the basic impacts of the stabilization plan.[95] We will show that the mechanisms put in place to address the critical balance-of-payments situation impose a high cost in terms of growth and income distribution. Second, we will examine in greater detail the adjustment processes of macroeconomic variables, seeking to highlight the short-term dynamics induced by the policy applied, particularly in relation to the evolution of prices.

Two features of the Argentine economy, largely ignored by the IMF, contribute to the recessive and regressive nature of the stabilization plan. The first is structural in nature and is related, on the one hand,

---

94 Numerous sources can be cited in this regard. However, two are particularly clear: the document presented to the military authorities by what would become the new government's economic team, published in *Mercado*, no. 343, April 1, 1976, and the speech given by Minister of the Economy Martínez de Hoz on April 2, 1976, *La Nación*, April 3, 1976, 1–16.

95 The vision of the Argentine economy presented here is developed in A. Canitrot, J. L. Machinea, and R. Frenkel, *Cambio estructural e inestabilidad en la economía argentina* (mimeo) (Buenos Aires: CEDES, 1977), and A. Canitrot, "La experiencia populista de redistribución de ingresos," *Desarrollo Económico* 15, no. 59 (October–December 1975). Several authors have described the Argentine economy in similar terms: C. Díaz Alejandro, *Ensayos sobre la historia de la economía argentina* (Buenos Aires: Amorrortu, 1973); A. Ferrer, "Devaluación, redistribución de ingresos y el proceso de desarticulación industrial en la Argentina," in *Los planes de estabilización en la Argentina* (Buenos Aires: Paidós, 1969); R. Mallon and J. Sourrouille, *La política económica en una sociedad conflictiva: El caso argentino* (Buenos Aires: Amorrortu, 1973); E. Eshag and R. Thorpe, "Las consecuencias económicas y sociales de las políticas económicas ortodoxas aplicadas en la República Argentina durante los años de postguerra," *Desarrollo Económico*, no. 16 (January–March 1965); and O. Braun and J. L. Joy, "A Model of Economic Stagnation: A Case Study of the Argentine Economy," *The Economic Journal* LXXVIII, no. 312 (December 1968).

to the nature of exportable goods as the main source of wages and, on the other, to the weight of consumer demand by wage earners in overall demand. The second is dynamic and refers to the process of economic adjustment in the face of a reduction in effective demand. Both features and their consequences can be analyzed by conceiving of the Argentine economy as composed of two distinct productive sectors: exportable goods and goods for the domestic market. Exportable goods are mainly agricultural products, which in turn constitute the main consumer goods of wage earners. Given the low share of Argentine production in world markets, it can be assumed that international demand for Argentine exports is perfectly elastic with respect to prevailing international prices. Consequently, the export goods sector remains at full employment, regardless of the situation in the rest of the economy. Employment of wage earners in the export sector is low and demand for imported products is practically nonexistent. On the other hand, the domestic market sector consists of industrial and service activities, and its exports are limited, while its demand for imports consists almost entirely of inputs and capital goods. This sector is the main employer of labor. The consumption demand of wage earners and retirees accounts for about two-thirds of total consumption demand. Wage earners save practically nothing, so their consumer spending is directly determined by their wage level. The demand for agricultural goods, as essential wage goods, is inelastic with respect to price: when prices increase, the quantity in demand decreases, but spending on these goods increases; at the same time, total spending decreases, which in turn reduces the effective demand for industrial goods.

Let us now look at how prices are determined. The price of exportable goods (assuming subsidies and taxes) is determined by their price on the international market and the exchange rate set by the government. The prices of goods imported by the domestic market sector are determined by the same mechanism. The prime costs of this sector depend, in the short term, on the nominal wage and the price of intermediate goods imported or purchased from the export sector; consequently, given international prices, these costs depend on wages and the exchange rate. The price-cost ratio of the domestic market sector (the markup of that sector) is a crucial variable in the short-term behavior of the economy; for the moment, we will assume that this markup is constant in the short term,[96] so that the prices of the domestic market sector are determined by the nominal wage and the exchange rate. Therefore, given the international prices, the exchange rate policy and the level of nominal wages define the system of relative prices, including real wages.

Assuming that private and public investment, government consumption, and consumption by the non-wage-earning sector are fixed in the short term, the level of activity in the domestic market sector depends on the demand from wage earners, which in turn depends on real wages. Considering the previous observations on price determination in the domestic market, this implies that, given the non-wage components of expenditure, the exchange rate and nominal wages determine—through the multiplier effect—the level of activity and employment in the domestic market sector and, consequently, in the entire economy. Note how levels of activity and employment depend positively on real wages. Non-wage consumption does not depend on current profits; moreover, public expenditure on investment and consumption can be considered independent of the price system in the short term. Private investment is determined by long-term expectations, which may depend on current profits and activity levels, but it is hard to imagine that the relationship between the two is such that increased investment would be able to exactly offset the decline in wage-earner consumption in overall effective demand.[97] As a result, effective demand for industrial goods depends on wage-earner spending, which in turn depends on real wages.

Since wage employment in the export sector is insignificant, three different types of income recipients can be distinguished: two capitalist sectors—those of the export sector and those of the domestic market sector—and wage earners in the domestic market sector. The

---

96 This is a provisional assumption made in order to simplify the explanation of recessionary and redistributive impacts. We will return to this point and its implications for domestic market pricing below.

97 In contrast, the Argentine experience appears to confirm a positive relationship between wage consumption and private investment in the domestic market sector.

distribution of income among these recipients is also determined by the relationship between the exchange rate and wages. The higher the ratio between the currency price and wages, the lower the real wage and the greater the share of income appropriated by the export sector. An increase in the exchange rate translates into a proportional increase in the prices of exportable goods. If nominal wages remain constant or grow at a slower rate, the costs of the domestic market sector grow less than those prices. The variation in the earnings of domestic market entrepreneurs therefore depends on the behavior of their markup on prime costs and the magnitude of the decline in their activity.

The trade balance is also regulated by the relationship between the price of currency and the price of labor. An increase in the exchange rate has positive effects on exports in two ways: directly, on production in the export sector, and indirectly, through a reduction in domestic demand and a consequent increase in the balances available for export. On the import side, the recessionary effect on the level of activity in the domestic market sector leads to a corresponding reduction in demand for imported intermediate goods.

The simplified features of the Argentine economy that we have outlined are sufficient to show the basic impacts of the stabilization program based on the IMF's vision. It is worth summarizing its mechanisms and emphasizing their relationship with the most defining features of the Argentine economy. The devaluation of the exchange rate increases agricultural and livestock prices and causes a fall in real wages. This induces a recession in the activities of the domestic market sector. The recessionary impact of the decline in effective consumer demand is not offset by a sufficient expansion in economic activity, resulting in a fall in GDP.[98] Imports are then reduced and exportable balances

---

98 This is not a question of the logic of the model but of facts. Theoretically, it would be possible to determine in all circumstances the expansion of exports capable of offsetting the recessionary effect of the fall in wages. But in practice this is difficult to achieve, both because of the comparatively small share of exports (and investment) in overall demand and because of the lower multiplier effect of these expenditures in relation to wage expenditure. As we will see below, the experience we analyze is a good illustration of this general consideration.

increase. Devaluation greatly alleviates the balance-of-payments situation through its recessionary effects and its impact on income and wage consumption. The magnitude of the recession depends on the amount of the devaluation and the evolution of prices in the domestic market sector. On the other hand, the reduction in public spending and in the credit that accompanies changes in relative prices intensifies the recessionary effects. The greater the reduction in effective demand caused by the devaluation (further reinforced by fiscal and monetary policy), the greater the recessionary impact of the stabilization program. Regressive income redistribution is another significant social impact of the program's implementation; the measures cause a sharp drop in wage income, while at the same time increasing the income of export sectors, especially the earnings of landowners in the Humid Pampas region.

This stabilization program, the impacts of which we wish to analyze, was first implemented in March 1976 under the economic policy of the new military authorities.[99] At that time, the economic situation

---

99 The new authorities faced urgent external payment problems. They immediately obtained $300 million from commercial banks for 180 days and an extension, from the second to the fourth quarter of 1976, of public sector maturities worth $350 million. The economic program was presented to international financiers for the first time at the annual meeting of the Board of Governors of the Inter-American Development Bank in Cancun in early May. On May 27, missions from the IMF and the World Bank arrived in Buenos Aires. The World Bank was asked for several long-term loans and issued a public report that was highly favorable to the program. In mid-June, Minister of the Economy Martínez de Hoz traveled to the United States, where negotiations with the IMF were finalized to obtain the first tranche immediately and two-thirds of the second tranche by April of the following year, pending the Argentine government's presentation of the program for the first half of 1977. On August 6, the agreement with the IMF was signed, and $180 million was transferred, corresponding to $160 million SDRs. Alongside the negotiations with the IMF, a stand-by arrangement was negotiated with international private banks. In October 1976, a pool of North American, European, and Japanese banks, led by Chase Manhattan Bank, granted the Central Bank of Argentina just over $1 billion for four years at an interest rate of 1 1/3 above LIBOR. Negotiations with the IMF culminated in April 1977 when it approved the program for the first half of the year and released the balance of $100 million from the aforementioned agreement. Cf. *Boletín Semanal del*

was critical: there were significant difficulties in relation to payments abroad, with a clear danger of defaulting on commitments, and from mid-1975 onward, inflation started to accelerate, reaching peaks of around 30 percent per month. This acceleration was to a large extent the result of the previous government's frustrated attempts to enforce a stabilization program similar in certain respects to the one described above, but under conditions in which the unions had considerable bargaining power over wages. This led to an intense dispute over the appropriation of income, with the state acting as arbitrator in a rapid succession of recurring conflicts. However, during the first quarter of 1976, the Peronist government's devaluations increased the exchange rate-wage ratio by just over 70 percent,[100] while real wages fell by 22 percent over the same period. In other words, some of the main elements of the stabilization program were already underway when the new government began to develop its policy. In this regard, the most significant elements of the new stabilization program are—along with the increase in the exchange rate—the virtual elimination of price controls in the domestic market and the freezing of nominal wages.

Putting off consideration of the inflationary process for the moment, let us examine some of the instruments and impacts of the stabilization policy, beginning with relative prices. During the second quarter of 1976—the first quarter of the program's implementation—the initial wage freeze and the subsequent prohibition on increases above those officially determined led to a 37 percent reduction in real wages. By the end of this quarter, wage levels represented only 60 percent of those at the end of 1975 and just over two-thirds of the real wage level of 1960. Table 1 shows the evolution of the minimum wage for industrial laborers, based on its average value in 1960. This series gives an indication of the evolution of income in sectors with less bargaining power, although in the second half of 1976, and to an even greater degree in 1977 and 1978, actual wages exceeded the levels recorded by the index. Although there is no reliable

---

Ministerio de Economía, various issues from 1976 and 1977, and *Mercado*, various issues from 1976.

100 During the first quarter of 1976, the exchange rate for traditional export products rose by 137.6 percent.

information on this subject,[101] an estimate that includes the evolution of family allowances and a 40 percent drift—the maximum allowed by the authorities—leads to the conclusion that real wage levels in the first quarter of 1978 were equivalent to those of the third quarter of 1976.[102] Consequently, the impact on real wages after two years of implementing the stabilization program would be a reduction of between 30 and 40 percent compared to the already deteriorated level of March 1976.

During the initial stages of the program's implementation, prices in the export and domestic markets moved in line with the stated policy objectives.[103] As can be seen in Table 2, by the end of the first half of the year, agricultural prices had risen 30 percent relative to industrial prices, and this new price ratio tended to hold steady during the first year of the plan despite the resurgence of inflation, which we will discuss below. Subsequently, the new relative price scheme tended to weaken due to the effect of the reduction in international prices of exportable goods, the exchange rate policy, and the behavior of prices in the domestic market sector.

The movements induced in relative prices had a strong impact on demand, which was predictable. As shown in Table 3, during 1976,

---

101 Starting in the second half of 1976, workers with greater bargaining power were likely to have obtained wage increases higher than those recorded in the statistics. Subsequently, the so-called wage flexibility policy allowed companies to grant increases above the officially set rates up to a certain maximum percentage.

102 Calculations made by the Institute of Economics and Finance of the Faculty of Economics of the Universidad Nacional de Córdoba, *Comentarios Económicos*, Córdoba, April 1978.

103 While between March and December 1976 non-agricultural wholesale prices increased by 100 percent, the effective exchange rate for wheat exports increased by 360 percent and for corn and sorghum by 330 percent. Figures from the Central Bank and spreadsheets from the Foundation for Latin American Economic Investigations (FIEL, for its acronym in Spanish), *Indicadores de coyuntura*, various issues. In this comparison, and in other tables, we have used the March 1976 figures as a base. This is so we can compare the program's impact with the prevailing conditions at the time of its implementation and in no way implies that we attribute characteristics of normality to these basic figures.

despite a 40.7 percent growth in exports, total demand fell by 4.6 percent, driven by reductions of 8.1 percent in consumption and 6.2 percent in gross domestic investment.[104] Taken together and viewed from the perspective of the first quarter of 1978, application of the plan over two years had a distinctly retractive effect on demand. However, during 1977, especially in the second and third quarters, investment demand and export growth led to an expansion that caused the total demand for the whole of 1977 to grow by 5.3 percent. This expansion was short-lived, collapsing in the last quarter of the year, leading to a very recessive climate in early 1978. This is worth mentioning because it highlights an important aspect of the impact of the stabilization program on the Argentine economy. First, despite the strong increase in investment and export demand, these factors barely had a multiplier effect on consumption. Consumer demand fell by 4.1 percent during 1977, demonstrating its ties to real wage levels. Second, export and investment growth figures for 1977 were exceptionally high,[105] but the intensity and duration of their expansionary effect were poor. This experience tends to confirm the recessionary nature of the stabilization program: even in the case of favorable investment and export performance, it is still insufficient to offset the trend established by the decrease in wages.

The indices of economic activity follow the trend determined by the evolution of effective demand. GDP fell 2.9 percent during 1976, grew 4.4 percent during 1977 in an expansion concentrated in the second and third quarters, and returned to a recessionary trend beginning in the fourth quarter of 1977. Table 4 shows the evolution of quarterly GDP; it reveals the differential effect of the stabilization program on the export sectors and the domestic market. While the agricultural sector maintained an expansionary trend until the fourth quarter of 1977, manufacturing was the main driver of the recession. In the fourth quarter of 1976, after nine months of implementing the program, industrial production levels were on average 11 percent lower than in the same

104 It should be noted that 1975 was a recessionary year, during which GDP fell by 1.3 percent.

105 See Table 3.

Table 1. Real Basic Wage Index (Industrial Laborer) (Base 1960=100)

1976	
JANUARY	125.7
FEBRUARY	107.3
MARCH	97.8
APRIL	72.6
MAY	64.2
JUNE	71.8
JULY	68.8
AUGUST	66.0
SEPTEMBER	66.8
OCTOBER	62.0
NOVEMBER	66.5
DECEMBER	58.0
1977	
JANUARY	64.4
FEBRUARY	59.3
MARCH	69.0
APRIL	65.1
MAY	61.1
JUNE	56.8
JULY	61.4
AUGUST	55.2
SEPTEMBER	51.9
OCTOBER	47.6
NOVEMBER	43.7
DECEMBER	40.8

Source: Analysis of figures from the National Institute of Statistics and Censuses (INDEC, for its acronym in Spanish), *Boletín Estadístico Trimestral*, various issues

quarter of 1974; the brief expansion in 1977 brought activity indices at their peak—in the third quarter of that year—to figures similar to those of 1974, and the subsequent recession meant that industrial output in the first quarter of 1978 fell by 11.5 percent compared to the same period of the previous year. The level in the first quarter of 1978 represented 83 percent of industrial activity in the first quarter of 1974.

Although the entire industrial sector was affected by the recession, demand fell more significantly in sectors producing goods directly associated with consumption by wage earners. Table 5 shows the gross output of the manufacturing industry broken down by subsector. The impact caused by the fall in demand on production in the industrial sectors corresponding to foodstuffs, textiles and clothing, and wood and furniture can be seen in this table; in these cases, in order to find levels of activity similar to those of the last months of 1977 and the first months of 1978, we must go back in the statistics to the early 1970s or late 1960s.

The balance-of-payments reacted as predicted by the program. Exports increased by just over 30 percent during 1976, reaching a value of close to $4 billion (in U.S. dollars); imports fell by 23 percent, dropping to just over $3 billion dollars. The $900 million trade surplus, along with a net capital inflow of around $600 million, made it possible to meet financial service payments and increase foreign exchange reserves by approximately $1 billion. During 1977, import levels remained low, staying at nominal values similar to those of 1975, while exports, mainly due to the exceptional harvest of 1976–77, exceeded $5 billion. The evolution of trade between 1974 and 1977 is shown in Table 6.

Table 2. Sector Price Indices

	March **1976**	September **1976**	March **1977**	March **1978**
Agricultural wholesalers (1)	100	210.7	309.0	725.0
Non-agricultural wholesalers (2)	100	161.5	244.9	617.1
(1)/(2) (%)	100	130.4	126.2	117.5

Source: Analysis of figures from the INDEC, *Boletín Estadístico Trimestral*, various issues

By the end of 1976, it could be said that the objective of the stabilization policy with respect to the external sector had been achieved. By that date, the monetary system's reserves stood at $1.812 billion,[106] equivalent to almost two-thirds of the imports for that same year. However, the persistence of the policy and its own success with respect to the external sector placed the Argentine economy and the stabilization program in a paradoxical situation. During 1977, in addition to the $1.5 billion trade surplus, there was a net inflow of noncompensatory capital of another $1.5 billion, attracted in part by the differences between domestic and foreign interest rates. This meant that the monetary system's reserves reached $4.038 billion by the end of 1977,[107] a figure equivalent to the total imports for that year. The paradox is that this exceptional external liquidity and the increased indebtedness are occurring alongside a severe recession that is keeping a significant proportion of industrial production capacity idle in a country where the external sector has traditionally been an obstacle to growth.

We will now explore the impact of the stabilization program on the inflationary process. We feel it necessary to address this issue separately because the program's failure to achieve its stated objective in this regard has exacerbated the decline in real wages, the resulting redistribution of

106 Fundación de Investigaciones Económicas Latinoamericanas, *Indicadores de coyuntura*, Buenos Aires (March 1978). Based on data provided by the Central Bank.

107 Ibid.

Table 3. Total Demand (Percentage Change Rates Compared to the Same Period in the Previous Year)

	1976	1977					1978
	Year	Year	Quarter				Quarter
			I	II	III	IV	I
Total demand	-4.6	5.3	1.8	7.2	9.4	2.9	-6.2
Total consumption	-8.1	-4.1	-10.3	-5.7	-0.9	0.5	-2.4
Investment							
Durable equipment	-0.4	26.6	31.3	39.5	33.0	5.4	-30.1
Construction	-12.7	9.8	3.2	8.1	16.2	11.6	8.1
Exports	40.7	51.4	87.3	76.7	51.8	7.9	-9.4

Source: Central Bank of Argentina, provisional figures

income, and the depth of the recession. The combination of high inflation rates and a sharp contraction in effective demand constitutes an exceptional economic situation, similar to the results of another IMF-guided stabilization program, the Chilean experience after 1973.

In order to consider the impact of the stabilization program on the inflationary process, it is worth reexamining the model of the Argentine economy presented above. According to its hypotheses, the initial impact is always inflationary: the prices of exportable goods increase in the same proportion as the price of the currency, and the same occurs with the prices of inputs imported by the domestic market sector. Therefore, even if wages vary, the prime costs of the domestic market sector increase, albeit at a lower rate than the prices of exportable goods. The rate at which prices in the domestic market sector increase therefore depends on the behavior of their markup.

If companies tend to keep their markup constant—the provisional assumption we made above for explanatory purposes—prices in the domestic market sector rise at the same rate as their prime costs, and as a result, the average price indices of the economy rise at a rate lower than the rate of devaluation. In conditions of weak demand, the markup in the domestic market sector should be expected to remain passive in the face of rising prime costs; that is, it should tend to remain constant

Table 4. Gross Domestic Product (Percentage Changes Compared to the Same Period of the Previous Year)

	1976					1977					1978
	Year	Quarters				Year	Quarters				Quarters
SECTOR		I	II	III	IV		I	II	III	IV	I
Gross Domestic Product	-2.9	-4.4	-5.2	-1.7	0.2	4.4	0.9	0.9	9.1	2.5	-7.2
Agriculture, forestry, hunting, and fishing	3.5	7.9	-0.1	0.8	5.9	7.1	5.1	5.1	9.7	-2.1	-7.9
Mining and quarrying	0.8	-6.0	-2.5	3.3	8.3	8.8	9.0	9.0	11.0	3.4	-1.6
Industrial manufacturing	-4.5	-6.7	-6.3	-2.9	-2.0	3.8	0.3	0.3	11.5	2.6	-11.5
Construction	-14.1	-26.7	-15.0	-10.7	-0.8	13.3	6.3	6.3	19.7	16.7	9.2
Power, gas, and water	3.4	4.2	1.6	4.8	3.4	5.0	4.3	4.3	5.4	5.9	-0.7
Commerce, hotels, and restaurants	-5.9	-9.8	-9.2	-2.4	-2.1	5.5	1.1	1.1	10.0	3.8	-6.0
Transportation, warehousing, and communications	-4.3	-5.3	-10.2	-2.0	0.5	5.8	3.6	3.6	9.7	2.1	-4.6
Financial institutions and real estate	3.5	6.7	3.5	2.0	2.1	0.2	-1.8	-1.8	1.2	2.1	1.5
Community, social, and personal services	-0.2	1.1	-0.1	-0.1	-0.1	-0.4	-4.0	-4.0	4.0	-0.5	-6.9

Source: Central Bank of Argentina, provisional figures

Table 5. GDP of the Manufacturing Industry (Percentage Changes Compared to the Same Period of the Previous Year)

SECTOR	1976					1977					1978
	Year	Quarters				Year	Quarters				Quarters
		I	II	III	IV		I	II	III	IV	I
Foodstuffs, beverages, and tobacco	0.3	-1.2	5.6	-1.1	-2.1	-3.5	-4.5	-6.7	-1.0	-1.8	-8.1
Textiles, clothing, and leather	-4.6	22.7	-5.4	-6.1	-2.5	-6.0	-11.5	-5.9	-1.2	-5.7	-22.0
Wood and furniture	-27.8	-26.3	-35.5	-26.0	-21.0	-11.5	-24.9	-19.0	-3.0	-0.6	-22.0
Paper, printing, and publishing	-7.3	-10.5	-7.5	-2.9	-8.2	-4.8	-1.5	-4.6	-10.8	-4.2	-2.7
Chemicals and petrochemicals	-0.7	-1.3	-0.4	00.0	-0.4	44.1	11.2	22.5	7.3	5.2	-4.5
Non-metallic minerals	-4.5	-3.4	-8.9	-3.3	-2.3	-0.6	-3.7	-1.5	3.9	-1.8	-1.6
Basic metals	-24.1	-25.4	-30.2	-19.7	-19.1	115.4	00.5	7.3	25.0	28.0	-5.2
Machinery and equipment	-3.8	-12.1	-8.1	-0.6	4.1	110.4	7.3	99.0	21.6	3.7	-17.8
Other industries	-3.4	-0.9	-4.9	-7.4	0.0	2.4	33.3	22.0	6.6	-1.6	-7.6

Source: Central Bank of Argentina, provisional figures

or decrease by a certain proportion. Following the initial inflationary impact, one logical consequence of this behavior would be the slowing of inflation, even if successive devaluations maintained the relative prices desired by the stabilization program. If the economy behaved in this way, the stabilization program would induce cost inflation, but with a tendency toward slowdown.

This hypothesis of constant markups in the domestic market sector is based on the Keynesian assumption of a mechanism for adjusting the goods market by quantity: when effective demand falls, companies tend to maintain their prices, reducing the quantities sold and the level of activity. In inflationary conditions, the reduction in demand takes place at the same time as an increase in prime costs. Under these conditions, companies tend to maintain the price-prime cost ratio in the short term. Argentina's extensive experience prior to the current stabilization program reflects this assumption fairly closely.

However, with the current stabilization program, prices in the domestic market are exhibiting new patterns. The first measures of the program—particularly the elimination of subsidies, regulations,

Table 6. Argentine Trade (in Millions of U.S. Dollars)

Year	*Exports*	*Imports*	*Balance*
1974	3,930.7	3,634.9	+295.8
1975	2,961.3	3,946.5	-985.2
1976	3,916.3	3,033.0	+883.1
1977	5,610.0	4,100.0	+1,510.0

Source: INDEC, *Boletín Estadístico Trimestral*, various issues, and Central Bank of Argentina, preliminary figures

and direct controls—led to a sharp increase in prices. After this initial impact, the first months of the program revealed a downward trend in the monthly inflation rate, from approximately 35 percent in April to less than 5 percent in June and July 1976. During these first months, prices appeared to follow the historical model, with a trend consistent with that of wages and the exchange rate. However, at the end of the first six months of the program, prices in the domestic market sector began to accelerate again: in the following six months, the cost of the living index increased at an average rate of 8.2 percent per month, and the industrial price index (non-agricultural wholesalers) at a rate of 7 percent per month. During the following year—the period from March 1977 to March 1978—inflation tended to accelerate and take on a "spasmodic" pace, fluctuating between monthly rates of 8 and 12 percent.

The inflationary trend has had a significant impact on income distribution and may have an even deeper and more persistent effect on the long-term trends generated by the implementation of the stabilization program. The depth of the contraction in the domestic market induced by this policy is directly related to inflationary trends. The persistence of a "monetarist" vision and diagnosis of inflation justifies the renewed application of contractionary measures. This, reinforced by the policy of "opening" the domestic market to imports of manufactured goods, may imply, as it did in the recent Chilean experience,[108] the dismantling of a significant portion of the industrial sector and the crystallization of an actual wage level that sets back the income distribution pattern by several decades.

Hyperstagflation is a novel phenomenon. However, in order to examine the impact of IMF-oriented programs under such circumstances, we should point out certain elements at the core of the process. The phenomenon appears to result from the combination of certain stabilization program measures with the particular circumstances of the economy at the time of their implementation. As noted above, the balance-of-payments crisis that the program sought to address was compounded by accelerating inflation that had begun in mid-1975 and had reached peaks of around 30 percent per month. State price controls were overwhelmed, and black markets had become widespread, with the economy functioning as a set of highly speculative markets.

---

108 For an important contribution on the Chilean hyperinflationary process, see Joseph Ramos, *The Economics of Persistent Inflation and Hyperstagflation: Lessons From Inflation and Stabilization in Chile* (Santiago de Chile: PREALC, 1977).

One of the characteristics of this situation is the reduced capacity of economic agents to make medium- and long-term forecasts, with the corresponding reduction in investments in assets with those maturities. Another factor is the significance of short-term expectations and the resulting assessment of all information that contributes to facilitating their formulation. With inflation rates of this magnitude, short-term expectations must take into account not only future demand but also future prices of inputs and goods that form part of the company's assets. The key to this process seems to lie in the relationship between the time required for production and sales and the rate of change—increase per unit of time—in the prices of those goods. The short period of production and sales is less than the time required to receive information on significant variations in the prices of inputs and assets.[109] This means that the company's sales prices must necessarily include estimates of the future prices of these goods. Errors in predicting these future prices can be very costly, significantly affecting the capital of companies that underestimated their trend. On the one hand, these market characteristics give rise to an urgent demand for information for the formation of short-term expectations. On the other hand, a risk-averse policy on the part of the price setter will probably tend to overestimate future prices, increasing the expected inflation rate with a consequent rise in the markup on their current costs.[110]

The measures of the stabilization program respond to these demands for information, with consequences that run counter to the anti-inflationary objectives pursued. First, the disappearance of state price regulations, invoked as a key measure to enable the free action of the "invisible hand," increased the already high level of uncertainty in the economy. This measure eliminated one of the main sources for the formation of short-term expectations, reducing the visibility of the price setters while stimulating information requirements. In this context of reduced visibility and increased sensitivity, public sector prices and

---

109 Variations that affect expected returns and, in certain cases, capital.

110 In addition to its self-accelerating effect on inflation, this has an impact on sales and activity levels, as well as on income distribution.

Table 7. Price Trends (Monthly Variations [%])

1976	*Consumer prices*	*Wholesale prices*
JANUARY	8.9	19.5
FEBRUARY	19.0	28.6
MARCH	37.6	54.1
APRIL	33.9	26.3
MAY	12.1	4.8
JUNE	2.7	4.7
JULY	4.2	6.1
AUGUST	5.5	8.0
SEPTEMBER	10.6	8.8
OCTOBER	8.5	4.4
NOVEMBER	8.0	6.8
DECEMBER	14.3	6.5
1977		
JANUARY	8.0	13.8
FEBRUARY	8.3	7.0
MARCH	7.5	3.9
APRIL	6.0	5.7
MAY	6.5	6.3
JUNE	7.6	6.6
JULY	7.4	5.7
AUGUST	11.3	12.6
SEPTEMBER	8.3	7.3
OCTOBER	12.5	13.6
NOVEMBER	9.0	7.9
DECEMBER	7.3	4.2
1978		
JANUARY	13.4	10.1
FEBRUARY	6.2	5.3
MARCH	9.5	9.0

Source: INDEC, *Boletín Estadístico Trimestral*, various issues

tariffs and interest rates—determined directly or indirectly by program policies—“inflate” expectations, accelerating the inflationary cycle in the domestic market sector. In effect, both the evolution of public sector prices and tariffs and the interest rate are the result of having made the control and restriction of the money supply the primary objective of the anti-inflationary program. In relation to public enterprises, the reduction of the fiscal deficit implied a pricing policy that sought to “stay ahead” of inflation through periodic increases. The rates of adjustment of public sector tariffs and prices thus constituted an expansionary factor in generating expectations. In the financial area, the objective of controlling monetary variables led to a transformation of the sector and its operating methods. Policy in this area has shaped a financial market with a wide variety of very short-term assets that, given the elevated and fluctuating inflation rates, operates under highly speculative conditions. Directly or indirectly, interest rate increases were encouraged as part of

Table 8. Interest Rates on 30-Day Transactions (%)

	Passive	*Active*	*Wholesale price growth rates*
1977			
JUNE	6.1	7.4	6.6
JULY	6.6	7.2	5.7
AUGUST	7.3	8.2	12.6
SEPTEMBER	8.0	9.2	7.3
OCTOBER	9.4	12.2	13.6
NOVEMBER	10.3	13.7	7.9
DECEMBER	10.6	13.6	4.2
1978			
JANUARY	10.3	13.5	10.1
FEBRUARY	8.1	11.2	5.3
MARCH	7.0	9.2	9.0
APRIL	6.8	8.3	9.5

Source: Interest rates: Latin American Economic Research Foundation. *Informe Financiero Mensual*, various issues. Prices: INDEC, *Boletín Estadístico Trimestral*, various issues

the anti-inflation program. Intensive use of private credit was called for as a source of financing for the fiscal deficit, while fiscal contributions to provincial governments and agencies, public enterprises, and municipalities were reduced, urging them to finance their deficits through taxes or loans taken out on the financial market. Real lending and borrowing rates rose, with the latter reaching 8 percent per month in some periods. The following table shows the evolution of interest rates in the last half of 1977 and the first months of 1978. As can be seen, the real monthly interest rate fluctuated in some periods by as much as seven points.

With regard to the inflationary pressure of high interest rates, it is likely that this will not be limited to its contribution to the generation of short-term expectations, but will also put pressure on prices via growth in the financial costs of the inter-market sector. During the severe recession in late 1977 and early 1978, which coincided with a boom in interest rates, these rates reached real figures of around 30 percent per quarter for some industrial sectors, relative to their own prices. Table 9

Table 9. Relationship Between Short-Term Lending Rates and Growth Rates for Certain Wholesale Prices: Third Quarter of 1977

Sectors	%
Foodstuffs and beverages	25.7
Tobacco	10.6
Textiles	25.8
Clothing	17.0
Wood	30.4
Paper	16.2
Chemicals	16.8
Petroleum	34.5
Rubber	-0.2
Leather	38.2
Minerals	-1.5
Metals	6.1
Vehicles	7.5
Machinery and tools	6.3

Source: Prepared by the author based on data from the INDEC, *Boletín Estadístico Trimestral*, various issues

provides some indications of this, where the thirty-day lending rate has been deflated by the monthly growth rate of certain wholesale prices, accumulating the resulting rate for the last quarter of 1977.

A summary of the main impacts of the stabilization program we have outlined concludes that, of its explicit short-term objectives, only the one referring to the elimination of difficulties in international payments was achieved. The other aspects of stabilization are far from being achieved. Inflation continues to be high and erratic, and "pricing freedom," apparently imposed for anti-inflationary purposes, has meant a loss in state regulation and control. There is a similar situation in the capital market, where, under the cover of inflation, intense speculation is taking place, now with significant participation by foreign financial capital,[111] creating an unstable financial situation that reduces the state's room for maneuver. Productive investment has fallen, and the conditions generated by the program do not appear to have attracted direct investment from transnational companies. The long-awaited reestablishment of long-term "confidence" on the part of the local bourgeoisie and transnational investors has not been achieved,[112] nor does it seem achievable in the near future, given domestic market trends and inflation. The counterpart to these results is recession, a sharp reduction in wage income, and the consequent regressive redistribution of income.

It is not easy to find industrial sectors that can be considered beneficiaries of this economic policy.[113] Although, as in all recessions, some

---

111 During the last quarter of 1977 and the first quarter of 1978, private financial capital inflows exceeded $1 billion. See Central Bank of Argentina spreadsheets.

112 During 1977, capital inflows for direct investment amounted to only $52 million. See ibid.

113 This assessment focuses on companies in terms of sectoral activities and the short term. There is no doubt that many industrialists have amassed substantial profits during this period through commercial and financial speculation. However, we do not intend to refer here to the long-term accumulation strategy that could be implicit in the short-term measures of the stabilization program. In this regard, our assessment in this text is limited to the framework of objectives explicitly stated by government authorities. An example of these objectives is formulated, for example, in the memorandum

groups have expanded at the expense of others, the contraction of the domestic market has affected industrial activity to such an extent that in some sectors one has to go back ten years to find production levels similar to those currently being recorded. The direct beneficiaries of this economic policy should be the traditional export sectors, which the program cites as the backbone of the economy's reorganization. However, inflation and the most recent exchange rate policy have significantly eroded the advantages initially granted by the program. The sectors involved in financial speculation are certain to benefit, as a significant proportion of corporate profits have flowed into these areas.

While it is difficult to identify direct beneficiaries of the stabilization program among domestic social actors, this is not the case at the international level. The critical balance-of-payments situation was quickly overcome by the stabilization program, allowing for the comfortable payment of $1.1 billion for financial services during 1976 and 1977.[114] International creditors can point to the "success" of the Argentine stabilization program as an example. Not only have they been paid on time, but they have also been provided with a guarantee in the form of foreign exchange reserves equivalent to fifteen months of imports.[115] They could hardly be more satisfied with the success of the recommendations spelled out in the IMF's vision.

We will now turn to the internal political processes through which, with the establishment of a BA state, the stabilization programs agreed upon with the IMF are being carried out.

---

that forms the technical basis of the agreement with the IMF for the first half of 1977; *Boletín Semanal del Ministerio de Economía*, no. 179, May 2, 1977.

114 Figures from the Central Bank of Argentina.

115 Up to March 31, 1978. Considering the level of the reserves as of December 31, 1977, and the imports for the year 1977, Argentina ranks first in the world in terms of external liquidity ratios (reserves/annual imports). Argentina's ratio is double that of the country that follows it in the ranking. IMF, *International Financial Statistics* (March 1977).

IV. Internal Political Processes

Roberto Campos, Otávio Bulhões, Jorge Cauas, Guillermo Vega Villegas, Adalbert Krieger Vasena, and José A. Martínez de Hoz—the heads of the stabilization programs undertaken by contemporary Latin American central banks—all had something in common: before taking up their respective ministerial posts, they belonged to a circle that, in each of their countries, had fluid contacts and personal dealings with international financial institutions, both public and private. In fact, they were part of those circles at the local level. That was one of the reasons they were appointed. Beginning in 1964 in Brazil, the abrupt implementation of the BA[116] was an attempt to end what many saw as a deep political and economic crisis. This involved, with varying degrees of severity from case to case, high inflation and an acute balance-of-payments crisis. To resolve this crisis, it seemed crucial to agree with the "international financial community"—starting with the IMF—on a package of policies that would make it possible to obtain the necessary contributions to alleviate the crisis. Who better than these ministers to head north with these programs? They already enjoyed prestige there and shared the belief that the measures and goals of these programs embodied an economic rationality that was essential to pulling their countries out of crisis. We will explain various issues raised by these statements, but it is worth noting that the above remarks point to a complex problem of causality. It is simplistic to believe that "someone" imposed these programs from the outside. But it is also simplistic (or diplomatic) to claim that a particular government "freely" chose a certain program that was then approved by the IMF. What we have in reality is a confluence of determinations or, if you will, an overdetermination: we believe that without the need to receive the IMF's blessing, the stabilization program adopted by these ministers would have been similar to the one they agreed upon with the IMF. On the other hand, even if the respective economic teams had been unconvinced of the

116 On this state, see Guillermo O'Donnell, "Reflexiones," and "Tensiones en el Estado burocrático-autoritario y la cuestión de la democracia," CEDES/GE-CLACSO, no. 11 (1978). [The latter is included as Chapter II of this book.]

wisdom of these policies, the need to formulate a program that satisfied the IMF and the "international financial community" would also have led to a program similar to the one that was actually agreed upon. This confluence is one of the points we are interested in exploring here.

There is no need to repeat the analyses carried out in other works already cited. We will simply outline a few points that are essential to the topic at hand. The implementation of the BA occurs as a fearful response to what many see as a deep economic crisis. On the political side, it is seen as a great "disorder" and, consequently, as a decline in the state's ability to guarantee the current system of domination, that is, as a threat of societal collapse. This sense of threat unites the bourgeoisie around its fundamental interest in reproducing itself as a class and propels it to support a coup that, imbued with notions of "national security" that converge on the same result, is unleashed by the armed forces. In addition, the sense of "disorder" and "insolence" among previously passive sectors and the economic uncertainties they suffer also motivate a large part of the middle classes to support the abrupt interruption of that process. This sets the stage for the two major tasks that the resulting government sets out for itself. The first of these is the reestablishment of "order." This involves adopting measures to dismantle the threatening popular political mobilization, eliminate its forms of political expression, and control the unions. This, along with the concomitant dismantling of institutions of political democracy, results in the political exclusion of the popular sector and its allies. The second major task is the "normalization" of the economy: that is, stabilizing some crucial variables and, in the longer term, supposedly reactivating economic growth based on a more efficient and "healthy" productive structure. But these goals come up against serious obstacles.

First, the political and economic uncertainties of the preceding period led almost everyone—including the bourgeoisie—to engage in speculative behavior, which in turn fueled the crisis. This resulted in a decline in investment, capital flight, and a disruption of the circuits of capital accumulation. Second, this was reflected in and reinforced by inflation that, especially in the cases of Chile in 1973 and Argentina in 1976, grew at a rate that was as fast as it was erratic. On the other hand, there was a tendency to slow down the overall growth rate of the economy, which, in turn, was approaching its breaking point on another front—that of the balance-of-payments.

It is in this context that the aforementioned stabilization programs are introduced. As mentioned above, they are primarily aimed at relieving pressure on the most manageable aspect of the economy: the balance-of-payments. This involves not only the urgent inflow of essential credit for this purpose, but also the possibility of renegotiating an external debt that the previous crisis has made more urgent, and the restoration of more fluid conditions for other real and financial international transactions. To the extent that the crisis, in one of its most immediate manifestations, appears on the balance-of-payments side, and that its relief requires some kind of solution at that level, the problem "naturally" falls within the IMF's purview. From this point, policies follow—based on the logic we have examined—, and adopting these policies is a requirement to receive the requested support from the perspective of the IMF and the "international financial community."

It is crucial for new governments and their internal contributions to restore "international confidence." This is no easy task. For now, it is a matter of reversing a previous situation that generated deep pessimism about future prospects. That assessment was not only of a particular government but also with respect to a "country" that had such explosive potential that it ended up in that situation. Given this, and despite efforts to reimpose order, restoring confidence in the future of that economy also requires a guarantee that order will be maintained for as long as those who decide to risk capital in those countries are willing to do so. The political exclusion of the popular sector and its allies is the main component of that guarantee. But the guarantee of the future continuity of this situation also implies that the popular sector—especially the working class and public employees—will lose the ability to participate in decisions about their income. This leads to complementary measures on the part of the government to control unions, such as the suppression of the right to strike and the freezing of wages, and others that we will not describe in detail here, that lead to a severe negative redistribution of income. The consequence of this is the economic exclusion of the popular sector. This issue (which is one aspect of the imposition of a class-based order) involves the guarantee that these controls will be maintained for as long as those assessing the new economic situation deem necessary.

After all, the history of these countries shows repeated attempts to establish "strong" governments and, with or without them, to carry out stabilization programs that were aborted by political activism and the ability of the popular sector and its allies to formulate economic demands. That is why, in order to build the trust that is needed, a new "strong" government, a "sound" economic program, and "prestigious" ministers are not enough. These things are necessary, but it is also essential to convince people that "this time" all of it will last.[117]

Somewhat perversely, the very depth of the preceding crisis lends credence to this argument. The greater the crisis, the greater the efforts and costs required to impose "order," making it seem more likely that a point of no return has been reached in terms of returning to the "demagoguery" of the previous period. But this is not enough. Those who occupy the highest positions in the state apparatus are those who have earned them by having imposed the rupture: the armed forces. And they are, institutionally, the segment of the state and the social group that is, in principle, least consistent with the stabilization policies to be undertaken and with their executors. How can the socialization of the armed forces, reinforced by conceptions of national security centered on the empowerment of the nation, be reconciled with the orientations—and consequences—of an economic policy that in so many ways implies the opposite? Internationalization of the productive structure, criteria of "efficiency" taking precedence over considerations of origin or location of capital control, and dismantling of part of industry, especially its most fragile part, which is, not coincidentally, the part that is unequivocally in national hands, among others. This enigma cannot be deciphered at the level of the actors' orientations and discourses. Nor can it be fully deciphered here. Suffice it to say that, for the period we are concerned with in this essay—that of the adoption and initial implementation of stabilization programs—there is

117 Should further proof be needed, Argentina's previous bureaucratic-authoritarian experiment of 1966–70 serves as a clear example. After the successes achieved by its relatively unorthodox stabilization program (which in turn was related to a significantly less severe preceding crisis), the major social upheavals of 1969 led to a swift erosion of trust and an exacerbated recurrence of the crisis that the 1966 coup had been thought to have eliminated.

one factor that, despite the differences noted, is shared by members of the armed forces and economic "technocrats" alike. That is, the feeling that the depth of the previous crisis demands action without concessions or hesitation. The nation appears to the armed forces as a sick body that needs an occasionally terrible surgery to be saved. For those "technocrats," it appears, at the same time, as an opportunity to introduce another scalpel: that of a vision of the economy in which the suppression of "politics" saves it from "demagogic temptations" and from the pressures that for so many years prevented them from acting "as they should," thoroughly and for as long as necessary to achieve results. Therefore, for a short period, while both approaches believe they are facing a similar evil, they can understand each other by speaking of the similarity of the difficult tasks—order and normalization—that each, with its own tools, has had to undertake.

The second major problem with these policies is that not only do they not benefit the excluded, but they also severely punish many of those who supported the coup. From the above, it is clear that the beneficiaries of these programs are far fewer than those who support the implementation of the BA. The imperative to reduce the fiscal deficit leads to a sharp drop in the incomes of public employees and promotes layoffs that highlight the uncertainty of their precarious incomes. On the other hand, the recession, the shortage of liquidity and credit, and the advances in the concentration of the productive structure punish a broad swath ranging from small businesses (thus uniting—through their shared fate—nearly the entire petty bourgeoisie that had recently mobilized against the "disorder") to, as we have already pointed out, a large part of the industrial and commercial bourgeoisie. It is not only a question of the decrease in their income or the increase in bankruptcies. The problem also arises from the lack of protection afforded to various bourgeois fractions in the face of the oligopolistic—and more internationalized—layers of the bourgeoisie itself. Many companies find that they have lost the state, which was certainly "demagogic" but also nationalist and protective in previous periods, and that this has happened at a time in which the recession is greatly reducing their economic space.[118]

118 For an initial overview of these issues, see Guillermo O'Donnell, "Notas para el estudio de la burguesía industrial local en sus relaciones con el capital

It is not just a matter, then, of ensuring the continuity of these policies against the opposition of the excluded. It is also a question of ensuring continuity in the face of the complaints of those who were part of the alliance that promoted the establishment of that state. Furthermore, some of them are bourgeois strata that are difficult to repress and unlikely to have promoted the threatening processes of the past. In addition, the middle classes and the local bourgeoisie can put forward an argument more in line with that of the "technocrats" than with the orientations of the other great pillar of the state, the armed forces. Indeed, how can we think about strengthening the nation if, in the long-term extrapolation of those policies, we find a productive structure dismantled in the name of cold "efficiency," with a local bourgeoisie so weak and—in terms of the statements of those " technocrats," not in terms of the results that have since been observed—with a state apparatus that is also dismantled? How, on the other hand, is it possible to reconcile these goals with a process that, as we have seen, seeks to favor export-related sectors and promotes financial capital to the detriment of productive activities that, for better or worse, were generating an industrial and commercial bourgeoisie that—after the exultations of the month that followed the coup—discovers it has to fight hard to find a place for itself in this new state? How, too—a strong argument for anti-subversive concerns—is it possible to guarantee that masses of people employed in this way will remain silent indefinitely given that this is not a credible scenario?

However, with the exception of Argentina in its previous bureaucratic-authoritarian experience, the "technocrats" of the stabilization programs and their policies have remained in office much longer than a survey of their main allies in the state apparatus would suggest. Why? Despite the opposition of the excluded, of the complaints and fissures of many of their original allies, and of the ambiguities of a significant portion of the armed forces, this defiance of the law of gravity can be attributed to two main reasons. The first, which is only an apparent paradox, is that these policies are failing even according to their own

---

internacional y el aparato estatal," CEORS Document, no. 12 (1978), and Latin American Institute for Transnational Studies (ILET, for its acronym in Spanish). [Included as Chapter IV of this volume.]

premises. The second is that the convergence or overdetermination that we postulated at the time of the adoption of these policies continues to exist. We will now turn to these issues.

V. The Successes and Failures of Stabilization

In section III, we showed how stabilization policies tend to favor sectors associated with exporting primary products and financial capital.[119] We also saw that these policies alleviate previous balance-of-payments constraints but are much less successful in terms of inflation. However, and for reasons discussed above, these policies exacerbate a recession in which negative income redistribution also heavily penalizes wage earners. This leads to an economy that, despite official rhetoric, continues to be driven primarily by financial speculation. What does this mean with regard to our topic? It means that there continues to be little room for productive investment, even from the much-desired transnational capital, and that the functioning of the economy is fundamentally governed by financial speculation. Or, to summarize: (1) The adoption and implementation of policies deemed "reasonable" by the IMF and the "international financial community" is a necessary condition for obtaining balance-of-payments relief at the time of the introduction of the BA state; (2) such relief is all the more urgent given the depth of the preceding crisis, which means that these policies and their implementation must be stricter and more orthodox in order to "deserve" such support; but (3) this leads to the reproduction of a speculative economy, at the cost not only of the economic exclusion of the popular sector but

119 One effect that we will not examine here—mainly because it tends to appear more in the long term—is that, although they often bear the brunt of violent market contraction, the upper echelons of the industrial and commercial bourgeoisie, due to the recession mentioned above and the resulting increase in the mortality rate of the most vulnerable companies, tend to make significant gains in their level of control over their respective markets. This further consolidates the already high degree of concentration in the urban productive structure.

also of the suffocation of the internal productive structure; although (4) the improvements obtained in external payment capacity are perfectly consistent with the interests of transnational financial capital.

The international approval that these policies receive and their tenacious implementation are not only evident in the stand-by arrangements and additional credits that typically follow them. This approval is also evident in short-term foreign capital inflows. But the limits of the confidence that these programs can inspire are revealed, conversely, in their inability to attract significant transnational capital inflows for direct investment into these economies in recession facing numerous uncertainties.

The only thing resembling "success" that these "stabilization" policies, which are far from being such, manage to show is relief in the balance-of-payments.[120] But for this to be maintained, the codes of supposed economic rationality that permeate the IMF's vision and are reflected in the agreements analyzed here must be respected. This is because a loss of short-term confidence in the stabilization program would expose, even to its own supporters, the failure of policies that have already been so costly in many ways. So what can be done about this? Assuming that there has been no significant change in the existing balance of power,[121] the best answer—unfortunate for many—seems to be to do more of the same. That is, to insist a little more with such policies, in the hope that tenacity will attract long-term foreign capital and that, by increasing the efficiency of the productive structure (which is largely a euphemism for dismantling it), more powerful drivers of growth will reappear than those that can be provided by the hypertrophy of the

---

120 Of course, this assertion presupposes an interest in safeguarding and eventually expanding the domestic productive structure. From the point of view of the IMF and international creditors—who, as we have already argued, are primarily interested in a "solid" balance-of-payments position and the free international movement of capital—domestic misfortunes matter much less than outcomes in these last areas.

121 For a variety of reasons, in addition to those presented here, we do not believe that this can be achieved through the internal dynamics of this state, but rather through impulses "from outside" the state that are tightly controlled, especially in the first stage, which is our focus here.

financial sector and possible booms in the primary-export sector.[122] This may help explain the continuity of a policy such as the one adopted by Chile starting in 1973 (and, with its own particular characteristics, by Argentina in 1976), which has little social support and, in terms of those it punishes, includes many of the sectors that supported the implementation of the respective BA. It follows from the above that it is not true that these policies have no social base or beneficiaries: what happens is that they are an extremely small segment and impose on the economy a particularly perverse mode of reproduction, not only for opponents of the process but also for a large part of the bourgeoisie itself.

This is one of the points where the interweaving of economics and politics is clearly evident. In Latin America, numerous stabilization programs have been implemented during more or less democratic periods. However, their implementation broke down earlier than in the cases that interest us here; not only did the now-suppressed capacity of the popular sector to fight for their wage levels come into play, but the bourgeois fractions punished by those attempts also moved in a similar direction.[123] It has only been since the BA state that the implementation of these policies has been stubbornly maintained. Why? The answer is complex, and we can only address it partially here. It is fundamentally due to the depth of the previous crisis, which not only brought with it a greater disruption of the economy but, above all, a greater sense of impending doom for capitalist society. The resulting fear remains in the memory of the bourgeoisie in the subsequent period, as a memento of the fact that this state, beyond affecting the economic interests of a large part of the bourgeoisie itself, has saved it as a class. This, in turn,

---

122 It may be worth noting that in this essay we have focused on the short term, involving the period following the implementation of the BA state and the stabilization program. However, short-term stabilization programs deserve specific attention, if only because their impacts contribute decisively, as we argue here, to the rearticulation of society as a whole with a marked bias toward a small—but obviously powerful—group of economic actors.

123 On this point, see Guillermo O'Donnell, "Estado y Alianzas en la Argentina, 1956–1976," CEDES/GE-CLACSO, no. 5 (1977) and *Desarrollo Económico* 16, no. 64. [Included as Chapter I of this volume.]

limits, in the short and medium term, the possibility of an alliance with the popular sector (which has emerged as the bearer of that threat) and increases the harshness of the imposed order. This tends to turn these fissures within the bourgeoisie into bureaucratic struggles within the state apparatus, aimed at minimizing the costs of these policies in a fragmented way, but—for that very reason—unable to present themselves as an alternative. In other words, the opacity, bureaucracy, and fragmentation of the defensive attempts of nearly the entire bourgeoisie (sectors, groups, and even companies) prevent these attempts from appearing as a plausible argument of general interest, notwithstanding vague invocations of a nationalism without the people that the BA, with its mission of "order," excludes. The bourgeoisie as a whole is grateful to the BA for having saved it as a class and, largely because of this, limits itself to vague complaints when, in the first stage of this state, the "technocrats" of the normalization crucify no small part of it in homage to an "efficient" and internationalized capitalism. Thus, bound by their gratitude as a class, but reeling from the damage to their economic interests, a significant portion of the bourgeoisie discovers that, in the period preceding the BA, there was a state that contributed to their reproduction under conditions (demagogic and ultimately almost overpowering, but also protective) that the initial period of the BA denies them. However, in a context that presupposes the exclusion of their potential ally—the popular sector—these economically hard-hit segments of the bourgeoisie also discover their inability to promote an alternative within the BA's palace politics. That potential ally is still too close to having deeply threatened them and, moreover, has the coercive power of the state strongly focused on itself. Therefore, the popular sector can, at most, be piously invoked by the bourgeoisie—once again demonstrating the fragmented and small nature of its schizophrenia in the face of the BA—as a decisive variable, in the form of falling wages, of the recession that is suffocating it. But this is nothing more than complaints and rumors that, locked into the dynamic imposed by the tasks of order and normalization undertaken by the BA, cannot seriously be presented as alternatives to the current economic program.

The fissures and discord within the armed forces are no less significant, especially as the passage of time reveals the costs and failures of these policies and the dismantling of the productive structure, particularly in areas that—not coincidentally in these dependent capitalist economies—are most specifically national. Additionally, the efforts of the local bourgeoisie to minimize the costs of these policies and explore the possibility of a less burdensome alternative are directed at the armed forces. In societies where little can be learned through mass media, this leads to a flood of rumors, including doubts and opposition to the economic policy of this or that group within the armed forces. This is the reflection of intra-bureaucratic struggles focused on the continuity of these policies, which echo the complaints of the local bourgeoisie. However—and despite the fact that to the uninformed who add up the correlations of forces algebraically these rumors would indicate that the stabilization program is about to be reversed—it is repeatedly reaffirmed. To understand this, we must also take into account a factor that affects the armed forces themselves, despite the fact that among their ranks dissenting opinions regarding the program prevail. That is, the initial authorities of the BA, driven by the need for the rapid approval of the IMF and the "international financial community," are deeply committed to the economic program, as well as to the "technocrats" who embody it. This commitment by the top authorities of the BA, the military, is, as we have already seen, one of the fundamental conditions, apart from the imposition of order, to create the confidence necessary to secure urgent support for the balance-of-payments: that "community" has ample experience with recurrent "acceptable" programs that proved impossible to implement due to a lack of the necessary political and coercive support. From that initial moment on, there are few options left for those BA authorities, at a time when so much discord and doubt—a significant short-term concern—is being expressed among their own colleagues, who do not support the insistence on these policies, in the hope that the low inflation, at least moderate expansion, and efficient economy promised by the executors of the economic program will not take long to materialize. After announcing *urbi et orbi* that the stabilization program, accepted as the epitome of economic rationality, is the armed forces' own program and that, therefore, they would back it on the arduous path to its implementation, the highest authorities of the BA are bound to uphold its continuity. This, of course, gives rise to the aforementioned dissonance and opposition, but the real alternative—a change of course in the economy, with the concomitant reconstitution of alliances—puts the continuity of these authorities in play to an even greater degree. Why should this new stage not be led by the military leaders who have been arguing against this program and have been forging relationships with the bourgeois fractions who, like them, believe that a BA that is no less concerned with order but more benevolent in economic matters is possible?

Furthermore, the armed forces, like the bourgeoisie, have seen the precipice that appeared in the previous period and have also institutionally taken on the complicated responsibility of establishing order. As a result, they tend to share the fear of the significance and responses that may be developing behind the curtain of silence that this order imposes on a large part of society.[124] For this reason, the decision points of any policy alternative, including and above all economic policy, must contain a credible guarantee that they will not trigger processes that risk reactivating threats that they have worked so hard to suppress.

Another no less important factor comes into play here, contributing to renewed support for the stabilization program. That is, repeated expressions of international support—conveniently publicized domestically—for the program and those implementing it. Added to this are warnings that abandoning the program would lead to a loss of the "international confidence" that has been achieved and, with it, the collapse of the efforts that have already been made with such great sacrifice. The drumbeat of applause and the warnings of the abyss that would appear if the mistake of prematurely abandoning the stabilization program were made, sacrificing the domestic and international support that has been achieved, are an important part of the internal political game in this state. There, external support that helps ensure the continuity of these economic teams and their policy guidelines is woven together in a way that suggests full awareness. The rest—alternatives that are possible in principle—are either not expressed by the excluded sectors or appear,

124 This is one of the reasons for the search for mechanisms of mediation and "participation," as well as for the emergence of democratic proposals, however surreal, from this state. For more on this topic, see Guillermo O'Donnell, "Tensiones en el estado burocrático-autoritario," CEDES/GE-CLACSO, no. 11 (1978). [Included as Chapter II of this volume.]

in the complaints of numerous bourgeois fractions and groups within the armed forces, as understandable but premature concerns that could, in any case, be addressed "in due course" when the economic program in question has finally yielded the results that, contrary to all evidence, are still being promised.

In short, even within objectives consistent with the constellation of forces supporting the implementation of the BA, there is nothing inevitable about stubbornly maintaining policies that can only boast success in the balance-of-payments against a long list of failures. However, once the BA is implemented and there is a need to rush to the IMF to obtain some respite in the most urgent matters, it is essential that the BA's economic apparatus be controlled by a team that is clearly consistent with the IMF's vision and that the leadership of the armed forces be deeply committed to supporting that program. From that point on, the dice are loaded so, despite significant grumblings from even important allies, the program will continue far beyond what its undeniable failures would lead one to believe. Certainly, the dice are also loaded because this is a game of palaces and bureaucracies to which the sectors excluded by the BA have no access and in which, consequently, the misfortunes of the weakest and most national fractions of the bourgeoisie tend not to move beyond a mere chorus of lamentations or simmering hostilities over minor advantages.

Thus, this conjunction of factors served to ensure, in contrast to what any unsuspecting (or innocently mechanistic) inventory of those harmed by the programs in question would predict, that they were kept in place, in the cases discussed here, long after their overwhelming cost balance and rather meager list of successes had become evident. The underlying reason, once again, is the policy of bureaucracies that determines the exclusion of the popular sector and the elimination of channels of representation in which, at the very least, the demands must be presented as being in the general interest. Given this—during the first stage of the BA, which is the focus of this work—and given the recent history that precedes it, one begins to understand the portent of this clearly capitalist state that nevertheless punishes so much of its own bourgeoisie economically and is deaf to demands that, for the reasons already outlined, the latter is only able to stammer. The resulting void filled with rumors creates the conditions for the continuation of an economic program so antagonistic to the national society as a whole that it seems, nevertheless, to be the only way to continue skirting the precipices that have opened up in the still recent past.

VI. Variations on a Single Theme

Perhaps our argument will become clearer if we turn to a case that in some ways contrasts with the contemporary situations in Chile, Argentina, and Uruguay: the normalization program launched in March 1967 during the previous bureaucratic-authoritarian experiment in Argentina. That program achieved successes that went far beyond relieving the balance-of-payments, but it has also been the only one to date that was aborted, following the events of May 1969 and their aftermath. That conjunction of success and termination, as can be seen from what we have analyzed so far, is not accidental.

The 1967 program began under more favorable conditions than those of the 1970s. The level of political threat was lower, and the economic crisis and inflation had not reached the proportions they later did in Chile, Uruguay, and Argentina. In large part because of this, the stand-by arrangement with the IMF, as well as subsequent loans from transnational banking consortia and the U.S. government, stipulated less stringent conditions than in those cases. In particular, and notwithstanding the preservation of many of the items analyzed in section III, this arrangement recognized that the main driver of inflation was related to costs and the expectations of economic actors, rather than demand. This allowed for the implementation of an expansionary policy, contrary to the prescriptions that would result from an inverse diagnosis. Nevertheless, the weight of orthodoxy was evident in the inclusion of the typical imperative to eliminate the fiscal deficit, despite the fact that this was inconsistent with the accepted diagnosis of existing inflation. However, this could be solved by resorting to a resource enabled by an important aspect of Argentina's structure: the existence of an agricultural sector—in the pampean zone—that benefits from a high differential income appropriated by the state through withholdings on the export prices of its products. This meant antagonizing the pampean bourgeoisie, but it had the fundamental advantage (which the other cases did not) of allowing, on the one hand, a substantial reduction in the fiscal deficit and, on the other, the simultaneous launch of a major public investment program.[125] This enabled the emergence, through these investments, of the dynamic momentum that, for the reasons noted above, had been lacking in other cases until then. The result was that by 1968 inflation had fallen sharply, overall economic growth had recovered, and although the process continued to reproduce familiar characteristics of bias in income distribution, as well as the concentration and internationalization of capital and negative income redistribution (albeit less severe than in other cases), the fact is that the successes achieved went far beyond an improvement in the balance-of-payments.

And this was precisely the "problem." Indeed, why go on incurring the aforementioned costs and "denationalization" if these successes made it feasible to return to policies more concerned with the national interests of the bourgeoisie that, supported by an improved balance-of-payments, could promote a greater revival of the domestic market through wage increases? These questions allowed the local industrial and commercial bourgeoisie to do what had not been possible up to that point. That is, to find within the state apparatus, mainly in the armed forces, interlocutors willing to promote what appeared, under those conditions, to be a viable alternative (and more consistent with their orientations) for a more "fair" and "national" capitalist development. Additionally, the lower threat level posed by the popular sector had not subjected it to such severe controls as had been the norm in other cases, presenting it as an ally that did not awaken deep fears. All of this meant that, although each of these sectors had contributed less financially to normalization than in other cases, the key political event that had been hitherto lacking could take place: the successful merging

125 Nor is this the case in contemporary Argentina. Here—demonstrating once again that the issue is far from being merely "economic"—following a previous, more profound crisis, the ruling coalition has had to incorporate the pampean bourgeoisie at the cost of not taxing it, and therefore, losing the source of revenue on which the previous experience was based.

of their political tactics into a consensus around replacing the current economic program.

The main point is that contemporary cases, starting from a deeper crisis and threat level, have been less successful, within their explicit premises and goals, than the Argentine case of 1967–69. And it is not despite this but precisely because of this that these programs have been maintained: their failure seems to close off any possibility other than to insist on maintaining the status quo. Success in substantially reducing the inflation rate and regaining some overall growth is precisely what *politically* erodes the likelihood of the continuation of these programs. This is not only due to the negligible opposition from the popular sector, but also to the possibility that many allies from the BA perceive of redirecting their policies without any substantial risk toward areas that are more consistent with their immediate interests.

There is no stronger guarantee, despite the fissures and rumors, for the continuity of stabilization programs and the "technocrats" who implement them than their own failure, which is at the same time, as we have seen, their success and the fundamental reason for the considerable support they receive from the IMF and current and potential creditors in the "international financial community." Nothing is riskier, apart from challenges that may come from outside the established power system, than their own success in achieving the anti-inflationary and economic growth goals they declare. Nothing, on the other hand, helps as much to subordinate these capitalisms and a large part of their own ruling classes to the dysrhythmias imposed by their subordination to financial speculation. Few things, too, so clearly illustrate the political importance that it has had—and, for a time, continues to have—that even if it was in this way, these cases seem to have saved capitalism.

The tentative and partial nature of this work that we noted at the outset should now be evident. Much remains to be done, both from the center and on the periphery, to better understand the institutions, processes, and impacts that affect more than complex economic issues. We hope to have at least demonstrated the intrinsic intertwining of economics and politics in the issue at hand. Among other things, these economic programs are supported by a narrow (albeit powerful) social base, and the soundness of their postulates on the free functioning of markets is undermined by the iron-fisted state control established over wages. This, in turn, means that these programs can only be implemented by a state that is sufficiently authoritarian to stifle opposition arising from the high social costs incurred. Of course, the technocratic argument about the neutrality of this or any economic policy is a fallacy. However, extending this reasoning beyond the obvious, it seems clear in these cases that perhaps only this type of state can back the arduous implementation of programs such as those we have discussed. In this regard, it may be worth discussing the resulting contradiction: while some countries in the core seek to safeguard certain values, some of their institutions, either directly or through organizations such as the IMF, actually support policies that, like those analyzed here, are only possible under a very particular type of state. Whether this support results from explicit decisions or—more likely and frequently, we assume—from the belief that for certain conjunctures there is only one economic rationale—namely the one embodied in the IMF's vision—matters little in terms of the impacts of these programs. Yet, thinking in the long term, the force of the seemingly obvious and of beliefs reinforced by the authority of "the" science points to an intellectual and ideological field that has been sorely neglected by those who might raise doubts and concerns such as those outlined here.

CHAPTER IV

Notes for the Study of the Local Bourgeoisie, with Special Reference to Its Ties to Transnational Capital and the State Apparatus

Introduction

Although it sets a bad example for the new generations of scholars, I must say that this is another project that, like the one in the previous chapter, we were unable to complete due to various circumstances.

Like the others, it revolves around a number of central concerns. One is to historically recover the rebellious Argentina that the BA viciously attacked and which was outlined in "State and Alliances" (Chapter I of this volume). Another is to ask myself what was and could be an entity that was sometimes mythologized, sometimes reviled, and sometimes denied in its very existence: the domestic or local bourgeoisie (or "national" bourgeoisie, according to the most positive views of it). This is the fraction of the bourgeoisie that we saw "in action" in Chapter I, on its own and institutionally embodied by the CGE-CGI [Confederación General Económica-Confederación General de la Industria], at the time constantly allied with the popular sector and its representation in the unions and in Peronism.

However, this fraction, like the rest of its class, alarmed by the "disorder" and "subversion," supported the 1976 coup, although it soon found itself trapped in a state that attacked it economically and ideologically, without the recourse of realigning itself with a popular sector that was not only being subjected to harsh repression but of which it also had recent memories of its threatening political activation prior to the coup.

So what kind of actor is this and—a topical subject—what kind of actor could it become, economically and politically? This text does not answer these questions in the abstract, nor would I be able to do this in the present. Nevertheless, I believe that what remains valid is that the answer cannot be found through an economic perspective; it can only be found in politics as a result of the alliances in which this actor is involved and that the context offers as a possibility. Another conclusion that emerges from what I argue in this chapter is that, though in some circumstances it can become dynamic and democratizing, the domestic bourgeoisie remains, in several important ways, subordinate to international circuits of capital accumulation and, as part of the class that it is, will never support projects that seek to transform the capitalist parameters of society: this is less pressing and more evident today than in the 1970s, but it is perhaps worth keeping in mind.

Notes for the Study of the Local Bourgeoisie, with Special Reference to Its Ties to Transnational Capital and the State Apparatus[126]

I.

This text is a preliminary approximation to the topic of the local industrial bourgeoisie in Latin America. I have limited myself here to presenting the main theoretical and methodological criteria that I believe should be taken into account when studying this social subject, without attempting to provide an exhaustive analysis of the issues involved. This essay is a tool developed for use in ongoing research and therefore reflects a degree of conceptualization that will be refined as future work progresses.[127] In the final part of this essay, I illustrate some of the applications of this conceptualization by taking a quick look at a case study, that of contemporary Argentina. Despite these limitations, it may be of use to share these reflections in the hope of contributing to the national and comparative case studies that are so sorely lacking in this area.

---

126 CEDES, *Estudios Sociales*, no. 12 (July 1978). Prepared for the research program of the Latin American Institute for Transnational Studies (ILET) and presented to the Congress of German Latin Americanists, Bielefeld, March 1978. The research mentioned in this paper has received support from the Social Science Research Council.

127 This research was carried out at CEDES, with the participation of Laura Golbert.

I choose to speak of the local bourgeoisie rather than the "national" bourgeoisie in order to avoid making assumptions about complex questions concerning the concepts used and their referents;[128] the question of whether or not the bourgeoisie can properly be called "national" should be the corollary and not the premise of an analysis that we are far from having adequately developed. Within the local bourgeoisie, I will refer exclusively to the urban bourgeoisie and, within that, to the industrial bourgeoisie and only tangentially to the commercial bourgeoisie. This means leaving aside not only the agrarian bourgeoisie but also the financial and, to a large extent, the commercial fraction of the urban bourgeoisie. Of course, this does not imply negating the importance of any of them.[129] The limitation noted is due to the fact that we have not found it empirically possible to extend our research beyond the local industrial bourgeoisie; moreover, it would not be valid to generalize what we have learned about this fraction to the others.

By local industrial bourgeoisie, I mean the section of the bourgeois class that owns and governs the organization of production in industrial capitalist enterprises, the capital of which belongs entirely or mainly to national entities, and whose senior decision-making centers are located within the same national territory.[130] According to this definition, the social subject in question cannot be understood dichotomously as

---

128 The choice of terminology is irrelevant, provided that the reader adheres to the definition set out above. I could equally have referred to this group as the "domestic bourgeoisie" or, following the terminology of Nicos Poulantzas (*Las clases sociales en el capitalismo de hoy* [Mexico: Siglo XXI, 1976]), as the "internal bourgeoisie." This author's contributions to the topic are extremely interesting, but I believe that—since his referent is the bourgeoisie of core capitalist countries, which he regards as subordinate to the United States—extending the use of this term to the bourgeoisie of peripheral or dependent countries would only add to the existing confusion.

129 No less important than the study of the fraction chosen here is that of local and international financial capital, about which very little is known.

130 This criterion implies including only strictly capitalist enterprises, thus excluding sectors of great importance in our countries, such as artisanal activities and small businesses in which the owner combines their personal labor with that of a small number of workers.

national or non-national (or, according to the terminology proposed here, as local or non-local). Indeed, the definition aims to allow for the analysis of situations that fall into a "gray area" between those two poles, not only in terms of the obvious (shareholding) but also in terms of the effective control of the process of production and accumulation. That said, this definition is a first step in addressing an issue that I want to emphasize here: the role that even unmistakably local companies can play in a process that is more complex than what can be detected at the level of companies or the subjectivity of members of the bourgeoisie: the transnationalization of capital.

The lack of studies on this topic is surprising.[131] The reason, however, is not hard to discover. In the 1950s and 1960s, there was a wave of studies that included the industrial bourgeoisie as part of the "emerging middle classes" that would bring about modernization and jointly produce economic development and political stability. These studies gave rise to several manifestos heralding this fortunate event, as well as surveys of businesspeople aimed at determining the degree of "traditionalism" or "modernism" in their attitudes as a predictor of their ability to contribute to that outcome. These conceptions have been widely criticized. They have also been disproved by facts that showed that, whatever their contribution to "development," both the "emerging middle sectors" and the industrial bourgeoisie appeared determined to contradict the (real and supposed) political behaviors of their predecessors in the core capitalist countries. Additionally, in many cases, they became active promoters of a political instability that only appeared to be "resolved" through the resurgence of increasingly severe and prolonged authoritarian regimes. Thus, the hopes placed on these individuals were transferred to others, especially the armed forces, which seemed capable of ensuring economic growth (albeit not the improved distribution of resources that

131 There are important exceptions, including Fernando Henrique Cardoso's book, *Ideologías de la burguesía industrial en países dependientes: Argentina y Brasil* (Mexico: Siglo XXI, 1971), and Philippe Schmitter, *Interest, Conflict, and Political Change in Brazil* (Stanford: Stanford University Press, 1971), as well as ongoing research by Ricardo Cinta (Colegio de México) and Renato Boschi and collaborators (Instituto Universitário de Rio de Janeiro, IUPERJ).

was originally implied in the idea of development) and a certain degree of political stability (of course without the other factor of the original equation, namely democracy).[132] With this transfer of hopes from one actor to another and the consequent "realism" in reducing those hopes, the erroneous stream of studies mentioned above was cut off, and thus the social subject we wish to recover here disappeared from view.

On the other hand, despite the rich sense of complexity that we find in the main approach to the problem of dependency as well as subsequent works by Fernando Henrique Cardoso and other authors,[133] "dependency" also became fertile ground for numerous simplifications.[134] One of these was to conceive of international capital and imperialism as all-powerful demiurges that imply, among other things, the lack of any autonomy on the part of the local bourgeoisie. In these versions, the latter was eliminated as a social subject in its own right, which did not require further study since its behavior appeared to be determined by those "external" actors.

This does not imply denying aspects that, in fact, I wish to emphasize. In particular, the significant degree of subordination of the local bourgeoisie with respect to transnational corporations (hereinafter TNCs) and, even more decisively, with respect to the global process of capital transnationalization. However, the phenomena of subordination I will explore in this chapter do not prevent the local bourgeoisie from

---

132 Perhaps the best example of this shift is the difference between John J. Johnson's two books, *Political Change in Latin America* (Stanford: Stanford University Press, 1958), with its prophecies about the "emerging middle sectors," and *The Military and Society in Latin America* (Stanford: Stanford University Press, 1964), with its hopes transferred to the armed forces. Certainly, the changes in these currents signal the distance between the initial euphoria of the Alliance for Progress—based largely on the premises mentioned above—and President Johnson's current administration.

133 Fernando Henrique Cardoso and Enzo Faletto, *Dependencia y desarrollo en América Latina* (Mexico: Siglo XXI, 1969).

134 See especially Fernando Henrique Cardoso, "The Consumption of Dependency Theory in the United States," a paper presented at the 1977 annual meeting of the Latin American Studies Association, containing a sharp critique of some of the simplistic assumptions employed in the use of the concept.

having sufficient autonomy to constitute a social subject in its own right or from maintaining significant points of potential friction with transnational capital.

There is an issue that has remained implicit in the above statements. That is the question of what it means to study a class or, more precisely with respect to the topic in question, a fraction of a class. Without attempting an exhaustive answer here, it seems to me that, in the case in question, this implies dealing with three levels: (1) An initial structural level, understood as the position of that fraction in the productive system. And this can be considered in two main directions. One is the position of that fraction in terms of its economic relations in the broad sense (including technological) with other bourgeois segments (including the TNCs), with the subordinate classes, and with the state apparatus. The other direction, "inward" from that fraction, aims to establish its own structural differentiation. It is clear that, even after excluding companies that are not fully capitalist, the local industrial bourgeoisie includes a wide variety of situations ranging from small, capital-poor companies forced to operate in highly competitive conditions to an "elite" of companies—the upper echelon of this fraction—that participate in oligopolistic markets and may have rates of capital intensity and technology incorporation that are no lower than those of TNC subsidiaries operating in the same market. These and other factors determine positions in the productive system and, potentially, divergent interests that require caution when making statements about this fraction as a whole. (2) The level of the corporate organization of the industrial bourgeoisie as a whole.[135] I am referring to chambers of industrial companies—which tend to represent quite specific interests, almost always determined by the finished product they offer—as well as more aggregated associations or federations, which claim to represent the interests of groups in the sector and, even more broadly, the entire industry.[136] At

---

135 When I say "industrial bourgeoisie as a whole," I am assuming that both local companies and subsidiaries of TNCs coexist at this corporate level.

136 In other words, as is often the case—including in Argentina—we can distinguish three basic levels of corporate organization. The first and most specific brings together companies based on their final product (e.g., production of wire); a

this level, as at the previous one, there are significant variations, both over time and from country to country. These variations can occur in dimensions that are highly relevant to our topic (and highly illustrative of differences in the underlying processes that I will discuss later), such as the mode of articulation between these organizational levels, the degree of presence (or absence) of TNC affiliates in them, their ties to the state apparatus, and even, as in the case of Argentina until 1976, the existence of more than one organization at the national level that aspired to represent the industrial bourgeoisie as a whole.[137] (3) The level of specific political action by these organizations. By this I do not mean what I mentioned above, the corporate level of specific articulation of industrial interests, although this in itself makes these organizations political actors. What I am referring to here are interventions in which, either directly or through state bureaucracies, political parties or movements, and alliances with other social sectors, these organizations appear to transcend the articulation of specific interests and act as bearers of general interests involving some kind of proposal for the political and economic organization of society.

The levels mentioned above could be referred to as structural, corporate, and political-ideological, respectively. However, in order to avoid confusion, a few clarifications are necessary. The first is that class is not only structural. A class or fraction is constituted as such on all three levels simultaneously; it is what it is as a result of its specific mode

---

second generally brings together trade associations that share the same main input (e.g., the Association of Metallurgical Industrialists of Argentina), which includes interests as diverse as those of wire producers, steel rolling mills, and producers of durable consumer goods for the home, among others; and finally, there is a third level in which one or more associations seek to represent the industry as a whole.

137 The comparative history and morphology of these and other forms of representing interests is the main focus of a study currently being carried out by Philippe Schmitter on several European countries, the United States, and Japan. Clearly, similar studies in our region would be of great importance.

of being and manifesting itself jointly on those three levels.[138] This means that similarities between fractions from one country to another, observable at the structural level, are not created by the same social subjects if differences that can be considered significant appear at one or more of the other levels. The second caveat follows from the above: there is a presumption that structural position limits the degrees of freedom that exist, for example, in the modes of capital accumulation and in the political behavior of that fraction. However, the remaining degrees of freedom are sufficiently broad, and the resulting probabilities are co-determined by other factors, so it is not valid to "deduce" the other levels from the structural position. The third point is that the concept of class or fraction, and the segment of social reality to which they refer, are relational. A social subject cannot be understood in isolation, as something that "intrinsically is"; on the contrary, at the three levels mentioned above, they are constituted as such through networks of relationships that, by connecting them with other social subjects, insert them into the plexus of relationships of society as a whole, from which they acquire their specific characteristics.

Put more simply, what constitutes the local bourgeoisie in each case does not arise solely from its structural position, but also from its modes of connection with other social subjects at that level in the corporate and political-ideological spheres. This essay is particularly interested in its relations with transnational capital and the state apparatus; I will occasionally refer to its ties to the subordinate classes. Therefore, I hope it is once again clear that this is only a partial approximation of the many issues involved in the study of the industrial bourgeoisie.

138 From this perspective, even the "non-presence" of a class on the political-ideological plane is a way of constituting itself through the absence of politics, which co-determines not only the characteristics of that class but also the global field of forces in the political arena.

II.

A core argument of this paper is that the issue of the local bourgeoisie must be addressed from the perspective of the broader and more dynamic problem of the transnationalization of capital. Thanks to excellent studies,[139] considerable progress has been made in understanding the performance, relative weight, and impact of TNC subsidiaries in our countries. This is a fundamental dimension of the dynamics of these societies. It is also key to understanding various aspects of our topic. However, irrespective of studies in which the unit of analysis is these subsidiaries and/or the aggregation of their impacts on a national context, it is important to place them in a broader and more analytical perspective.[140] In other words, to view the expansion of these subsidiaries as one of the manifestations, in a dependent or peripheral national context, of the transnationalization of capital.

Certainly, the rates of expansion of TNCs worldwide and in our markets are an indication that, at the level of economic actors, they are the dynamic forefront of capitalism on a global scale.[141] However—as

---

139 Notably, Fernando Fajnzylber and Trinidad Martínez Tarragó, *Las empresas transnacionales: Expansión a nivel mundial y proyección en la industria mexicana* (Mexico: Fondo de Cultura Económica, 1976); Juan Sourrouille, *El impacto de las empresas transnacionales sobre el producto y el empleo: El caso de Argentina*, (Geneva: Organización Internacional del Trabajo, 1977); Carlos Doellinger et al., *Empresas multinacionais na industria brasileira* (Rio de Janeiro: IPEA, 1975); and Constantino Vaitsos, *Intercountry Income Distribution and Transnational Enterprise* (New York: Oxford University Press, 1974).

140 For a similar suggestion in this regard, see Fernando Fajnzylber, "Oligopólio, empresas transnacionais e estilos de desenvolvímento," *Cadernos Cebrap*, no. 19 (January–March 1977). For a very interesting outline of the problems generated by the transnationalization of capital in relation to the nation state, see Norbert Lechner's introduction to his book, *La crisis del Estado en América Latina* (Buenos Aires: El Cid Editores, 1977).

141 I will not bore you here with overly familiar references. Suffice it to say that the studies just cited, among others, have shown with overwhelming regularity that the subsidiaries of TNCs in our markets, as well as TNCs as a whole on a

I will argue—, they are only the tip of the iceberg of a broader process that must be understood analytically, in contrast to the specific study of actors to which they may be subjected. When I speak of capital, I am not referring to a thing that can be appropriated due to its concrete nature. Following an old line of thought, I conceive of capital as a social relationship arising from an unequal and contradictory connection between social subjects. As such a relationship, capital is not only a set of objects or what appears represented in papers that support the exclusive claim of ownership of a productive unit. It is, in essence, a certain mode of production through the aforementioned connection between social subjects. It is also a certain systematic bias in the tacit conception of society's needs, originating in the dynamics of capital reproduction as a process of privately appropriable accumulation. This form of production is also expressed in technology, including that embodied in the means of production. Despite their reified condition, these are traversed by networks of social relations: on the one hand, the conditions of capitalist-worker relations implied and specified by that means of production, and on the other, the type of product and its tacit definition of the range of social demands or needs it serves. Production (including means of production and technology), relations of production, and circulation are moments of capital as a process of accumulation, which as part of this process "dispatches" to the market products that—beneath their appearance of neutral thingness—embody the specificity of what in essence is a particular form of production based on a particular kind of relationship between social subjects. The relationships implied in all this constitute the fundamental fabric of society, which they shape not only in terms of the resulting structure of production, classes, and power, but also—and I want to emphasize this point—in terms of the tacit yet decisive definition of which "needs" are met, with their corresponding prioritization of socially backed values.

From this perspective, what is meant by the transnationalization of capital? The term refers to something more than the immediately

---

global scale, tend to record the highest rates of growth, profitability, product diversification, capital intensity, privileged access to credit, and other factors that clearly show them to be at the forefront.

apparent, such as the participation of TNCs in production and accumulation. It also implies the permeation of a society by specific modes of interaction between social subjects, by modes of production, by the means of production and technology, by products, and by a tacit definition of prioritized needs and values, which are the result of conditions existing at the points of the irradiation of this permeation: the centers of global capitalism. This is alluded to, albeit too narrowly, by terms such as the internationalization of the productive structure, even though this phenomenon is a central aspect of the process. The idea is to point out that a certain mode of capital reproduction, historically specific to the social conditions of the countries from which it radiates, is "imposed" on the "receiving" countries, while retaining its own basic characteristics. That is, in areas that, not corresponding to those original impulses, incline all of their social relations, including their modes of capital reproduction,[142] toward replicating that original specificity that was foreign to them, and even toward a tacit definition of needs and values largely induced by the products that they also tend to replicate.

Of course, this derivation interacts with specificities that ensure that the replication is partial. What is important to note at this point is that the process of the transnationalization of capital is one of its reproduction on an increasingly universal scale, according to modalities that are neither neutral nor "natural," but rather the result of the historical specificity of its centers of influence.[143] Note that, at this level, it does not yet matter who the specific economic actors are, where they operate, or the specific nationality of those whose behavior drives this process. This does not imply denying the importance of this level. However, I suggest that, in the analysis, this should come after some positioning of

---

142 Or, to put it in more current terms, its "development style."

143 One challenge in approaching this topic is the tendency to slip into a view of archetypal capitalism (that of the core countries), from which ours would be seen as a kind of deviation or distortion. As Lechner rightly suggests in *La crisis*, it is a question of understanding the transnationalization of capital as a global process, whose pattern of deployment derives from the specificity resulting from the partial limitation of that space by certain national states (and markets).

the global process in which these actors are inserted. It is in this process that the TNCs, with their subsidiaries located in peripheral markets, are the dynamic vanguard, but it also encompasses various strata of the local bourgeoisie, even though a high proportion of their companies are national. We will see that this national ownership is important in many respects. On the other hand, this bourgeoisie is incorporated, as a bearer and co-promoter of the process of capital transnationalization irrespective of its subjectivity. This, which I have presented abstractly so far, will be further explored in the next section with an example that will allow us to begin to see how the constitutive ambiguity of the local bourgeoisie (especially its industrial segment) underlies its relations with transnational capital, its tensions and conflicts with TNC subsidiaries, and the limits imposed on it by its subordination to those subsidiaries. We will also see how this same ambiguity affects its relations with the state and, correspondingly, how it influences certain characteristics of the latter.

III.

Let us now consider what a successful national company looks like. It produces goods for final consumption, is part of an oligopoly in its sector, and appears to be completely independent of transnational capital (in other words, it has no shareholding or contracts for technology, brands, or management). Rather, this company competes with subsidiaries of TNCs and does so successfully, as it holds a significant share of its market and achieves profits that allow it to maintain that share. This company appears to be a tangible contradiction of dependency: it seems to be, and in many ways is, an example of the dynamism and viability of a local bourgeoisie that competes with subsidiaries of TNCs and does not limit itself to operating in the gaps that they may leave.

But what is the basis for the expansion and success of this company? It is a copycat of the goods offered by transnational corporations, including subsidiaries with which it competes in its own market. In other words, a necessary condition for the success of this company is that its products resemble those of transnational corporations. And this even applies to the foreign allusions of the designs, packaging, and brands that this company tends to use in order to lend "prestige" to its products. Note that this often has consequences that cast some doubt on its fully national character: even if it is not paying for technology services, it is likely that the production equipment it uses has been imported from core countries, at least its most complex components.[144] The technology integrated into this equipment tends to narrow the range of options for the final product, directing it toward goods that replicate those offered in core countries. For this reason, concerned with mimicking their competitors' offerings, the company's executives have acquired this equipment.

What is the aim of these observations? In order to explore less trivial territory, a digression is needed. It is clear that the main way for TNCs producing end-consumer products[145] to grow and maintain their dynamism is through the continuous introduction of products that incorporate innovations,[146] driven by research and development activities made possible by the enormous scale of the operations of a TNC. This innovation enjoys monopoly conditions for a time, during which

---

144 In addition to the limited production of capital goods in Latin America, even in its most industrialized countries, a recent study shows that a large proportion of those produced in the region are simple goods and that the industrial equipment itself continues to be largely imported. See Ayza et al., *América Latina: Integración económica y sustitución de importaciones* (Mexico: ECLAC and Fondo de Cultura Económica, 1976).

145 The argument I am developing refers strictly to companies that offer consumer goods, whether durable or perishable, on the market. It does not, therefore, consider the case of companies that produce capital goods—which are of little importance in our countries for the reasons just mentioned—or intermediate goods. As for the latter, although they involve markets that are different from those of final consumption, as well as forms of competition that are also different from those I will point out for the former, I presume—admitting that there is a serious lack of knowledge here—that their specific characteristics are generally determined by the type of final supply for which they are intended as consumables.

146 Of course, the innovation need not be substantive in any sense. It can also be a different way of presenting the same product.

it is aimed primarily at high-income sectors that are less price-sensitive and whose "needs" it satisfies. This is usually the period of highest profitability for the product, which declines when other competitors appear with a similar product and when, moreover, its supply must be directed at lower-income sectors whose purchasing habits are more price-elastic. The decline of that product until its eventual "death" through its replacement by another is offset by the introduction of other innovative products, which thus restart the cycle described above.[147] To the extent that the comparative advantages of TNCs emerge from their capacity for continuous innovation, as the literature cited above indicates, it is therefore economically rational—from the perspective of long-term profit maximization—for them to orient their strategy toward the reproduction of these product cycles. For the same reason, the trend toward the globalization of their production is rational. Indeed, after the implementation of a variety of customs and exchange barriers in much of the world closed the path to direct exports from the core, the response was to bypass those barriers by establishing subsidiaries that began to act as domestic producers in those markets.[148] Why? Because the access achieved this way allows new product cycles to be launched, with the advantages described above, when the product introduced into these peripheral markets has already entered into decline in the market of origin and, most probably, in the core countries as a whole.

Thus, product p_1, which in period t_1 generated monopoly profits in its country or countries of origin, enjoys a similar situation in period t_n in a group of peripheral countries, while in the former it has already been replaced by product p_n, which in turn begins its own life cycle. The

147 I am summarizing here from the literature on the "product cycle." See in particular the groundbreaking book by Raymond Vernon, *Sovereignty at Bay* (New York: Basic Books, 1971), and, for its interesting implications for peripheral markets, John Knickerbocker, *Oligopolistic Reaction and Multinational Enterprise* (Cambridge, MA: Harvard University Press, 1975).

148 On the characteristics and speed of the expansion of TNCs since the 1950s, see Myra Wilkins, *The Maturing of Multinational Enterprise: American Business from 1914 to 1970* (Cambridge, MA: Harvard University Press, 1974).

logic of this growth pattern indicates that, *ceteris paribus*,[149] among the markets to which they can thus gain access, TNCs will prefer the larger ones, since they offer the greatest probability of maximizing the profits resulting from these "resurrections" of products that are no longer novel in core countries. Therefore: the larger the market size of Latin American countries, the greater the number of industrial TNCs that establish themselves there with a greater number of activities.[150] In this way, and without detriment to subsequent "resurrections" of the same product in smaller or, for other reasons, less attractive markets, it is possible to achieve the long-term maximization of the consolidated profits of TNCs at a global level. So it is as if the TNCs were being dragged along by the logic of their comparative advantages and resulting pattern of growth, toward the globalization of an activity whose products are introduced at different times as a result of the stratification of the world market into two fundamental layers: the central layer, where innovations originate and are introduced, and the peripheral layer, where TNCs "resurrect" their products.

This is well known. So are some of the consequences. (1) In the periphery, the supply of innovations that require high purchasing power intersects with a more unequal distribution of income than in the core, which tends to be accentuated by the displacement of the resources needed to sustain demand from a relatively small sector of the population. (2) The levels of concentration of industrial property, mainly benefiting TNC subsidiaries, tend to be higher in the periphery than in the center.[151] (3) The ways in which subsidiaries are linked to their parent companies involve a high import ratio. As that industrialization progresses, in contrast to the center, it contributes to stifling the precarious

---

149 *Ceteris paribus* refers to the more or less "friendly" and guaranteed stable political conditions of those markets.

150 See CEPAL, *Estudio económico de América Latina, 1970. Estudios especiales: La expansión de las empresas internacionales y su gravitación en el desarrollo latinoamericano* (Santiago and New York: 1971).

151 See Fajnzylber and Martínez Tarragó.

balance-of-payments of peripheral countries.[152] (4) Competition between products, following the same logic as the cycles outlined above, is based on differentiation in terms of presentation, brand, supplier "image," and similar factors. In other words, the product is sold primarily on the basis of its novelty, which usually requires the support of a large advertising apparatus aimed at motivating sales through the product's distinctive features, rather than through price-focused competition that, as Fernando Fajnzylber points out[153]—by removing the logic of the continuous introduction of innovations—would completely alter this pattern of growth and many of the comparative advantages of TNCs.

Having briefly outlined the above, I would like to highlight a few points that are relevant to our topic. First, as this growth pattern spreads as the dynamic pillar of the economy, its products generate a "development style." In other words, they not only determine who will be its main drivers and which social sectors will have access to its "benefits." They also, and more decisively, imply a determination of social needs (and, beyond them, the prioritization of values) that must be addressed with the resources available at any given time. Whatever its inadequacy in the core, on the periphery this tacit definition appears in all its irrationality in the face of much more widespread and basic needs that remain unmet, in part—and not insignificantly—due to the pumping out of resources necessary to reproduce that pattern of growth.

The aim of this paper is not to lament the consequences of this development style. What is important is to highlight a logic that operates on two fundamental levels prior to the subjectivity of the actors. The first is that the pattern identified is economically rational for the expansion of the TNCs themselves. The second is that for the national company in our example to be successful, it must fit into this pattern of growth, incorporating itself into it as fully and mimetically as possible: it must maintain a certain pace with respect to innovation; its products must resemble those of TNCs; and its brands and advertising must evoke the

---

152 On these points, see in particular the works previously cited by Fernando Fajnzylber, Trinidad Martínez Tarragó, and Constantino Vaitsos.

153 Fernando Fajnzylber, "Oligopólio empresas transnacionales y estilos de desarrollo," *El Trimestre Económico* 43, no. 171 (1976): 625–56.

prestige of what is expensive and accepted in core countries. In other words, by being successful, that national company becomes a co-driver of the way transnational capital expands in its own market, that is, a co-driver of the transnationalization of capital. In this way, the process spreads like an oil slick, beyond the activities of the TNCs themselves and beyond the most obvious cases of local companies linked to them upstream or downstream.[154] In all of these ways, the company in our example bases its success on promoting the development style that is predetermined by the core through the pattern of the growth and supply of goods of its most dynamic units, the TNCs, and through which the broader process of the transnationalization of capital is expanding. For that same reason, however, the condition for the success of that company is also the continuous reproduction of its organic weakness vis-à-vis the subsidiaries that the TNCs have established in "their" market. I would like to expand on this point, which I believe to be crucial.

The company in our example is part of the oligopoly in its sector and has growth and profitability rates similar to those of the subsidiaries with which it competes. However, a closer look reveals several important differences. First, the mimesis on which its success is based can hardly be complete. We must remember that it is not the originator of the new products it imitates. What does this mean? It must enter into some kind of agreement with a foreign company, not based in its market, in order to have access to its innovations, in which case it ceases to meet our assumption of a company that is truly independent of international capital. Or it must be attentive to new products being developed in the core, so that it can copy and/or adapt them in order to introduce something similar into its market more or less simultaneously with the subsidiaries based there.[155] Obviously, this mechanism

---

154 It is important to remember that the replication carried out by the company in our example does not occur solely at the level of circulation. In order to be successful, it has also had to mimic the level of production, most likely by importing capital goods from the center and reproducing the social relations implied and induced by those goods.

155 The adaptation of technology generated at the core to local conditions is giving rise to interesting research that, among other things, demonstrates the creative

has risks and limitations that do not apply to those who have generated the innovation, but what allows our company to succeed would seem to be the beneficial effect brought about by the delay with which TNCs tend to introduce innovations previously launched in core countries.[156] A second limitation results from the fact that, regardless of its size, such a company is not only small in relation to each TNC but also, whether it exports or not, the situation of its own market tends to play a decisive role in its fate. On the other hand, for the consolidated balance sheet of the TNC, a period of recession and/or low profits in that market is scarcely significant. In third place, the smaller size of that company, compared to the resources that a TNC can mobilize, in addition to the limitations resulting from acting imitatively, mean that even the largest and most successful local companies tend to produce—as suggested by abundant but unsystematic evidence—a smaller range of goods than the subsidiaries. This, like the previous point, is a source of vulnerability and, presumably, affects the long-term profitability of both types of companies.

---

capacity available in the periphery. See Jorge Katz, "Precios de transferencia, rentabilidad y esfuerzos de investigación y desarrollo: Un estudio de casos en el mercado farmacéutico," *Desarrollo Económico* 16, no. 62 (July–September 1976); Jorge Katz, *Creación de tecnologías en el sector manufacturero argentino* (Buenos Aires: BID-CEPAL, 1976); and Jorge Katz and E. Ablin, "Tecnologías y exportaciones: Un análisis microeconómico de la experiencia argentina reciente," *Desarrollo Económico* 17, no. 65 (April–June 1977). However, these innovations and adaptations are based on what I would like to emphasize here, namely the extrinsic origin of the technology and/or product that is adapted to the local context, as well as the fact that success in achieving the resulting adaptive imitations involves reproducing and promoting the transnational pattern of TNC expansion.

156 This statement is merely a hypothesis based on my knowledge of some companies that can be compared to the example in the text. If this were the case, the TNC's profit-maximization logic, which drives it to first exhaust its monopolistic possibilities for each new product in the (more profitable) core markets, would give its competitors in the periphery time to learn about and attempt to replicate innovations that only later will the TNC's subsidiaries introduce into their markets.

Additionally, if the condition for the success of the local company in our example is the replication of innovations, and if these require some degree of access to its production technology, it will usually have, at the very least, ties to international capital as a supplier of its production equipment. On a macroeconomic level, this means that this company will be an importer of such equipment and will have little interest in promoting its local manufacture. Obviously, it will be even less interested in this than the TNCs (which will be more interested in "selling" equipment to their subsidiaries that is obsolete in the core but still suitable for production in the periphery). Therefore, this pattern of growth, both for the subsidiaries and for the national company, discourages the production of capital goods and, thus, the likelihood of domestic innovation that would lend dynamism to this "development style" in the periphery.[157] So this pattern of growth, while leading to extensive industrialization (whose most dynamic component is the array of goods aimed at high-income demand), consolidates it as an acephalous productive structure, lacking the autonomous impulses that come from the production of capital goods and its concomitant generation of creative technology for new products. This is one aspect of economic dependence that, as we can see, is not the result of subjectivity or astute conspiracies, since even in our example—the closest to a situation of autonomy—it is not cut off at the point where its growth would be truly endogenous. On the contrary, if the company in the example is successful, it is because it replicates a microeconomic pattern of growth and co-drives a global economic pattern of growth that leads precisely to that structurally acephalous situation that, along with the type of supply already mentioned, is, through the local inability to endogenously drive that "development style," an expression of the dynamics of transnationalization that starts from the core.

In other words, the way in which the company in the example achieves its success has two main consequences. Macroeconomically, it contributes to maintaining the disorganization of the productive structure in which, in contrast to the TNCs, it is almost completely

---

157 The data used here is from Juan Ayza et al., *América Latina: Integración económica*.

embedded. On the other hand, at the microeconomic level of the company, this success, achieved through its imitative incorporation into the pattern of growth of the TNCs, confirms its relative organic weakness. The resulting vulnerability does not usually manifest itself during periods that are more or less normal but, as recent experience in the Southern Cone shows, it appears in periods of prolonged and/or acute recessions. During these periods, this weakness, which is often compounded by more costly and difficult access to external financial resources, is reflected in the high mortality rate, not only of the most fragile domestic companies but also of quite a few others, such as the one in our example.

I have so far focused on an example that is at the edge of the oil slick through which the transnationalization of capital spreads. We can now turn to more obvious and better-known cases: those of local companies embedded in the networks upstream and downstream of TNC subsidiaries. Both (upstream) suppliers of inputs and parts and (downstream) purchasers of inputs and marketers of products from TNC subsidiaries are subordinate parts of economic power subsystems centered on those subsidiaries. I do not feel it necessary to discuss this point in depth, but I would like to highlight two issues.[158] First, the high degree to which the activity of these linked companies is controlled by those subsidiaries; in terms of production and distribution, these companies form part of circuits run by subsidiaries that, for various reasons, have chosen to divest themselves of some of their activities. The second point is that these subsystems often consist of numerous linked companies negotiating in varying ways, depending on the case, with monopolies/oligopolies or monopsonies/oligopsonies. Here, the formal-legal criterion, based on the owners' nationality and the company's location, is

158 On this point, Raúl Trajtenberg makes an important theoretical and methodological contribution in *Un enfoque sectorial para el estudio de la penetración de las transnacionales en América Latina* (Mexico: ILET, DEE/D/1, 1977). For an attempt to conceptualize these networks of relationships as subsystems of (primarily but not exclusively) economic power, see Guillermo O'Donnell and Delfina Linck, *Dependencia y autonomía* (Buenos Aires: Amorrortu Editores, 1973).

more misleading than in our previous example: in contrast to the latter, linked companies are part of the production process of TNCs. They are part of the expansion of TNCs and the broader phenomenon of the transnationalization of capital, to which they contribute segments of activity that only make sense as parts of the processes of the production, circulation, and accumulation of capital led by TNCs. The importance of the decisions made by TNC subsidiaries for these local companies is greater than in our previous example. This is also clearly evident in recessive situations, in which subsidiaries use their power in the subsystem to transfer a large part of the costs and uncertainties to satellite companies and, through them, to the workers employed by them.[159]

But that is only one aspect of this question. If we exclude the successful competitive companies from our first example and the companies linked upstream or downstream to the TNCs,[160] what do we have left? Basically, we are left with the least dynamic, least profitable, least capital- and technology-intensive layers of the local industrial bourgeoisie,

---

159 A country like Argentina, with its recurring economic crises, recessions, and efforts to attract transnational capital, has a rich history of complaints from companies linked in this way when faced with TNC subsidiaries. Perhaps the most transparent are those of auto parts manufacturers, on the one hand, and auto dealers, on the other, regarding the ability of auto factories to pass a significant part of the costs of recessions on to them. As expressed by the association that unites the latter: "In our industry, there is a pyramidal organization in which decisions are made in a single sector: that of the [automotive] manufacturers." *La Nación*, January 29, 1978, section 2, p. 2.

160 It should be noted that I am not concerned here with cases in which the control is internalized, rather than being wielded by transnational capital, as it is in companies linked to them externally through the establishment of the process of production and circulation. This is the case for companies that are only formally national, linked to transnational capital through shareholding (even if minority) and/or through management contracts. Whatever the legal formalities, it seems clear that here we are dealing with cases in which effective control of the company is no longer in local hands. With regard to companies linked to transnational capital exclusively through the provision of technology or the use of trademarks, the broad range of existing situations—which can be similar to both the "independent" company in our example and those I have just mentioned in this note—prevents me from addressing them here.

which are also subject to a high mortality rate. In other words, with the weakest and most fragile of the bourgeoisie: those who ultimately have less capacity for accumulation precisely because they have ended up on the sidelines of the oil slick of transnationalization. On the other hand, despite their organic weakness and subordination, the companies we have discussed so far are those that tend to have the highest rates of growth and accumulation within the local industrial bourgeoisie. This is, in my view, a fundamental characteristic of "dependent and associated development."[161] On the one hand, the strata of the local bourgeoisie that participate in it are, for that very reason, its most dynamic and privileged elements. The flip side of the coin that reveals the structural ambiguity of the most dynamic layers of the local bourgeoisie of an independent capitalism is that this same participation helps reproduce a pattern of growth and a process of the transnationalization of capital that restores these strata to their condition of organic weakness with respect to transnational capital, which—through it—reproduces itself as the dynamic vanguard of this process on a global scale. This, in turn, repeats the conditions that generate the structural ambiguity of that local bourgeoisie. Macroeconomically, this fosters an industrialization skewed toward the confiscation of particularly scarce resources and the decapitation of its productive structure.

In this chapter, we have begun to examine the corporate organization and political-ideological action of the local industrial bourgeoisie, which we can summarize in two statements. The first is that organic weakness and subordination do not always imply a harmony of interests with TNCs. The second is that the privileged situation resulting from participation in a "development style"—in any of the ways mentioned so far—sets the parameters within which these conflicts tend to unfold. But before we explore this topic further, it may be worth revisiting some of the conclusions that emerge from what we have observed in this section on a more abstract level.

---

161 Fernando Henrique Cardoso, *Estado y sociedad en América Latina* (Buenos Aires: Nueva Visión, 1973).

IV.

In the contemporary world, relations between social subjects unfold in political and economic spaces established by nation states. These states seek to define a sphere of privileged loyalties—the nation—, exclusive control over a territory, and relations of production and circulation—the market—, whose performance would depend fundamentally on state policies and the "private" subjects located within its territory. But that state, in the cases of the dependent and associated development that interest us, must not cease to express the ambiguities and contradictions resulting from what we examined in the preceding sections. As an attempt to delimit one space from others, the state apparatus tends toward the construction of a truly national society. On the other hand, the state is also a co-driving force behind the transnationalization of capital both in terms of its policies and in relation to the classes of whose domination it is a complex synthesis. This is the contradictory way in which the transnationalization of capital occurs in the contemporary world, through nation states that bow to its dynamics.[162]

I cannot enter into a theoretical reflection on the state here,[163] but I would like to point out some characteristics related to the present work. We will begin with the observation that the history of Latin American countries, which have more or less stumbled along as capitalist societies, reveals a series of pendular swings between nationalist periods and others in which there has been an eager attempt to promote an increasingly influential role for international capital. During the former, a nationalist discourse is typically accompanied by policies that limit the scope of action that TNCs are permitted (without ruling out certain expropriations) and seek to promote the expansion

162 See once again Norbert Lechner, *La crisis*.

163 For further reading on this topic, see Guillermo O'Donnell, "Apuntes para un teoría del estado," CEDES/GE-CLACSO, *Documento*, no. 9 (1977). [Included as Chapter VI of this volume.]

of "national entrepreneurship."[164] However, regardless of the degree to which these decisions advance in each case, what is not usually questioned is the development style pursued. It seems that during nationalist periods, the aim is to continue doing the same thing, but—thanks to the restriction or exclusion of TNCs—with a change in the economic actors who would most benefit. Yet this is like trying to contain a great river within the narrow wall of a state apparatus ill-suited to resolving and, above all, implementing these policies, supported by a local bourgeoisie that is rather ambiguous about what is being proposed. First, insofar as the development style is tacitly ratified,[165] this limitation tends to generate a poor replica of TNC-led growth, since its drivers—the local bourgeoisie and the state apparatus, including public enterprises—remain incapable of incorporating the sources of new products, technology, and production equipment that give precisely that role to the centers of capitalism and their TNCs. Second, nationalist policies are diluted by their difficulties of implementation in the midst of the great river of transnationalization, and TNCs once again fulfill their leading internal role despite the continuity of a nationalist discourse that is increasingly detached from reality.[166] Third, it is possible, as recent history in the Southern Cone shows, that these policies may "overreach" and interact with a popular political awakening that appears to call into question the continuity of society's capitalist

---

164 As they are not directly relevant to our topic, I have not mentioned other fundamental aspects of these periods, such as their policies toward the agrarian oligarchies or the relative impact that primary activities and the insertion of TNCs in them may have in each case.

165 An important feature of these policies is the attempt to produce positive income redistribution, at least for the benefit of the urban poor. However, the available evidence shows that these effects, when achieved, were short-lived and later reverted to more regressive patterns.

166 The case of Mexico is quite important here. Despite decades of nationalist policies—in the sense indicated in the text—the role played by TNCs in its market, as well as the general pattern of resource distribution, is remarkably similar to that of Brazil, a country of similar size and market characteristics that, in contrast, has for long periods pursued policies aimed at attracting transnational capital with few restrictions.

parameters. Contrary to cases in which nationalist policies occur in a context where a high degree of control is maintained over autonomizing and rebellious movements of the subordinate classes,[167] in the cases I have just mentioned, there is a profound shake-up of confidence in the future situation of these markets.[168] Thus, political uncertainties feed back into an economic crisis that has two important components: one, the hollowing out of the existing productive structure, either due to the disappearance of the companies that occupy its most decisive positions or because their microeconomic logic drives them to speculative behavior in anticipation of the great apocalypse of the revolution or coup d'état. The other component of the crisis appears in the disconnection of these economies from the global capitalist system and, in particular, from financial capital. That is, one of the only remaining channels is allowing for "capital flight," while the political and economic crisis, together with the negative assessment of the policies undertaken, is contributing to the suppression of external financial flows that are needed more than ever by these economies, which are almost always short of foreign currency.

In other words, periods of acute political and economic crisis—usually involving a coup d'état—tend to lead to policies that, seeking to adjust to the real or presumed requirements of transnational capital, usher in other periods in which the latter is invited, first, to financially support the "reconstruction" of the economy and, then, as expected, to

---

167 Once again, the example of Mexico is relevant, as it suggests that it is not nationalist policies per se—at least up to a certain point, which it seems would be hard to implement without strong impulses "from below"—but rather the fear of the "excesses" that could be triggered by their combination with a political crisis that destroys the confidence of international capital.

168 I regret that the ramifications of this topic require that I refer to other works in order not to make this one even longer. I have discussed the topics mentioned in this text in "Reflexiones sobre las tendencias de cambio en el estado burocrático-autoritario," CEDES/G. E. CLASCO, *Documento*, no. 1 (1976) (also published in *Revista Mexicana de Sociología*, no. 1 [1977]) and CEDES, "Tensiones en el Estado burocrático-autoritario y la cuestión de la democracia," (1978). [Included as Chapter II of this volume.]

once again become the main driver of domestic growth. In this way, a strong swing toward one extreme tends to rebound toward situations in which, on the contrary, there is an eager effort to promote transnationalization and the leading role of TNC subsidiaries.

Why—if that capitalist state does not seem in the long run to be able to swim against the tide of transnationalization—is it also a national state, even in the sense of carrying out, with varying intensity but with regularity, various nationalist measures—that is, policies—aimed at dividing up its market for the main benefit of the classes that originated in its territory? I have already mentioned the logic of a state that must identify a political space in relation to others. But it is important to emphasize now that part of the delimitation of a space is the identification of a national market; that is, of exchange relations linked to a productive structure, which unfold mainly within the limits of the space delimited by the state. This is the domain of the classes of civil society, which—as a result of the interweaving of state, territory, and market—exist as national classes.

Given, on the one hand, the division of the world into nation states and, on the other, a transnationalization of capital whose specific modality presupposes this division, the bourgeoisie tends to want (and need) some delimitation of the sphere to which it has privileged access and in which it fundamentally carries out its accumulation. The nation implicated by the state is not only a field of subjective loyalties; it is also a market, a plexus of relationships to which privileged access is usually granted to those who in some way belong to, or have entered, the territory also implicated by that state. That nation-being is the legitimizing referent of the state, whose general interest it usually appears to serve, among other things, by promoting the economic growth of that bourgeoisie. This, in turn, presupposes that the state apparatus has the capacity to govern the main variables of the economy, including the behavior of the economic agents who have the greatest likelihood of influencing the overall economic situation, which can only be done to a limited extent with regard to the TNCs. As far as the bourgeoisie is concerned, the reinforcement of the national economy is the panoply with which it legitimizes its accumulation. This interweaving of the general interest of the nation and the driving force of bourgeois accumulation reappears, at the level of the state apparatus, in the form of policies that usually demarcate for "its" bourgeoisie a national market,[169] a hunting ground to which it would have privileged access. In this sense, the state is a national state and many of its policies are nationalist, in that they stand in the way of what would otherwise be the direct transnationalization of capital.

However, as we have seen, the cases that interest us here have their most dynamic layers in TNC subsidiaries and local companies that are, in one way or another, part of the vast oil slick of transnationalization. This does not prevent the local bourgeoisie from needing and demanding a national state.[170] On the contrary, it is precisely its condition as a potentially opulent but structurally weak bourgeoisie (due to its insertion into an acephalous productive structure) that reinforces this need. We can see an indication of this in the complaints and losses of the local bourgeoisie when state policies swing toward criteria of "international efficiency" and "non-discrimination against foreign capital." Reductions in customs and exchange rate protection, the recessionary effects of policies aimed at equilibrating the balance-of-payments and mitigating inflation, the corresponding "austerity" in public spending and monetary policy, and the offer to TNCs of generous conditions to operate in fields that were previously off-limits to them are some of the phenomena that lay bare what I have stated in the preceding pages. In other words, the fragility of a local bourgeoisie that, as a whole, must also contribute its share to restoring the economy to its "normal" patterns of growth and transnationalization. This fragility appears not only in the economic suffering of that bourgeoisie but also in the fact that the state appears unconcerned about limiting its privileged sphere of accumulation, even if it is for relatively short periods of time. This is felt by companies located outside the large oil slick. But it can also be felt by companies linked in

---

169 Note that I am referring here to the bourgeoisie as a whole, regardless of its origin, local or otherwise.

170 This is even evident in the behavior of some subsidiaries, typically in their use of the state apparatus, including nationalist arguments, to prevent the entry of other TNCs or those that, by deepening import substitution, would force them to purchase inputs locally that they currently import.

one way or another to TNCs, which find that they must negotiate with them under conditions in which the latter can, and often do, bring into play an economic power that is no longer constrained by a protective state apparatus. And this usually occurs in a recessionary context in which the cost of wielding that power is higher than ever for the local satellites of the TNCs. The situation also affects companies, such as the one in our first example, that are subjected to tougher than usual competition, both from established TNCs and from imports.[171]

In general terms, this suggests something more permanent and profound: this bourgeoisie, whose most privileged strata are co-drivers of the transnationalization of capital, must reproduce itself as a class that needs a national state to protect it, even though, for its part—as the capitalist state of a dependent society—that state tends to be, at least passively, a co-driver of the "development style" that determines the fragility of that bourgeoisie. The reproduction of its status as the local ruling class is, therefore, at the same time and for the same reasons, the reproduction of the conditions that place it in a subordinate position with respect to the transnationalization of capital and the expansion of TNCs in its own market. As for the state, its condition as a national state, with the concomitant of privileged access to its market, is at the same time—with exceptions that have culminated in political crises that have further "denationalized" that state—the introjection of processes and actors that, on the one hand, reproduce the fragility of its bourgeoisie and, on the other, overwhelm the state's claim to effectively govern social relations within its territory.

State protection of the bourgeoisie and, ultimately, of a class structure as national, even though it makes the state and the bourgeoisie

171 The basis for this assertion is weaker than for other segments of the local bourgeoisie. However, in the case of Argentina, it is plausible with respect to some companies of this type that I have been following. Indeed, when the economy is booming and the state apparatus is receptive to protecting these bourgeois segments as national entities, the subsidiaries of TNCs have adopted moderate positions on competition (to the extent that their top executive in Argentina told me that it was in the interest of that TNC for some significant national companies in its sector to survive in order to avoid the "political complications" that would have resulted from becoming a monopoly).

co-drivers of the transnationalization of capital, is not limited to policies aimed at such protection, nor to bourgeois demands to circumscribe the scope of action of TNC subsidiaries and non-domestic international capital. This is also expressed in the institutional spheres of the state to which sectors of that bourgeoisie have access, formally or otherwise, seeking both to steer measures that provide the protection they seek and to veto or halt the implementation of "anti-national" decisions. This need to enter the state apparatus—particularly keen for a bourgeoisie aware of its fragility—is one of the main drivers of its corporate organization. But another level at which this protective role of the state is expressed is in the expansion of its own apparatus. This takes the form not only of regulatory institutions that seek to patch up the countless crises and imbalances that tear apart a society subject to this pattern of growth, but also of state-owned enterprises that tend to become a key economic player. It is, above all, in the more industrialized and structurally complex peripheral countries that large investment projects reveal the fragility of a local bourgeoisie lacking the resources and initiative necessary to undertake them. Only the state apparatus, apart from TNCs, can mobilize sufficient resources. To do so, it often splits into public enterprises that, along with their subsidiaries, constitute the "elite" of the largest and most dynamic enterprises in the region, with the local bourgeoisie in a distant third place. This aspect of state expansion sometimes aims for greater vertical integration of the productive structure, while at other times it is the result of bailing out local companies that have been unable to survive the advances of this pattern of growth. The result is that even in this acephalous productive structure, the top positions are not usually occupied by the most privileged strata of the local bourgeoisie. This bourgeoisie, whether prosperous and dynamic or not, remains in a weak position, not only with respect to the TNC subsidiaries and policies of the central state apparatus, but also in relation to the behavior of public enterprises, whose criteria play a decisive role in their fate and, as such, are also focal points for their corporate organization.[172]

---

172 For more on the topic, see Atilio Borón, "Una nueva forma de estado capitalista en América Latina," paper presented at the World Congress of Sociology,

I hope that the above provides some insight into the complexity of the issue: in particular, and returning to the crux of the argument, the peculiarity of a local bourgeoisie whose reproduction as a class implies subordinating itself to the TNC subsidiaries and state apparatus. This involves presenting itself (and effectively re-creating itself, in real and in diverse ways) as a national class, despite the fact that the very reproduction of a transnationalizing pattern of growth subordinates it to transnational capital and confirms society as a whole as an acephalous and, therefore, economically dependent productive structure. The resulting contradiction between these national impulses of the state and the local bourgeoisie, and their co-driving results of the transnationalization of capital, lies at the root of the nationalist and transnationalizing vacillations of that state and that bourgeoisie. Due to the contradiction they express, they cannot definitively establish themselves at either extreme, nor, in terms of the sectors we have considered so far, can they be overcome.

V.

It follows from what has been said so far that there is nothing that makes the state or the local bourgeoisie of these societies intrinsically national or transnationalizing, nor are they "instruments" of transnational capital. In neither their structural consequences nor their behavior can the bourgeoisie or the state apparatus be, as their eulogists and detractors believe, consistently nationalist or drivers of transnationalization. This is because both the state and the bourgeoisie are simultaneously and contradictorily both things. Both are focused on a nation and a market that are the setting, for the state, of its claim for control and legitimacy and, for the local bourgeoisie, of its accumulation. However, they are not outside a process of the transnationalization of capital, which consists of inserting itself into and—at the same time—continuously exceeding the boundaries of the national. Moreover, as we have seen,

---

Uppsala, Sweden, 1978.

their participation in this process does not come strictly "from outside"—as a criterion based solely on specific economic actors, such as TNC subsidiaries, might indicate—but rather the national state and the local bourgeoisie themselves are the bearers of the contradiction that makes them the co-drivers of transnationalization.

The degree to which the state and the local bourgeoisie oscillate toward one side or the other of this contradiction, both over time and on a case-by-case basis, depends on factors that are more concrete and historically specific than those considered thus far. These factors depend on the characteristics of society as a whole, especially the relationships established with the subordinate classes. Said factors are also a function of the particularities of each productive structure and, likewise, of the alliances and conflicts with which the local bourgeoisie constitutes itself in the political-ideological field. The degree and modes of oscillation of the local bourgeoisie toward one side or the other are also expressed in the characteristics of its corporate organization. The resulting particularities cannot be deduced linearly either from the position of that fraction with respect to transnational capital and the state, or from its patterns of structural differentiation. I have argued that a class is also constituted at the corporate and political-ideological levels, and that although the structure sets limits on it—which, as a bourgeoisie, it can only transpose catastrophically—both levels have, analytically and historically, significant degrees of freedom with respect to the former.

The level of detail involved limits me to illustrating the argument with a few characteristics of the Argentine case. This is only a first step in a task that has yet to be undertaken: comparing, at the three levels mentioned above, the local industrial bourgeoisie in different national contexts. However, the Argentine case may be interesting because it is, among the Latin American countries, the one where some of the tensions potentially contained in the position of that fraction with respect to the state and transnational capital played out most fully. It can therefore serve as a contrast to cases in which these tensions have remained within limits that are more compatible with a less turbulent reproduction of the pattern of growth and transnationalization that we have been analyzing.

It seems clear that linked companies have interests that are not always easy to reconcile. On the one hand, they must support the expansion of the subsidiaries on whose accumulation they ultimately depend, and on the other, they must achieve conditions for negotiation (state protection and a "political climate" that is sensitive to nationalist arguments) that compensate as much as possible for their low bargaining power due to the significant imbalance of economic power between them. As for the bourgeois strata marginalized by transnationalization, the pattern of growth has other consequences: the continuous destruction, absorption, and subordinate re-creation of their productive units. This may appear as an inevitable "normality" in relatively favorable periods, but in times of recession and other hardships, these phenomena not only become more acute but can also be perceived by these fractions—along with other actors, typically the middle sectors—as a consequence of the voracious action of two categories that largely overlap: "monopolies" and TNC subsidiaries.

Any of the above scenarios could lead these bourgeois strata to promote and support policies based on angry nationalist rhetoric and explicitly targeting transnational capital. But while integrated companies are unlikely to want to exclude TNCs, marginalized bourgeois strata may believe, along with other social sectors, in the possibility of a capitalist path to development that privileges them and at the same time involves a much more active role for the state apparatus, excluding TNCs from their market. In the case of the successful national company in our first example, none of the factors considered so far prevent it from potentially allying itself with a program of strong restriction or even exclusion of TNCs.[173]

But this is not decisive for the policies, except as structural limits that, in practice, are rarely brought into play. For the time being, before these or other bourgeois fractions support a policy of excluding TNCs,

---

173 However, due to its own needs to connect with the global capitalist system in terms of imitations and often financing, even at this level it seems unlikely that it would support a process that extends beyond protecting its own specific interests. Furthermore, its own imitative programming of the supply of goods by TNCs could be inconsistent with the change in development style that could result from this. Nevertheless, as we will soon see, the issue is much more complex.

popular movements with roots in the working class tend to enter the political arena, and their growing influence can come across as a subversion of the social order that this faction of the bourgeoisie, as the bourgeoisie, cannot help but fear above and beyond its immediate economic interests, especially when these movements have expressed goals aimed at the suppression of capitalism.

The above raises several points on which I would like to expand. The first is that the reality of the bourgeoisie as a class is its fragmentation into companies, groups, branches, associations, and penetrations into the state apparatus. This fragmentation reflects the differentiation of immediate interests and the resulting inter-bourgeois conflicts that in our countries are exacerbated by the particularly unequal pattern of economic growth to which they are subjected. Here we see the relevance of comparative studies to establish the history and morphology of the associative modalities of the bourgeoisie. Surely—as in the Argentine case—its origin lies in some association that sought to represent the interests of "the" industry against oligarchies, agro-export sectors, and segments of transnational capital then linked to those sectors. Furthermore, in contrast to what often happened in core countries, this association did not emerge as much as a response to extensive labor unionization, but rather as a differentiation of interests from other dominant classes, organized primarily within the state apparatus, so that the latter would begin to act as a guide for this incipient activity. However, regardless of whether these associations continue to exist at the national level, we find a continuous branching out of secondary chambers and associations that address more specific and complex issues. That is, organizational forms that have emerged in line with the intention of creating defensive fronts against other bourgeois strata,[174]

---

174 Typically, this revolves around interests arising from common dependence on upstream or downstream linkages to a state or private monopoly/oligopoly or monopsony/oligopsony. Frequent cases involve various state suppliers and, more recently, companies linked upstream or downstream to TNC industrial subsidiaries.

either as a direct or indirect effect of the state apparatus[175] or due to the need to present a common front against the unions.[176] Here, the key variable appears to be the extent and period in which each country expanded this organizational network, whether in response to conflicts between bourgeois factions, under the impetus of the state apparatus, or in opposition to subordinate classes, namely the working class.[177]

The interest in learning about these points does not stem from a simple curiosity in cataloguing comparative differences. The premise is that they are the crystallization, at the level of the organizational patterns of the industrial bourgeoisie, of a history of alliances and conflicts, both extra- and intra-bourgeois, which has made it what it is in each specific case, beyond possible structural similarities. Another probable crystallization is the degree of conflict that, based on the possibilities noted in the previous sections, has taken place in each case between fractions of the local bourgeoisie and transnational capital. Do TNC subsidiaries coexist with national companies in the same chambers, associations, and federations? Or, as in the case of Argentina, did the differentiation extend so far as to create two national associations, of which one (the Argentine Industrial Union, or UIA for its acronym in Spanish) sought, true to its origins in the nineteenth century, to represent the entire industry, including TNC subsidiaries, while the other (the General Economic Confederation, or CGE, and its main affiliate, the General Confederation of Industry, or CGI), created during the first Peronist

---

175 Cases in which the attempt to open up new economic activities as a state policy decision and the search for the consolidation of the resulting support to carry them out encourages the creation of associations of the respective interests being promoted.

176 Not only as defensive measures against what may appear to be their "excessive" power, but also in situations, such as in Argentina for a number of years, where these associations have been the legal counterpart to TNCs in negotiating collective bargaining agreements.

177 For example, it seems reasonable to assume that in cases such as Chile and Argentina, the latter aspect must have been more important than in countries where the challenges coming directly from the working class have been less significant and more sporadic.

era, invoked the interests of the national business sector?[178] The reality of who each organization represented was much more complex. What matters at this point, however, is that, unlike other cases in which the potential conflicts between the local bourgeoisie and TNC affiliates—and, in general, the group of companies that hold the most privileged positions in each sector—were less acute, in Argentina this dual form of association led to situations in which these conflicts erupted to such a degree that they approached the structural limits already mentioned.

Furthermore, insofar as the interests and orientations of certain fractions of the bourgeoisie differ corporately, this can promote the individuation of these fractions on the political-ideological level as well, even as antagonists of other bourgeois fractions or strata, thereby reinforcing this differentiation. This creates a specificity that cannot be captured by structural data. In effect, the CGE gave a corporate and political-ideological voice to what in other countries has been subsumed indiscriminately under the joint representation of a bourgeoisie that includes its national monopoly strata and the subsidiaries of TNCs. By invoking the interests of a "national business sector" that is different from the "monopolies" and the TNCs, interests that the state must protect in the name of greater national autonomy and a "more just" path to capitalist development,[179] and by being recognized as the

---

178 The past tense used here is due to the fact that from 1973 to 1976, the UIA merged with the CGE under the leadership of the latter, and that one of the first measures taken by the current government was to intervene and dissolve the CGE and the association resulting from that merger.

179 Or, in the words of Pedro Cristiá, president of the CGE at the time: "The CGE has chosen its path. It declares the comprehensive development of the country and wants its businesspeople to be masters of their own destiny in the full sense of the word. These businesspeople do not want to receive orders by telex; they want to discuss and negotiate by telex, with a profound awareness of national goals and objectives. If we do not react in time, multinational companies will determine from their metropolitan centers what the country will produce, what the level of wages will be, our working methods and criteria for remuneration and promotion, safety and employment criteria, the nature of our social relations system, and even our living conditions." CGE, *Memoria e Informe Annual* (1968–69), 124.

representative of those interests, the CGE was a factor in the constitution of the industrial fraction of the local bourgeoisie as a political-ideological and corporative actor, something that has not occurred with this degree of specificity and organizational continuity in other countries in the region. On the other hand, it is interesting to note that, although its proposals presupposed the homogeneity of the interests it invoked, the leadership of the CGE remained in the hands of groups that did not come from the weak and marginalized strata of the bourgeoisie but from successful companies such as the one in our first example or those linked to TNC subsidiaries. During a turbulent history of recessions and sudden changes in state policy, these leaders were able to construct a nationalist discourse that, while seeking not to cross the hazy line separating a restriction on TNC subsidiaries from an exclusion they could not want, drew weaker—and more authentically national—bourgeois strata into that ideology and its arguments in defense of the domestic market and protection against "monopolies" and TNCs. This also materialized in the form of political alliances, where the CGE repeatedly allied itself with trade unions,[180] based on the nationalist argument that, while on the one hand it implied the expansion of the market for the benefit of those bourgeois fractions, on the other hand it brought with it the defense of a relatively high level of wages and employment.

It was this that allowed the CGE, along with the interests it invoked, to establish itself as a political actor in its own right, through its participation in the state apparatus,[181] its influential role within Peronism,[182]

---

180 This even took the form of formal "pacts" with the General Confederation of Labor (CGT, for its acronym in Spanish), which explicitly outlined their agreement on immediate demands (a combination of measures to reactivate the domestic market, including wage increases, and a demand for active state protection for the bourgeoisie), as well as through the proposal of an alternative path to development that would be supported mainly by the "national business sector" and the "organized working class."

181 This fluctuated over time, reflecting the changing balance of power between it and, on the other hand, the UIA and other associations linked to it.

182 For its part, it added an important bourgeois element without which it would be difficult to understand some of the ambiguities of a movement that, like

and its frequent alliances with the urban popular sector, especially the trade unions. This alliance, forged in an essentially defensive convergence against the "excessive" advances of transnationalization and against the control of the state apparatus by "liberal" groups, has shaped Argentine politics for the past two decades. On the one hand, by repeatedly bringing together a significant portion of the local bourgeoisie with the middle classes and the popular sector, it offered unusual resistance to what in other cases has been the much smoother advance of transnationalization and the expansion of TNC subsidiaries. On the other hand, it corralled the popular sector and, within it, the working class and its various organizations, into a multi-class alliance reinforced by a nationalist ideology of capitalist development. This multi-classism, which included the bourgeois element provided by the CGE and the consequent exclusion of any departure from capitalism, facilitated the successes achieved by that alliance. These successes culminated in 1973 with their greatest and most catastrophic victory: as part of the great wave of Peronism, it achieved a high degree of control over the state apparatus and from there, despite the precautions of the CGE and its leaders—who had captured the state's economic apparatus and forced the UIA to merge with it as a subordinate—, contributed to the unleashing of a crisis that exceeded the structural limits outlined above.[183]

It is possible that these fractions of the local Argentine bourgeoisie are structurally similar to those in other highly industrialized countries of the region. But I want to emphasize that, at the corporate and political-ideological level, their existence as a fraction and, ultimately, their manner of constituting themselves as a political entity, does not come from any attribute that they possess "in and of themselves." Rather, it is the result of a relationship—generally unusually conflictive—with transnational capital and—generally unusually cooperative—with the better-organized strata of the urban popular sector. It was this relationship

---

Peronism, was based mainly on the popular sector and the unions.

183 For a more detailed discussion of these issues, which are only briefly mentioned here, see CEDES/G. E. CLASCO, "Estado y alianzas en la Argentina, 1956–1976," *Estudios Sociales*, no. 7 (1977). [Included as Chapter I of this volume.]

with the upper strata of its own class and with the subordinate classes that gave the local industrial bourgeoisie in Argentina its specificity.

This resulted from a history that began with the particularities of Argentina's original insertion into the world market, which gave its popular sector relatively high degrees of autonomy and organizational density. In countries where these conditions do not exist,[184] the local industrial bourgeoisie has not generated its own organizational network nor has it become a differentiated political actor. In these cases, the corporate and political-ideological indifference of the bourgeoisie has deprived the popular sector—which is weaker and less organized than its Argentine counterpart for reasons that also date back to the respective modes of incorporation into the world market—of the bourgeois ally it had in Argentina. A lower degree of differentiation in the organizational and political-ideological forms of the local industrial bourgeoisie expresses and reinforces a greater degree of subsumption of that fraction with respect to the economic and political leadership of the more transnational and oligopolistic bourgeois strata. This, on the other hand, entails a balance of power, translated at the level of the state and the policies emanating from its apparatus, which tends to more steadily promote the transnationalization of capital in its market. This does not mean that the state ceases to be a national state or to exercise its usual role of protecting the local industrial bourgeoisie, but this is fundamentally carried out through negotiations and pressure from the top—Mexico and Brazil are relevant examples—unshaken by a system of alliances in which that fraction accompanies the dynamic entry of the subordinate classes into the political arena.

If the speculations—or, more charitably, the hypotheses—drawn from a case serve any purpose, then it follows that the extent to which the structural limits and potential conflicts between the local industrial bourgeoisie and transnational capital can be explained depends on a succession of political and economic circumstances. These, in turn, are constituted by a constellation of forces that mainly includes the types of relationships—alliances and conflicts—between various bourgeois

184 There are others that I cannot address here and for which I must refer to the material cited in the previous footnote.

fractions and with the subordinate classes. Only from this contextualizing—and historical—perspective can we extract the local industrial bourgeoisie from the quietude of its structural data and understand it properly as a fraction that is constituted by the simultaneous intertwining of the three levels I have been emphasizing.

VI.

An additional complication arises from the fact that situations such as those I have outlined based on the Argentine example are far from static. On the one hand, periods of acute global crisis can lead to drastic changes in the alignment of forces and in state policies. Thus, the current Argentine government has not only undertaken the implementation of an "order" that involves the political and economic exclusion of the popular sector. It has also directed its action toward one of the linchpins of the previously mentioned recurring alliance, eliminating the CGE and its organizational offshoots. Currently,[185] there is discussion not only about what to do with the unions but also about what forms of organization will be promoted or tolerated for the industrial bourgeoisie; but it seems unlikely that, as long as the current balance of power remains, there will be a resurrection of anything similar to the CGE. The dispersion of the interests of that bourgeois fraction at the specific corporate level of the trade associations is necessary to guarantee the continuity of policies that, since 1976, have shifted toward an explicit promotion of transnationalization and its consequent "development style"; that is, the absorption of these fractions into a nationally based organization that claims to represent "the" industry as a whole and, as a result, eliminates the political role that the other fraction and its organizations played in the previous period. It is not for us to speculate here on where a situation that is unlikely to stabilize under its current terms will lead, but the fact is that this has put on hold, and likely profoundly altered, the very condition of the fraction of the local

185 [Early 1978.]

industrial bourgeoisie. This has obviously occurred at the corporate and political-ideological levels. However, while these levels cannot be deduced from one another linearly, they belong to the same social reality that the concept seeks to capture, and these changes also serve the rapid process of destruction, absorption, and subordinate re-creation of the fraction that is being promoted.

The Argentine case, like the rest of the Southern Cone, illustrates another possibility for change in what is, in each case, the historical pattern of existence of the local industrial bourgeoisie. At a time when a political and economic crisis seems destined to bring about the end of capitalism, the fundamental interest of the bourgeoisie as a whole in ensuring the conditions for its reproduction erases its divisions and conflicts. Thus, the strictly corporate level of second-degree chambers and associations loses importance, since confrontations with the subordinate classes take place at a more global level and little can be expected from the fragmented tactics used to penetrate a state apparatus that is also in crisis and, at times, occupied by personnel hostile to those interests. The result tends to be the fusion of the bourgeoisie as a whole into its national organizations or ad hoc associations behind goals that, in seeking to save it from the dangers that seemingly threaten it as a class, can only aim at the abrupt interruption of the ongoing process. After that, and as can also be seen in the Southern Cone following the implementation of its BA, fragmentation reappears, benefiting the most economically powerful strata of the bourgeoisie and severely punishing a large part of the local bourgeoisie which, in order to save itself as a class, has had to support the political and economic exclusion of its allies—the popular sector and its organized expressions—which, in more "normal" times, helped it counterbalance the Darwinian pattern of economic performance promoted by the upper strata of its own class. But those moments of fusion reveal what the local industrial fraction has in common with the rest, including the TNCs: that is, being a fraction of a bourgeois class. In the same way, and concurrently, those moments of fusion and their abrupt "resolution" show that, rather than a national or popular state, it is a capitalist state that, in saving the bourgeoisie as a whole, must once again make room—in fact, more than in any other period—for the transnationalizing pole of the contradiction that permeates it as much as it permeates "its" bourgeoisie.

VII.

These pages are no more than what was anticipated in the first section: reflections to guide ongoing research, focused—moreover—on a rather unique case. I have had to leave out many details in order to keep this work within reasonable limits. Furthermore, the learning process involved in this research means that these reflections cannot claim any theoretical status. However, the purpose of these pages is to reopen the discussion on a topic that has been neglected or subjected to simplifications that do not do justice to the complex, changing, and contradictory segment of social reality that it seeks to capture. Although it has not always thrived, nor has it proven to be the developmentalist "elite" or the puppet of transnational capital envisioned by outdated prophecies, the local industrial bourgeoisie is alive and well. Its survival is based on the fundamental contradiction that permeates the three levels of its existence, which serve as the central points around which I suggest revisiting this topic.

CHAPTER V

Notes for the Study of Processes of Political Democratization in the Wake of the Bureaucratic-Authoritarian State

Introduction

This text is part of a research project, but more than anything else, it is an expression of hope: to the extent that the project itself was a direct consequence of that hope. The project, in which I participated from its inception and which was hosted by the Woodrow Wilson Center, resulted in four volumes co-edited by Philippe Schmitter, Laurence Whitehead, and myself and published in Spanish under the title *Transiciones desde un gobierno autoritario* (Transitions from Authoritarian Rule) I have recounted the history of this project on other occasions, so I will not repeat it here. I will only add that I wrote this chapter in 1979 as co-director of the project, with the aim of organizing discussions and framing and guiding the contributions we were going to request from the authors of various comparative texts and national case studies. This text also served as the main basis for volume IV of that work, by Schmitter and myself, subtitled "Conclusiones tentativas sobre las democracias inciertas" (Tentative Conclusions on Uncertain Democracies).

At the time that I wrote that text, in mid-1979, the fissures in the BA that I had discussed the previous year in "Tensions" (Chapter II of this volume) were already clearly apparent. Likewise, the transitions in Spain, Portugal, and Greece were underway, although their outcome was still very uncertain, and in Brazil a process of liberalization was taking place (certainly not democratization, according to the obvious intentions of those in power) which, as General Geisel said, would be "slow, gradual, and certain," but which was nevertheless permitting the resurgence of genuine opposition.

That is why this essay takes some distance from the anger with which I wrote the previous ones. It is an expression of hope, of believing that, although there were still many uncertain steps ahead in order to achieve democracy, it was worth thinking ahead, distilling what I believed I knew about those paths and, of course, the many ways derailment was possible, for which the recent history of our country offered many examples.

The incipient transitions mentioned above, although still uncertain in their course, were the empirical referents I had at the time. Of course, I also had the experience of the transition that took place during General Lanusse's government, which I had analyzed for a book that was already finished but for which, for obvious reasons, I was unable to find a publisher until late 1982, when the long-awaited collapse of the BA was taking place. From all this, I felt I had learned a few things that I still believe to be true. One was that the cracks within the BA led some of its sectors, "soft" sectors in my text, although they certainly did not become democrats, to seek support outside the BA, and that this implied promoting a kind of "opening up," which of course they tried to control and limit considerably before the result resembled a democracy. Second, that this position created serious conflicts within the BA, with the "hardliners," and that these conflicts were exacerbated by the course of events, which, albeit reluctantly, forced those I referred to as "softliners" to press ahead with the transition. Third, that on the opposition side there were serious risks if the "opportunists" prevailed in that camp, willing to unconditionally accept what the "softliners" wanted to impose. Fourth, there was another serious risk if the "maximalists" prevailed in the ranks of the opposition as they were opposed to any negotiation with the moderates and committed to ending the BA with a revolutionary leap that would not need to rely on a return to democracy, which they valued little anyway. Fifth, it was fundamentally important that those who, for circumstantial reasons, I refer to in this text as "moderates" prevail in the ranks of the opposition. Years later, when I wrote the respective text with Schmitter, I felt free to call them by their true name, "democratic opposition." I was impressed then, in anticipation, and I continue to be impressed, post facto, by the enormous difficulties, risks, and uncertainties of successfully navigating from a BA to a democracy.

This framework (or, as some have called it, though I dislike the term, "model")—particularly since its publication in the books cited above—has given rise to numerous discussions, which have accumulated as other transitions have occurred. This is not the place to comment on those discussions, except to say that I am surprised (and, I confess, displeased) when I read that this framework is "elitist," given that in it I placed so much emphasis on political reactivation and the "resurrection of civil society," both of which, along with victory in the field of democratic opposition, are necessary to achieve democracy.

Yet I cannot resist the temptation to recount my delight when, while traveling around the world, I was approached by people who had also lived under harsh authoritarian conditions (among others, I recall individuals from Poland, Czechoslovakia, Korea, Taiwan, the Philippines, and South Africa), telling me that they had read that outline—photocopied or mimeographed and circulated clandestinely—and that they were grateful because it had given them hope and ideas for their own struggles.

I thought it might be worth publishing the text in which I originally set out these reflections.

Notes for the Study of Processes of Political Democratization in the Wake of the Bureaucratic-Authoritarian State

I.

The present text does not pretend to offer substantive answers to the manifold questions raised by the exit from authoritarian situations. Instead, my goal is to propose several focal points around which the study and comparison of transition processes might be organized.[186] Despite the fact that they typically occur within a short period of time, such processes present a great number and variety of elements for analysis. Accordingly, the title given to the following pages is not entirely appropriate; the processes by which a BA terminates do not necessarily lead to stable political democracy, as is demonstrated by the case of Argentina during the 1970s. On the contrary, such processes may

---

186 This chapter first appeared as "Notas para el Estudio de Procesos de Democratización Política a Partir del Estado Burocrático-Autoritario," *Documento de Trabajo, CEDES* 2, no. 9 [1979]). It was edited by John Rieger for inclusion in this book. Strictly speaking, the present notes are a working paper, the first fruits of a Guggenheim fellowship granted to me for the study of the theme indicated by the title. I have prepared the present text for a project on the same theme that is being developed in the Latin American Program of the Woodrow Wilson Center for International Scholars. Basically, it is intended as material for discussion among program participants; my hope is that it will prove useful for authors of the case studies to be carried [out] within the project. Given the nature of this work, I have omitted detailed bibliographical references.

provoke relapses that intensify the characteristics of earlier authoritarian rule. Histories of success in the consolidation of political democracy, and their determinant factors, should be compared with histories of failure, in order to isolate the decisive elements therein.

Of course, to speak of "successes" and "failures" implies a value judgment. I consider intrinsically valuable the move away from authoritarian forms that leads to a regime of reasonably consolidated political democracy. From the normative standpoint I am adopting, the achievement of political democracy—both on the level of competition for governmental authority and of the effectiveness of basic individual and associative rights—is an immense advance over the conditions imposed by a BA.[187] Furthermore, under the circumstances resulting from the previous existence of a BA, the achievement of political democracy may present the most viable route, if not the only one, along which to address issues related to the expansion of democracy at social and economic levels.

Other prefatory remarks are in order. First, I will not be concerned with the dynamics of the BA nor, therefore, with the tensions that contribute to the termination of this type of political domination.[188] Second, I will discuss the transition from a BA toward another sort of rule focusing on properly political factors and processes and paying scant attention to an issue that merits separate treatment: the fluctuations and problems of economic policy that typically accompany the political processes that concern me here. The third remark is that the present notes refer only to the transition from one kind of authoritarian state—a BA—not to transitions from any kind of authoritarian rule. It is possible that some of the reflections presented here are valid for transitions from other forms of authoritarianism, but the BA has characteristics that correspond to social and economic specificities, which influence the kind of

---

187 See chapter 2 of this volume [*Counterpoints*] and the author's "Reflections on the Patterns of Change in the Bureaucratic-Authoritarian State," *Latin American Research Review* 13, no. 1 (1978). See also *Bureaucratic Authoritarianism: Argentina, 1966–1973, in Comparative Perspective* (Berkeley: University of California Press, 1988).—Editor's note to O'Donnell, *Counterpoints*

188 See chapter 2 of this volume.—Editor's note to O'Donnell, *Counterpoints*

political transition that may arise from this type of rule. In particular, it should be borne in mind that the emergence of the BA is an expression of the fear of the dominant classes and various segments of the middle class regarding what they perceive as a high degree of threat posed by a politically activated popular sector—a popular sector not only politically mobilized but also underpinned by an organizational network that, at least during the period directly preceding the inauguration of the BA, is notably extended and autonomous from the dominant classes. A popular sector with these features is characteristic of an economic and social structure endowed with large urban concentrations and extensive though immature industrialization. Such a structure generates a large and strategically located working class, along with many dependent layers within the middle class, especially public employees.[189] Furthermore, the existence of a popular sector (including a working class) that has "been there"—that is, fully incorporated into the political arena, and in such a way that in the period preceding the establishment of a BA it was perceived as a threat to the continuity of basic parameters of society (particularly, its international affiliations and its condition as a capitalist society)—signals important differences between the BA and other kinds of authoritarianism—oligarchic and populist—in which the political activation of the popular sector has not occurred and the economy has not attained the level of complexity and industrialization typical of cases of BA. In any event, these are speculations that it will be necessary to explore comparatively through case studies that examine transitions from authoritarian forms other than the BA.

We should now address the problematic foci that, to me, appear fundamental for a case-by-case and comparative study of transition processes: the first consists of some conceptual clarifications regarding

---

189 As part of an effort to distinguish the BA from other authoritarian forms (especially, traditional or oligarchic, populist, and fascist), I propose these and other specific characteristics of the BA in several works. See, especially, "Reflections," and *Modernization and Bureaucratic-Authoritarianism* (Berkeley: Institute of International Studies and University of California Press, 1972). See also the discussions and conceptual advances contained in David Collier, ed., *The New Authoritarianism in Latin America* (Princeton: Princeton University Press, 1979).

the "whence" and the "whither" implied by the very idea of political transition; the second focal point is the identification of the main coalitions involved in this process; the third, which complicates the strictly political analysis to which the earlier topics tend, is what I will call the resurrection of civil society. In a final section I attempt to bind up some loose ends.

II.

The first problem with which one is confronted in thinking about the transition from a BA to another political form is the analytical determination of a point of departure—the point at which such a transition is understood to begin. Here, a strictly circumscribed definition of the authoritarian state (or regime, depending on the theoretical orientation of each author) that precedes the transition to be studied is an advantage. The problem of beginnings is an important one; only in one contemporary case that I am aware of (Portugal) did a swift transition from authoritarian rule to political democracy occur. In other cases, the situation remains authoritarian during a not insignificant period; yet, in order to conceptualize the transition itself, we must be able to distinguish between the subsequent authoritarianism (itself in fluid transformation) and the BA that preceded it. With this in mind, I propose that we are dealing with a BA whenever all of the following conditions still hold:[190] (1) the maintenance of what in previous works I called the political exclusion of the popular sector manifest (in what directly interests us here) in the coercive prohibition of the formation of organizations that publicly claim to represent the interests of the popular sector and/or the working class, as well as in rigid state control of unions, (2) the nonexistence or merely formal existence of institutions of political

190 The following attributes are derived from the definition of the BA proposed in my previous works [See note 3 above [or note 189 in this volume].—Editor's note to O'Donnell, *Counterpoints*] with a view to the issues that concern us here.

democracy, and (3) the restriction of the political arena, basically, to processes internal to the state apparatus, the actors in which are members—civilian and military—of this apparatus, as well as leaders of large private organizations. The disappearance of any one of these three conditions implies that the BA has ceased to exist. Yet that this occurs is a necessary condition for the emergence of political democracy, not a sufficient one. One characteristic of the kind of transition I discuss here is that, beginning from the time one or all of the just-stated conditions ceases or cease to remain in effect, the situation remains authoritarian; the latter, however, is no longer the specific type of authoritarianism that we refer to as a BA. Furthermore—and this is part of what we must come to grips with—throughout the transition such an authoritarian situation bears within it the probability, which we should not underestimate, of reversion to further instantiations of a BA. Political democracy is only one of several possible outcomes of a process that entails much more than the elimination of certain characteristics of the BA.[191]

Of course, it is usually impossible to pinpoint an exact "moment" at which the transition from a BA starts, but I hope that the categories I have just proposed may facilitate the identification of the beginning of such transitions with adequate precision. What, then, would be the "point of arrival"—the threshold at which our analysis would end? Here it is important to recall that one of the issues at play during the transition is the building of a new political regime.[192] The BA has a political regime,

---

191 In these processes, as we shall see, the struggle to achieve what could be properly called political democracy—the fight against those who would like to limit the transition to a "decompression" of selected characteristics of BA—is one of the main axes around which the political game is constituted.

192 It is important to adequately distinguish between state, government, and regime. On the first of these, see my "Apuntes para una teoría del Estado," *Documentos CEDES/CLACSO*, Buenos Aires, 9 (1978). By "regime," I understand the set of patterns actually effective (though not necessarily legally or formally established) that determine the following: (1) modalities of recruitment and access to governmental roles, and (2) criteria of representation on the basis of which are formulated expectations regarding access to those roles and expectations regarding influence over their incumbents. By "government," I understand the higher positions in the

though usually not a formally institutionalized one, that may outlive this kind of state itself; but, at one moment or another, that regime dissolves,[193] and there begins, also at this level, a transition that may lead to political democracy. In any event, the degree of formalization[194] and other characteristics assumed by an authoritarian regime are among the fundamental issues put into play in and by the transition. Although history remains open, one may plausibly conclude the analysis of a transition whenever a new political regime—democratic or not—with apparently reasonable chances of enduring over the medium term emerges.

We now turn to more specific issues.

III.

The transition from a BA toward another type of rule may begin for various reasons: opposition activities that betray the fragility of a BA's social supports and coercive arm (Argentina during 1969–73, and Greece), a perception that the BA is so firmly consolidated that its leaders are lured into seeking legitimation by way of elections (Brazil), or prospects of the more or less imminent disappearance of a leader central to the regime (Spain) together, as in Brazil, with a perception of rather high regime consolidation.

---

state apparatus, access to which is determined by the existing regime and from which may be mobilized, by the respective national state, its coercive supremacy over the territory it delimits.

193 At the regime level, the BA is characterized by restriction of access to governmental roles to those at the pinnacle of complex bureaucratic organizations (both public and private), who are—according to a pillarized and/or corporatist vision of society—considered to be, if not representative, entitled to speak for their "respective" social sectors; these criteria obstruct channels of access and exclude demands for the representation of popular interests and aspirations, apart from those that each leadership group claims to embody in a corporatist fashion.

194 Whether or not a regime is formalized—and, if so, the extent to which it is—depends upon the degree to which that regime is crystallized and institutionalized in a constitution and other legal instruments.

The degree of control exercised by the ruling alliance over the transition—especially its capacity to impose the rules of the game under which the transition is to proceed—depends upon the manner in which the process begins.[195] If the transition begins for fundamentally extrinsic reasons (that is, as a direct result of opposition activities), as it did in Argentina and Greece, then the control of the ruling alliance over the process will be weaker. If the transition begins mainly at the initiative of the ruling alliance itself, then its degree of control over the subsequent process will be greater. Furthermore, given that the ruling coalition will typically prefer gradual advances, guaranteed against the risk of "a leap into the void," then, other things being equal, the more control the ruling coalition has over the transition the more protracted it will be.

As we will see, there are also important variations from case to case in the characteristics of the parties or groups that succeed in being recognized as the principal voice of the opposition. They may represent quite moderate stands, as did the Greek opposition, or, as occurred in Argentina during the period 1969–73, they may embody an even more threatening radicalization than that which preceded the emergence of BA. The ruling coalition's initial degree of liberalizing commitment also varies across cases: their intentions may be limited to re-coating the BA in a more legitimate hue (as in Brazil 1973–74), or, their intentions may extend to the establishment of what we might properly call a political democracy (as they did in Spain during the Suárez period).

There are equally important case-by-case variations in the institutional forms that survive the BA or are created during it. The restoration of the monarchy in Spain and, in Brazil, the survival of the parliament and the BA's own creation of two parties (which, although they sometimes appeared devoid of real significance, subsequently took on a life

195 I will use the term "liberalization" to refer to decisions that, while they imply a significant opening of the BA (such as the restitution of effective judicial guarantees for certain individual rights or the establishment of parliamentary forms not based on free electoral competition), nevertheless fall short of effecting what we might properly call a political democracy. As I have suggested, such liberalization warrants that, analytically, we consider the BA to have disappeared, but it does not eliminate the authoritarian nature of the overall situation.

of their own) contrasts sharply with the institutional devastation produced in such cases as Chile, Uruguay, and Argentina. These differences may be crucial in determining the rhythms, issues, and risks that each actor faces. But, without ignoring such differences (here I am only able to take into account some situations by way of example, until such time as a properly comparative study furnishes the requisite data) I wish to highlight several common characteristics that may be gleaned from a broad observation of transition processes. I hope that these remarks serve as a conceptual axis that helps organize the wealth of empirical material of the cases to be studied.

One common characteristic of the transition is the formation of a "liberalizing coalition" that cuts across the typical BA alignments in a new fashion. This coalition is formed, on one hand, by members of the ruling alliance in the BA who, for any of the reasons already mentioned, opt to lead a process of political liberalization—these I will call the BA softliners. Their partner in this coalition is a segment of the opposition that I will refer to as the moderate, or truly democratic, opposition.

While the type of state and regime that the softliners wish to move toward may still be authoritarian, their decision to liberalize[196] and, thus, dissolve the BA, places them in direct conflict with the hardliners within the BA—those opposed to any kind of political transformation. Such opposition to change may be based on their commitment to the BA's unlimited duration, or it may be rooted in the belief that the right moment at which to "decompress" the political situation has—"still"—not arrived.[197] For their part, the softliners must take into account not only the many actors within the state apparatus who remain undecided about these matters (principally, within the armed forces) but also, and

---

196 With the apparent exception of Spain (where the initial decisions of the softliners appear to indicate an intention to establish a political democracy), it is typical of the beginning of transitions from BA that the purposes of the softliners do not extend beyond certain liberalizing measures.

197 Hardline opposition may also be based on the view that the proper response to events is not liberalization but an accentuation of existing repressive features of the BA; this was the case in Argentina, as it was in Greece after the riots of Córdoba.

no less importantly, among the dominant classes. To all of the above, the softliners must present a plausible argument to the effect that the transition they propose is "better" than the alternative of continuity advocated by the hardliners. In cases of spectacular opposition emergence (such as those of Greece, and Argentina during the period 1969–73), the softliners argue that liberalization will neutralize the most threatening opposition elements and, as a result, more effectively safeguard the fundamental interests of the members of the BA alliance than would be the case under the hardline alternative. By contrast, when liberalization is initiated in decisions essentially internal *to* the BA, then the softliners' argument is that the rough edges of existing domination must be rounded off through the legitimizing reestablishment of certain electoral mechanisms and/or—as in the case of Spain—by filling in inevitable institutional vacuums.[198] In either case, the softliners must persuade themselves and be capable of convincing other members of the ruling alliance that their fundamental interests will not be less effectively safeguarded (and, in the long run, will be more effectively so) than they would under the continuist hardline alternative.[199] Most important in this respect are the "fundamental interests" of the armed forces and of the dominant classes that form the principal social base of the BA.[200]

---

198 In "Tensions in the Bureaucratic-Authoritarian State and the Question of Democracy," [chapter 2 in this volume.—Editor's note to O'Donnell, *Counterpoints*] I argue that, whatever degree of success a BA might have achieved, its undeniably antipopular origins and its obstruction of electoral channels pose to this type of rule an insoluble problem: a lack of mechanisms of legitimation and succession. With the characteristics proper to each case, what we have observed above about Brazil and Spain is an expression of this Achilles heel that afflicts even the most "successful" BAs.

199 As I have mentioned, here I will not deal with the internal tensions of BA, which include the ideological malaise—diffuse but operative—that continuist inclinations typically generate among the most sophisticated sectors of the ruling alliance. To the extent that they interact with such factors, circumstances and developments within the international context must also be taken into account.

200 In the works referred to above, I speak of the upper bourgeoisie as the principal social base of the BA. With this term, I designate the more

What are those fundamental interests? An a priori and abstract reply to this question is impossible; such interests cannot be determined outside of the transition process itself. Indeed, the ongoing redefinition of the content of such interests is one of the central themes of the transition. At its beginning, both the upper bourgeoisie and the armed forces typically define their fundamental interests very broadly. Later, following the rhythm of changes in power relations that the transition itself provokes (in reality, the transition *is* those changes) such interests tend to be redefined in a more limited way by the members of the BA alliance. Quite early in the transition, these actors find themselves adopting positions that they would have rejected outright at the start of the process. But even though the flexibility of these actors turns out *to* be greater than they themselves originally supposed, it is not infinite. For the armed forces, a point of non-negotiability seems to be reached if attempts are made *to* alter their hierarchical lines of discipline, especially those that separate officers from noncommissioned officers and soldiers. For the upper bourgeoisie (in addition, obviously, to the continuity of society *qua* capitalist) a fundamental point is to obtain a reasonable guarantee that it will retain its position at the dynamic vanguard of the economy; however, this bourgeoisie may be prepared to accept an outcome in which its supremacy is attenuated or partially relinquished due to advances in various forms of state capitalism and/or state tutelage of selected local capital sectors.[201] Another non-negotiable point—more fundamental because it applies to the entire bourgeoisie, not only to its upper fractions—is that its cellular domination in society remain beyond question. In other words, the bourgeoisie's prerogatives to control the organization of the workplace and decide about the allocation of the capital it accumulates should not be challenged. The remaining interests of the armed forces and the bourgeoisie remain vaguely defined

concentrated, oligopolized, transnationalized layers of industrial, financial, and commercial capital.

201 Non-negotiable points for the upper bourgeoisie apparently do not include a significant redistribution of income or an increase in the political sway of unions. However, neither one of these outcomes would make most of the bourgeoisie happy.

and are ultimately subject to the vagaries of the transition; but those that I have just mentioned seem to be the core, the bottom line that the armed forces and the bourgeoisie cannot even contemplate negotiating. Were this nucleus of interests put in play, the higher echelons of the armed forces and/or of the bourgeoisie, as the case may be, would feel that the transition was leading to a catastrophic outcome; consequently they would adopt behaviors sharply antagonistic to it.

Let us revisit the political game played by the liberalizing coalition. Among their allies in the BA, the softliners will always find some hardliners. Furthermore, neither the softliners nor the hardliners are homogeneous.[202] Among the softliners there will be differences regarding how far the liberalization should go; accordingly, different kinds of softliners will seek different interlocutors within different sectors of the opposition. Among the hardliners there will be those unconditionally opposed to liberalization and those who believe that it is "still" not the right time for liberalization. These latter will allow for limited negotiations with the softliners, as will other members of the BA alliance: prominent figures, groups, and organizations that remain undecided, fence-sitters disposed to "wait and see" what happens with liberalization. One of the central problems faced by the softliners is the potential fusion of the hardliners and the undecided, along with the thinning of their own ranks that would follow from this; such a convergence might be brought about by a convincing argument to the effect that the liberalization process, far from having generated the results promised by the softliners, has led to a situation in which catastrophic harm is about to be done to the fundamental interests of the members of the BA alliance (however broadly those interests happen to be defined at the time of an eventual antiliberalizing fusion).

---

202 At this stage, it is convenient to point out that these categories and those that I will specify in discussing the opposition camp are analytical; as such, they should not be regarded as fixed attributes of concrete actors. One of the features of the transition's fluidity is the displacement of actors from one position to another, as well as the reconstitution of actors' identities; it is precisely for the analysis of such matters that the categories I propose might prove heuristically useful.

The danger of this fusion (and the subsequent coup—military or otherwise—that it would provoke) is very real; indeed, it is one of the most important problems that the softliners must face. On the other hand, the threat of such a fusion is a trump card that the softliners hold over the opposition. It is on this very basis that they pressure the opposition to "not demand too much"; in this way, the softliners endeavor to ensure that, at each stage of a very dynamic and uncertain process, the opposition is satisfied with whatever is possible "under the circumstances" over the short and medium term. In their negotiations[203] with the opposition, the softliners may always argue that, were it in their power, they would pursue greater and swifter liberalization; however, goes the argument, this is impossible, because it would trigger a hardline reaction, setting the process back to a situation much worse than that implied by the "realistic goals" of the softliners. One variation on this type of case—which appears when the leadership of the softliners is in the hands of those who control the armed forces—is illustrated, although under very different political circumstances in each instance, by the actions of President Lanusse (1971–73) in Argentina (a liberalization imposed on the BA from outside), and by those of President Geisel (1975–79) in Brazil (a liberalization initiated by decisions taken within the BA). In this kind of variation, it is the leader of the softliners who brandishes the threat that, if the opposition fails to recognize and respect the limits of the situation, he "will be forced" to clamp down on the transition.

However, quite soon it becomes evident that the softliners are so committed to liberalization and, therefore, opposed to a hardline coup that, were such a coup ever to occur, it would be aimed as much at the softliners themselves as at the opposition. It follows that even though the liberalization advances considerably beyond the softliners' initial intentions, to the extent that the latter wish to preserve their governmental positions—among other reasons, in order to attempt "still" to lead the process back toward a path more in keeping with their own

203 The term "negotiations" implies that the softliners have found interlocutors in an opposition that is not maximalist; this is an issue that I will discuss shortly.

preferences—their efforts to forestall a hardline coup make them vigilant guardians of the transition.

On the side of the opposition the situation is no less complicated. There will always be an opportunistic opposition (or pseudo-opposition) ready to accept practically any proposal made by the softliners. Objectively, this part of the opposition is an obstacle to democratization; to the degree that it succeeds in becoming the dominant voice within the opposition, the transition process will grind to a halt at a stage that closely reflects the initial proposals of the softliners—which is to say, short of political democracy. Another segment of the opposition will be maximalist, unwilling to negotiate anything with any sector of the BA. If other members of the opposition do so, the maximalists will execrate them as traitors who have "sold out" to the BA. Furthermore, maximalists will typically depict the proposed liberalization as a trap laid by the softliners and opposition traitors. The maximalist position within the opposition and the position of the BA's hardliners feed on each other. It is the maximalists who, with their words and actions, offer the best reasons for the hardliners to reaffirm their views, and provide them with ammunition for persuading the undecided *to* take a stand against liberalization. If maximalists succeed in imposing themselves as the dominant voice of the opposition, the consequences are more complex than those that would result from the victory of the opportunists within the opposition camp. The first such consequence is that the risk of a coup increases dramatically because the maximalists explicitly refuse *to* extend guarantees *to* any of the interests of the BA alliance. But, as is demonstrated by the Argentine case of 1969–73, the deterioration of the BA may be so severe (as manifested in a high degree of factionalization of the armed forces and an inability on the part of the upper bourgeoisie to envisage minimally coherent political tactics) that a maximalist triumph in the opposition camp does not lead to a coup, despite the risk of the same continually surrounding the process.[204] In such a case, the short-term

204 For a detailed analysis of this kind of process, see the author's *Bureaucratic Authoritarianism: Argentina*.—Editor's note to O'Donnell, *Counterpoints*

result is speedy democratization extending beyond the purely political sphere; with the consequent demise of the BA, the barriers to radicalization at the microlevels of society collapse. In other words, in cases such as these, none of the fundamental interests of the BA alliance are safeguarded. Moreover, the resulting democratization tends to be more the byproduct of maximalist supremacy in the political and social arenas than the result of conscious efforts aimed at the construction of a politically democratic regime.[205] When such a regime nevertheless emerges, as did today's regime in Portugal,[206] it is due to vicissitudes of the process that I cannot discuss here. In other cases of transitions culminated under maximalist supremacy, such as Argentina in 1973, the resulting democratic regime could not be minimally stabilized. Yet, in both cases, a maximalist triumph in the opposition camp that is not interrupted by a coup entails not only the collapse of the BA but also, at a more profound level, an acute crisis of the state (understood as guarantor of the relations of domination, including the capitalist relations of production).[207] For its part, such a crisis signals that what has emerged is, at the least, a prerevolutionary juncture; a situation of dual power may ensue, in which power is shared between whatever remains of the repressive power of the state apparatus and the various organizational forms in which the maximalist opposition is embodied (among others, militias, guerrilla groups, and even sections of the state

---

205 In general, the maximalist opposition will accord little value to political democracy (except to the extent that it becomes a tactical necessity). At the beginning of the transition, this is so because the maximalist opposition views political democracy as a trap set by the BA alliance. Later on, when the BA has eventually collapsed and this opposition has imposed itself in its stead, the maximalists view political democracy as an unnecessary constraint on the pursuit of their own goals.

206 The author refers to the regime instituted in Portugal in 1979.—Editor's note to O'Donnell, *Counterpoints*

207 This assertion follows from the view that the state is primarily a condensation of relations of social domination, and is to be understood only secondarily as a set of bureaucratic institutions, as I argue in "Apuntes." [See also chapter 2 in this volume.—Editor's note to O'Donnell, *Counterpoints*]

apparatus that have passed over to the maximalist camp). Nevertheless, in none of the contemporary cases—and despite the fact that in Portugal the process extended to an advanced degree of expropriation of the upper bourgeoisie and of restructuring of the armed forces—has the triumph of the maximalists provoked a leap outside the capitalist condition of society. In addition to immense objective difficulties, this is due to the splintering and lack of strategic programs typical of an opposition that is better suited to destroying the BA than to governing over its ruins. As a consequence, the fundamental interests of the former BA coalition once again make their weight felt, accompanied by a backlash against what (after the initial euphoria) is viewed by many sectors of the population as excessive "disorder." Under these circumstances, it is inevitable that a highly speculative economy will emerge. The combined effect of these factors is to encourage the adoption of policies—either by the maximalists or by those into whose hands the government has fallen after the exhaustion of the former—that effectively ratify the capitalist nature of society. Such policies—basically, economic "austerity" and social "discipline"—mark the Thermidor of maximalist victories and portend their ejection from the positions of governmental and social power which they have attained. In a case such as the Argentine transition of 1969–73, and in every other case in which the fundamental social positions of the bourgeoisie and the armed forces have remained intact[208] (no matter how shaken and weakened by the transition these forces may have been), the violation of their fundamental interests provokes reactions that drag the situation back to conditions that are even more repressive than they were under the previous BA. In synthesis, the maximalist opposition may eventually cause the collapse of the BA and generate a prerevolutionary situation, but it does not seem capable of pursuing the transition to the point at which the capitalist parameters of society cease. This, in turn, implies that, in the best of cases, a transition in which the opposition is dominated by the maximalists tends to reach a democratic conclusion

208 This marks an important difference from those transitions, such as the current one in Nicaragua, where the correlates of a neosultanistic regime are a weaker bourgeoisie and less professionalized armed forces.

not very different from that at which the moderate opposition aims all along—only that, under the maximalists, the route is likely to be longer and more costly. In the worst and, I fear, most probable of cases, a maximalist-led transition leads to conditions even more regressive than those imposed by a previous BA.

Let us move on to a third sector of the camp opposed to the BA—the moderate opposition. First, the moderate opposition is a true opposition; moreover, it is a democratic one. That is to say, the moderates' goal is not only to put the BA and any authoritarian alternative to an end; their goal is to establish a political democracy, which they consider valuable in and of itself. This opposition is not homogeneous; some of its members do not want to go further than the achievement of a regime of political democracy while others (on its left wing) are committed to an expansion of democracy on other levels, economic and social. Yet the democratic goal that is shared by all members of this opposition distances them, on the one side, from the opportunists in their own camp and, on the other, from the BA's hardliners. Their pursuit of democracy also distinguishes the moderate opposition from those softliners whose aims are limited to a liberalizing transformation of the BA and do not extend to what would be, properly speaking, a political democracy. On the other hand, this is a moderate opposition, in the sense that its members are prepared to extend a serious and reasonable guarantee that, to the extent that the transition remains within their control, the fundamental interests of the BA coalition will not be violated in the process of establishing a democratic regime. The willingness of the moderates to provide such a guarantee places them in direct conflict with the maximalists, who, to say the least, find it difficult to distinguish between the moderate and the opportunistic opposition; the maximalists may even regard the moderates as their "main enemy."

On the basis of the preceding analysis, we can see that as soon as the liberalization is initiated a complex game begins, consisting both of confrontations between former allies and of potential alliances between actors previously located in sharply opposed camps. I argue that the outcome of the transition basically depends upon the moderate opposition and its conflictive and fluctuating coalitions with the softliners. In addition, if the outcome is to be a reasonably viable political democracy, the moderate opposition must comply with several requirements.

The first of these is that it put to use its condition as a true opposition, extracting from the BA alliance decisions that move the process ever closer to political democracy and, therefore, preventing the softliners from stalling the transition in a stage of tempered authoritarianism. In this respect, the basic issues are, first, the characteristics of the regime to be established (fundamentally, the legal-institutional rules in which such a regime would be formally embodied) and, second, the already mentioned redefinition of the fundamental interests of the BA alliance. Typically, at the beginning of the process, the definitions of these interests are very broad, so broad as to interfere with the democratizing goal of the moderate opposition. It is through very complex processes—what I am trying to describe is anything but linear—that the moderates elicit successive concessions not foreseen in the original decisions of the softliners. In fact, these "concessions" are important opposition victories; they involve successive redefinitions of the fundamental interests of the BA alliance, interests that the softliners have pledged themselves—before the hardliners and the undecided—to safeguard. I already mentioned the limits of these redefinitions when discussing the opposition maximalists. That these limits shall not be transposed, the moderates are prepared to guarantee; at the same time, in a complex process, they exercise their condition as a true opposition, impelling the entire BA alliance to accept a degree of democratization (political, at least) greater than that which the softliners envisaged at the beginning of the process.

The second requirement is that the moderate opposition succeed in becoming the dominant voice in its camp; that is, it must politically defeat its two wings, the opportunists and the maximalists. Were it not to do so, consequences that I have already examined would ensue. In the wake of the BA, a long list of unsatisfied demands and grievances will be brewing in many sectors of the population. The moderate opposition must take up a large part of these claims and transform them into issues with potential electoral resonance; their ability to do this successfully greatly affects the moderates' chances of becoming the dominant voice in the opposition camp. On the other hand, given that to take up such demands and grievances may threaten interests that the members of the BA alliance consider fundamental at any particular stage of the process, and given the fact that the moderate opposition should both be and appear to be an authentic opposition—the role of which cannot but be bringing to the fore a good many of such issues—the moderates tread a very narrow path. On one hand, excessive caution in taking up these long-suppressed claims would bring the moderates into a position too similar to that of their opportunistic counterparts; on the other hand, if they "exaggerate" such demands—especially during the initial stages of the process, when the BA alliance defines its interests more broadly and controls the process more tightly—the moderates run the risk of provoking a coup that would annul the transition.

The third requirement that the moderate opposition must meet is to behave in a reasonably predictable fashion; the commitments its leaders give to the BA alliance must be perceived as binding on the organizations they claim to control. For the latter purpose, the most adequate organizational form is probably a party (or a coalition of parties), disciplined enough for the moderates' interlocutors to safely assume the viability the commitments given to them. Even if the moderate opposition meets the two requirements already stated, if it fails to meet the present one, in not controlling the political organizations that it claims to speak for, it runs the risk of being defeated in its own camp by opportunists or maximalists. Were this to occur, the game that the moderates and the softliners are engaged in would change. The requirement of plausibility of the commitments made by the moderates during the transition highlights the advantages of a historical legacy that reemerges in the shape of political parties capable not only of becoming the dominant voice of the opposition but of guaranteeing to other actors the continuity of their leadership. Spain and, in the future, Chile are cases in point. Alternatively, the creation of an "official opposition party"—Brazil's MDB, for example—may also satisfy this requirement. At least, in the crucial initial stages of the transition presently under way, this party has fulfilled the important role of opening up room for the moderate opposition and assuring the continuity of its leadership. The most unfavorable situation appears to be that faced in present day Argentina and Uruguay where, on one hand (in contrast with Brazil), the entire former institutional system has been devastated by the respective BAs and where, on the other hand (in contrast with Spain and Chile), there do not appear to be parties that are both potentially majoritarian in the opposition camp and disciplined enough to plausibly guarantee continuity in their demands and commitments.[209]

The fourth requirement is that the moderate opposition enter into coalition—conflictively and tacitly, but very truly—with the softliners. On the one hand—as the case of Spain suggests and as that of Brazil begins to—if the transition advances sufficiently it is between these two actors that electoral supremacy in the incipient democracy will be decided. In order for such a coalition to be possible, the softliners must acknowledge their underlying continuity with the BA of which they have been part; at the same time, and to the fury of the hardliners among the hardliners, the softliners must abjure the most sinister aspects of that same BA. For its part, the moderate opposition will continually proclaim its credentials as an authentic opposition as against the whole BA alliance; but at the same time, it will metabolize existing grievances so that they are not expressed (either in themselves or in the policies demanded) in ways that could lead to the moderates being mistaken for their maximalist counterparts. While the present observations point to areas of real disagreements between the softliners and the moderates, both are strongly interested in neutralizing the hardliners and the maximalists. Depending on the initial intentions of the softliners regarding the extent of the transition—whether it is to be limited to the cosmetic legitimization of their rule (as in Brazil) or extend to the establishment of a political democracy (as in Spain)—the opportunists will present a

209 The Argentine case, especially during the period 1971–73, is a rather extreme example of this problem. The voice of the opposition was overwhelmingly captured by Peronism. A highly heterogeneous movement, Peronism included the most extreme forms of opportunism and maximalism, together with the seed of what might have been a triumphant moderate opposition. Such heterogeneity aside, a central problem was that no Peronist leader could offer a plausible guarantee that his commitments in relation to other actors in the transition would bind his party in the future; Peronism lacked (and, thanks to the current "freezing of politics," continues to lack) minimally institutionalized mechanisms of authority. This deficiency was mainly the result of the personalistic leadership of Perón and his strategy of rotating support among the most diverse elements of Peronism.

greater or lesser problem for the moderates and, especially, the more or less severe will be the conflicts between moderates and softliners regarding the point at which the transition should stop. Yet, in both kinds of cases, hardliners and maximalists create lines of conflict against softliners and moderates that are more acute than those that separate these last two from each other. In this sense, one may speak of a liberalizing coalition that—tacit and limited, but nonetheless operative—becomes the axis of the transition; BA softliners and opposition moderates join in a coalition that, mixing real conflicts and common interests, becomes the axis of the transition. Evidently, the game is subtle and complicated, above all for the moderate opposition. Working from an initial position of limited power, at each juncture the moderates must correctly ascertain the extent to which the softliners can be pushed toward democratization; the moderates must also remember the interest they share with the softliners in the ongoing viability of the transition itself. To these subtleties (and to the consequent advances and setbacks in the process that are not always easy to explain to a rapidly repoliticizing citizenry), hardliners and maximalists oppose the simplism of their positions and their indignation about the "betrayals" of their former allies.

It is evident that, under such conditions, the demands placed on the quality of political leadership are extraordinarily severe, when the repressive and depoliticizing characteristics of the BA have tended to impair the development of high quality political leadership. For the moderate opposition, it is not only a question of identifying the basic issues and chief adversaries at each juncture of the process; the moderates must also convince both followers and antagonists that their tactical flexibility is but an instrument in the service of a firm sense of direction in the journey toward democracy. But we should still consider matters that render the situation under discussion even more complex and dynamic.

IV.

In the period during which the BA appears firmly entrenched, civil society remains profoundly depoliticized. Apathy, "tacit consent," the corporatization of various class organizations and the reduction of others to mere mouthpieces for official decisions and ceremonies, the fear of rousing the repressive pathos of the BA, censorship and self-censorship, and cultural stultification: these are typical of the periods in which the BA appears able to impose its domination indefinitely. One aspect of such a situation is that, while political activity hardly ceases, it is hidden behind a technocratic and "apolitical" cloak. The main arenas of politics are the bureaucratic arenas of the state; typically, these are entered only by those ensconced at the apex of other bureaucracies—public and private—for the opaque articulation of their interests. These same bureaucratic arenas and the silence imposed by the political exclusion of a large part of the population discourage such actors from even attempting to dress their interests in arguments that appeal to some sort of general interest. The gray, opaque politics of the BA, a politics of bureaucracies and bureaucrats, public and private, is difficult to render in detail, but in the narrowness of its arenas and of the interests therein articulated, it is transparently simple.

The first steps of political liberalization usher in the resurrection, the intense repoliticization, of society—a process that soon outpaces liberalization itself. The resurrection of society is fundamental: it determines the rhythm of the transition no less than the events within the state apparatus and in the renewed political party arena that occupied us in the preceding sections; without reference to the resurrection of society it is impossible to understand the real force of the opposition.

Whatever might have triggered liberalization (but especially when the termination of the BA is extrinsically provoked), people suddenly lose their paralyzing fear of the coercive capacity of the state apparatus. Recently feared figures are now publicly ridiculed. After years of censorship, avid readers find themselves swamped in a flood of publications that—even from an apparently apolitical standpoint—antagonize the existing powers. Various artistic expressions symbolically distill long-festering grievances and demands. In other words, civil society, until lately flat, fearful, and "apolitical," reemerges with extraordinary energy.

Shortly beforehand, from the heights of the state apparatus it seemed possible to control most class organizations. Quite suddenly these organizations begin to move in their own orbits, pulling themselves out of the suffocating control of the state and again becoming voices with something to say about the general guidelines of the organization of the state, the economy, and society. This implies that many organizations of civil society have resuscitated as such. For this very reason, they become camps of struggle over who is to speak on their behalf and in support of what. In this way, politics reaches these organizations not only because of the claims they begin to make, but also because they become arenas of competition among groups that are often tied to the game that other actors are contesting at the level of parties and elections.

In addition, as we have seen in the transitions that have already occurred or are underway, together with those "old" organizations there emerge new associative forms bearing witness to the social dynamism that, appearances to the contrary, the BA is unable to suppress. Neighborhood committees, self-help organizations, grassroots and other social movements, popular institutions of the Catholic Church and other religions are some of the entries on a long list of organizational forms in which the popular sector distills the lessons of the harsh period of BA rule.

Old and new organizations within civil society, more or less informal and radicalized, in tandem with a generalized revaluation of politics, create from out of civil society an exultant atmosphere of expectant triumph over the BA—even though it may not yet be clear who will capitalize electorally on this anticipated but as yet uncertain victory. It is precisely this resurrection of civil society that sustains the opposition; in the absence of such a resurrection, or were the support that it affords not embraced by the opposition, the latter would be too weak to withstand the pressures and threats mounted by the various forces within the BA alliance.

In other words, if the political arena during BA was narrow and simple, liberalization widens and complicates it enormously: first, it involves the reentry of political parties onto the scene, which presupposes an electoral system that is, at the least—although the extent of liberalization may fall short of political democracy—a point of departure for the reconstruction of the institutions of a democratic regime; second—and, I think, more importantly, because it is here that the central dynamics of the process arguably lie—liberalization broadens and complicates the political arena because it triggers the politicized resurrection of civil society. Analytically speaking, these two developments signal that the system of exclusion that the BA is has ceased to exist. At this point, even though the state and the regime might remain authoritarian, it is no longer a BA but one with characteristics that continually oscillate until a resting point is found: either in an authoritarian relapse or in some form of democracy. The problem for hardliners, softliners, opportunists, maximalists, and moderates, then, is not simply centered around the distribution of forces within the state apparatus (which, for its part, is also penetrated by reverberations of the repoliticization of society) and the arena of party politics; a no less important problem, now, concerns the manner in which these actors articulate their relations with that immense arena of politics that civil society becomes.

The resurrection of civil society is also manifest in an explosion of long-postponed demands. Some demands that are of an economic nature, especially those made by the salaried sectors, function as bridgeheads for further claims that aim at resecuring control over unions or reorienting their activities; as a result, significant strike activity is unleashed. In addition—sometimes in combination with such economic demands, sometimes expressing themselves directly—middle-class movements and marginalized popular sectors vigorously present various demands (which are typically more difficult to negotiate than those made by unions) for autonomy from the state and the dominant classes.[210]

While they generate the jubilant, springlike mood characteristic of such thaws, developments of this kind are found disturbing by the many (not only the hardliners of the now-defunct BA) who, nostalgic for the "discipline" and "respect for hierarchy" that epitomized the

---

210 I especially refer to various types of religious movements, demands for participation in the governance of unions, public and private enterprises, and universities, as well as the previously mentioned grassroots movements that are based in the poorest sectors of the population.

triumphant moments of the BA, experience this atmosphere as one of profound disorder. One result is the appearance of hardline promoters of a coup, who spread their message amongst potentially repeat backers of a BA—the upper bourgeoisie, some segments of the middle class, and, of course, the armed forces. The success of such attempts, as we have seen, depends on several factors that in part remain beyond the control of coup advocates, but the risk of a coup looms throughout most of the transition. As we also saw, this same risk is the card with which the softliners attempt to regulate the pace of the transition. They also use this card for sometimes applying (although now with a bad conscience) harsh repression, and to support their pretension to be the institutionalized heirs of the transition and, as such, the only real guarantee against the excesses of the hardliners and the maximalists.

The role played in all of this by the working class is fundamental. We have already seen that the BA emerges in the context of extensive but unbalanced and dependent industrialization. In the large urban centers this lends considerable weight to the working class; on the other hand, the economy becomes fragile during the transition, due to the concerns of a bourgeoisie that is weaker than those at the capitalist centers and has become too accustomed to exploiting a working class silenced by BA repression. The consequent uncertainties—amplified by the repoliticization of middle-class employees that runs parallel to that of the working class—provoke sharp increases in inflation, swelling fiscal deficits, difficulties with the balance-of-payments, and, at least, strong fluctuations in public and private investment, both local and transnational. These are symptoms, on one hand, of the renewed capacity of the popular sector to press for some of its demands and, on the other, of what is at least the acute concern of the bourgeoisie about where the transition might finally lead. As the case of Spain shows, such tensions need not extend to a truly deep economic crisis; but the experience of Argentina in 1971–72—not to mention later events in that country—makes it clear that this possibility is very real. The emergence of a profound economic crisis is related to the tenuous control of economic and social policy that the softliners characteristically exercise when, as in Argentina, they attempt liberalization as a last resort in the face of an opposition explosion. This scenario differs from cases in which the softliners retain more real power, as in Spain and in the current Brazilian transition. Whether or not the economy will plunge into acute crisis is also contingent upon the degree to which the maximalists succeed in occupying the dominant position in the opposition camp. In the Argentine case of 1969–73, it was clearly and openly a matter of the terror of a bourgeoisie that not only saw the "political solution" offered by the softliners shipwrecked but, even more worryingly, was directly challenged at the level of its cellular domination. The fears of the bourgeoisie resulted from the confluence of a working class motivated by militant economism that was also challenging the control of the workplace, and a violent maximalist opposition that the state apparatus (itself shot through by these tensions) was unable to contain. In Argentina, the result of the combination of these factors was, among other things, the severe economic crisis of 1971–72 and a dramatic increase in violence; in these events, both hardliners and maximalists saw the irrefutable confirmation of their respective positions.

When compared with the Argentine case I have just mentioned, the distinguishing characteristic of Spain and Brazil is that the maximalist opposition has not taken the lead, nor, despite its concerns, has the bourgeoisie felt that a true social eruption of the popular sector, especially of the working class, is likely to occur. Furthermore, the case of Spain illustrates the possibility that an articulate and militant working class may express itself politically through parties of the left (especially, the PSOE and the PCE) committed to the camp of the moderate opposition. In Brazil, on the other hand, it is much more a question of the political weakness of the working class than of any politically metabolized presence of the working class in parties such as the Spanish ones. In effect—reflecting the social structure of Brazil and, in particular, the history of its working class and trade unions—the opposition is mainly based on the middle class and certain segments of bourgeoisie in large urban centers. Although the Brazilian working class is overwhelmingly concentrated in such centers, until 1978 (and, thus, only after the initial years of a transition that began with the elections of 1974 had passed) it mobilized itself little, whether in support of the transition or of more tangible interests such as wages and the control of its unions.[211]

211 Nor have there been important movements of rural organizations and peasant demands. In cases of BA that have large peasant populations,

Only now[212]—with the transition at a more advanced stage and more difficult to reverse—the engagement of various layers of the working class in pressing such demands is beginning to shake up and render more dynamic the process of Brazilian democratization.

The fears of the bourgeoisie and the hardliners were allayed in each case: in Brazil, in the earliest and most fragile stage of the transition, the working class was virtually absent from the political process; in Spain, the political representation of the working class has been undertaken by parties historically rooted in it that have identified themselves unequivocally with the moderate opposition. Similar developments are foreseeable in the future of Chile. By contrast, Argentina (and, to a lesser extent, due to the smaller relative and absolute weight of its working class, Uruguay) contains a working class of considerable weight that has been an important actor in national politics but that, at the same time, is not tied to parties such as those of Spain and Chile. Moreover, the Argentine unions cannot substitute for parties as actors in the overall political process or in the political representation of the working class and of middle-class employees. The very logic of the unions' role in society makes it extremely difficult for them to go beyond economic claims, and demands for corporatist participation in the state apparatus. Consequently, in all these respects the Argentine transition of 1969–73 did not enjoy the conditions relatively favorable to the progress of democratization that I have identified in other cases. In the future, this combination of factors may again emerge as a serious problem, unless there have been changes at the party level (Peronist or otherwise) that the current "prohibition against politics" momentarily veils.

For the most part, what certain cases demonstrate positively, while others do so negatively, is that the fundamental issue for a viable democratization (that is, a democratization that is neither mortally wounded from the beginning nor merely the cosmetic liberalization

---

were there to arise significant challenges to agrarian class domination in combination with the political reactivation of urban workers, a situation eliciting the greatest fears of the dominant class would arise and, with it, the higher likelihood of a coup.

212 1979.—Editor's note to O'Donnell, *Counterpoints*

of an authoritarian state) is the extent to which the moderates control the opposition camp; that they do so is essential, not only at the political-electoral level but also, to a considerable extent, with respect to the manifold expressions of the resurrection of civil society that is an integral part—and an especially dynamic one—of the transition.[213] These observations underscore the magnitude and the subtlety of the tasks of this opposition.

---

213 One theme that I am unable address here, but which should be studied as an important part of the transition, is that of the medium-term consequences that appear to flow from the success of the moderate opposition in controlling its own camp. At least in Spain, and with not a few symptoms already visible in Brazil, the to-and-fro of process, the various tactical concessions (necessary or not, depending on one's view of the matter), and the bureaucratization of the parties involved because of the broadening of their electoral bases and their access to governmental positions, among other reasons, tend to separate the moderates from not a few of the most dynamic opposition movements and militants within civil society. From this results a certain mood of disenchantment and cynicism regarding the sometimes less than brilliant realities of democratic politics, for whose advent these actors struggled so much and so effectively.

CHAPTER VI

Notes for a Theory of the State

Introduction

I am closing this collection with a text that I hesitated to include. It reflects a moment in my intellectual journey when, obsessed with the brutal type of capitalist state that is the BA, particularly "our" BA from 1976 to 1983, I focused on the state and paid little attention to its potential connections with other issues, especially that of democracy. This connection makes the issue discussed here even more complex; I will soon publish a book (aptly titled *Democracy, Agency, and the State: Theory with Comparative Intent*) in which I address these issues.[214]

Nevertheless, I believe that the text has some value, at least as a counterpoint to views that either deny the very existence of the state and reify it as merely a set of bureaucracies, demonize it as the source of all evil, or see it as a neutral entity that only needs technical or bureaucratic refinement. However, while the preceding chapters present more or less intellectually polished results, I hope that this one is read as a stage in an ongoing exploration.

---

214 Guillermo O'Donnell, *Democracy, Agency, and the State: Theory with Comparative Intent* (Oxford University Press, 2010).

Notes for a Theory of the State[215]

I. Introduction

I would like to clarify the intention and scope of this work. First, these are notes for a theory and not an attempt to develop that theory because I only develop some of the topics necessary for a sufficiently complete view of the problems of the capitalist state. Second, these reflections do not arise from a generic interest; they are the result of my efforts to understand a type of capitalist state, which I have called "bureaucratic-authoritarian" (BA), through a study of the contemporary Argentine case compared with similar Latin American experiences. That attempt, as well as various comments received on my previous works, revealed to me the need to rethink the underlying conception of the state in those works. From this, it became clear that the most problematic aspect is neither "state" nor "society" but their conjunction, the "and" that unites them in an ambiguous and, as will be seen, misleading way in several key respects. Third, since the BA was a historical type of capitalist state, I had to consider some of the more general issues of that state, at least those that would allow me to later return to the more specific level of the BA: this is one of the reasons, apart from my own shortcomings, that these pages are the "notes" announced in their title. These reflections are, therefore, a moment in the development of conceptual tools to better understand not only a type of state but also—and above all—historical processes marked

---

215 CEDES/GE-CLACSO, *Documento*, no. 9 (November 1977). Prepared for presentation at the Latin American Congress of Sociology, Quito, Ecuador, November 1977.

by struggles that shape the establishment, impacts, and collapse of that state. In doing so, however, I feel a need in this work to "start from the other side," outlining certain characteristics shared by all capitalist states in order to then sketch the main distinguishing features of a type of state that tends to correspond to the fabric of a society that is very different from the classic and more purely capitalist cases. In these pages, these differences can only be identified in their most decisive but also most general characteristics. A detailed exploration of their consequences, as well as the identification of more specific contrasts between different Latin American cases, is beyond the scope of this work. This is the subject of the above-mentioned study, and therefore these "notes" are also partial in the sense that they are truncated before they reach that level of historical specificity. However, as a tool developed specifically from, and to advance, a study placed on that level, my hope is that they can contribute to the connection between detail and theory that we so badly need, not only for the sake of intellectual progress.

II. Society and State

1. Preliminary Definitions[216]

First, a definition that we must unpack step by step. I understand the state to be the specifically political component of domination in a territorially defined society. By domination (or power) I am referring to the actual and potential capacity to regularly impose one's will on others, including but not necessarily against their resistance. I therefore

216 I will draw on numerous contributions here—both classic and contemporary—and touch on discussions that approach the subject from various angles. This involves an enormous bibliography, which would be too pedantic to cite in its entirety. For this reason (and others of a more circumstantial nature), I have decided to mention only recent and less accessible contributions that have had a direct impact on my reasoning.

understand the political in the proper or precise sense as an analytical part of the more general phenomenon of domination,[217] one that is backed by significant control over the means of physical coercion in an exclusively defined territory.[218] Combining these criteria, the concept of the state is equivalent to the definitively political sphere, which is, in turn, an aspect of the broader phenomenon of social domination.

Domination is relational: it is a form of interaction between social subjects. It is, by definition, asymmetrical, since it is a relationship of inequality.[219] This asymmetry stems from the differential control of certain resources, through which it is usually possible to bring about the desired adjustment in the behavior and abstentions of the dominated to the will—explicit, tacit, or presumed—of the dominant party. An

---

217 A crucial point for this and subsequent arguments: given a set, "concrete" parts are those that can be separated from it and still be perceived sensorially (for example, the leg of a table). "Analytical" aspects are those that can be abstracted intellectually but with which the previous operation cannot be carried out (for example, the shape of that table). Hereafter, when I refer to "aspects" the reference should be understood as analytical.

218 Other relationships of domination do not have this backing. That does not mean they are not relationships of domination, but they are not relationships of political domination as I am defining them. Of course, to the degree that they form part of the set of relationships of domination, they remain similar to non-political relationships of domination. This is reflected in everyday language and in certain intellectual currents, which consider relationships such as those established in groups like families or clubs to be political. In these relationships, it is possible to "engage in politics" in a sense that we have not yet addressed (that of competing for positions that allow one to wield power), but they lack the specific component of coercive supremacy over an exclusively defined territory.

219 A number of comments on an earlier version of this paper have led me to realize that a couple of clarifications are necessary. First, not every social relationship is one of domination; I am focusing on them here because the issue I want to explore is that of the state, which, as we will see, is a specific form of domination. Second, a situation of inequality does not per se or necessarily prevent the social subjects affected by it from undertaking cooperative actions from which each of them can derive benefits or advantages (albeit probably to varying degrees determined by their inequality).

exhaustive inventory of these resources is unnecessary, but it is useful to highlight a few of the most significant ones that sustain domination. The first is the control of the means of physical coercion, which can be mobilized directly or through a third party. Another is the control of economic resources. A third is the control of information resources in a broad sense, including scientific and technological knowledge. The last one worth mentioning is ideological control, through which the dominated accept the asymmetrical relationship they are in as fair and natural, and therefore do not understand or question it as domination. This formulation serves to highlight a few points that will allow us to move on to more pressing topics. The first of these is that the control of any of these resources enables coercion, which consists of subjecting the dominated to severe sanctions. The second is that the most efficient resource in terms of maintaining domination is ideological control, which involves the consent of the dominated to the relationship.[220] On the other hand, coercion is the costliest resource, because it explicitly exposes domination and suggests that ideological control—at least—has failed. As an *ultima ratio*, however, it is essential that it backs domination. The third point is that there is usually a high correlation in the control of these resources: whoever controls resources "A" and "E" is highly likely to simultaneously control "C" and "D" or, at least, has in the former an effective basis for extending the scope of their domination to the latter.

These resources are the basis of all domination, not only that of a political nature. The specific characteristic of political domination is the predominance of physical coercion within a strictly defined territory.[221]

---

220 This is the basis for the virtuality of severe sanctions arising from ideological control; questioning the fairness or naturalness of the given social order is to think the forbidden, to endure the dissonance of considering the sinful, or to incur "ingratitude" toward those who hold the highest positions in a just social order.

221 It should be emphasized that both the element of coercive supremacy and that of territoriality are necessary in defining the specificity of the political-state. A street gang and certain types of parents possess and exert coercive supremacy over the people subject to their sphere of interaction, but their domination

2. The Foundations of Domination

Control over the resources of domination is not randomly distributed. At any given moment, there are many different factors that determine unequal access to these resources. Not only is it useless to attempt to inventory these factors, but such casuistry would also cause us to lose sight—in seeking an empirical precision that is useless at the level at which I am writing—of the fact that there is a major differentiator in accessing the resources of domination, both directly and because it generates situations that in turn allow such access. This major differentiator is social class or, more precisely, the unequal (and contradictory) division of society into social classes. By social class, I am referring to, as a first approximation, positions in the social structure determined by shared modalities of work and the creation and appropriation of its value. We will see that the establishment of these modalities is not only economic but also intrinsically involves other dimensions, including what I have defined as the state or political dimension in the strict sense. The state that interests us here is the capitalist state. The modality of the appropriation of the value created by labor constitutes the fundamental classes of capitalism, through the social relationship established by said creation and appropriation. The most obvious mechanisms and consequences of this relationship are economic. The main—but not the only—relationship of domination in a capitalist society is the relationship of production between the capitalist and the wage worker, through which the value of labor is generated and appropriated. This is the heart of civil society, its great principle of contradictory order.

This appropriation is not simply a relationship of inequality. It is an act of exploitation, which implies that it is also an inherently conflictive (or, to put it another way, contradictory) relationship, regardless of whether or not it is recognized as such by the social subjects. This is one of the key points of ideological control: its validity masks the inherent conflictive nature of certain social relationships. This suggests

---

lacks the element of exclusive territoriality. On the other hand, political domination is not simply coercion plus territoriality; the latter is merely its specific component.

that, although its most ostensible aspects are economic, the relationship in question is also imbued with ideological control. This, like the economic, co-constitutes that relationship, not as something that comes from the outside to ultimately reinforce it, but as a component that is already there, from the outset, contributing to its validity. We will see that the same argument can be applied to the political.

In what sense are social classes the major differentiator in unequal access to the resources of domination? First, directly; class position in itself largely determines this inequality. However, this position also gives rise to the differential probabilities of achieving certain situations (social prestige, education, access to information, the ability to be socially "heard" and ideologically influential, the availability of resources to be used in the political sphere, among others), which in turn enable access to the control of other resources of domination. This is not, like the previous ones, a definitive stipulation. It posits certain causalities, ranked in importance and in terms of their contribution to the differential distribution of the resources of domination, for which there should be—if correct—reasonable empirical support. This is, in fact, the case.[222]

But let us return to politics in the strict sense. There are social relationships that are ostensibly required by orders that are backed by the supremacy of coercion over a territory, such as the regulations governing service in the armed forces or a judge's ruling. There are others that appear to be "private" relationships that link social subjects without the state and its coercive power coming into play. These are typically contractual relationships, understood as those that involve an agreement on a set of obligations and rights. But the private nature of these relationships is only an appearance. In the vast majority of cases, the parties can resort to "something more" that underlines the usual probability of the contract's validity and enforcement. That something *extra* is the state, the institutions of which can be invoked for the purpose

---

222 For a summary of the evidence in this regard, see Frank Parkin, *Class Inequality and Political Order* (New York: Praeger, 1971); see also J. H. Westergaard "Sociology: The Myth of Classlessness," in Robin Blackburn, ed., *Ideology in Social Science: Readings in Critical Social Theory* (Glasgow: Fontana, 1972).

of enforcing a certain interpretation of the contract, using not only coercive resources, but any resources they can mobilize. There are few contracts in which it is necessary to resort to this. But in all cases, the guarantee of their effectiveness comes from the possibility of making such an invocation, tacitly but fundamentally, since otherwise it would be impossible to enter into a contractual relationship, and, if it were somehow established, there would be no possibility of ensuring compliance. On the other hand, if this component were missing, the only way to ensure the effectiveness of the contract would be through coercion that the parties could apply directly, a law of the jungle that is antagonistic to the predictable intertwining of relationships inherent in a minimally complex society.

Contracts usually presuppose a voluntary agreement freely entered into by parties who, in relation to the relevant legislation, appear as equals. This equality is often referred to as "formal" because it does not prevent the actual relationship between the parties from being extremely unequal. The key case is the sale of labor power, an act of formal equality that enables the appropriation of the value created by labor. This contractual relationship is also underpinned by the guarantee implied by the possibility of invoking the state, in the event of a "breach of contract," to enforce this unequal and contradictory social relationship. This capacity for invocation (or, in other words, the tacit and underlying presence of the state) is constitutive of the relationship; it could not exist, "it would be something else," without this element. And this role is not only played in the—trivial—case in which the invocation is made, but also, more permanently and fundamentally, in all relationships that have the possibility of making that invocation. By making it clear that there are territorially delimited resources of power that sustain the relationship under threat of severe sanctions, it marks from the outset the limits of what the parties can agree on (and fail to comply with) and governs their expectations regarding the effective validity and modes of execution of the relationship.

What does this mean? It means that the guarantee provided by the state to certain social relations, including the relations of production that are at the heart of a capitalist society and its contradictory division into social classes, is not an external or *a posteriori* guarantee of that relationship. It is an intrinsic and constitutive part of it, as much as other elements—economic, informational, and of ideological control—which are aspects that we can only discern in this relationship analytically. And what does this mean? It means that the dimensions of the state, or of the political (or economic) sphere itself, are not a thing, an institution, or a "structure": they are aspects of a social relationship.

3. Concrete Aspects and Social Subjects

We must now address a point that has generated some confusion. It is true that social actors tend to experience "state intervention" as something external and retrospective, incorporated into their relationships when something in them has "failed." This reflects, at the level of ordinary consciousness, something that numerous authors have pointed out: capitalism is the first historical case of separation between economic and extra-economic coercion. Slave owners and feudal lords, among others, concentrated resources of economic power, information, and physical and ideological coercion. In contrast, in their relationship with the worker, the capitalist does not directly control all these resources. But this contrast has been overstated, and some necessary distinctions must be made. First, it is a mistake to deduce from this contrast that the capitalist retains only economic coercion. Although they do not monopolize it, they also tend to exercise ideological control, even if the content and form of this control differ from those of other historical situations. Additionally, their control over information resources may have increased, especially given the fragmentation of the situation in which workers find themselves, with the consequent difficulty of reconstructing from within this situation the social meaning of their work.

But what is important to highlight is that the nature of capitalism is not only that the worker is dispossessed of the means of production; it is also that the capitalist is dispossessed of the means of coercion. Several important consequences extend from this: the separation of the capitalist from the means of coercion does not imply that coercion is absent in the social relationship that links the capitalist to the wage worker. As we have seen, coercion is a virtual presence that is usually brought into play when something has "gone wrong." This action is the enforcement of a guarantee of its validity through the mobilization of resources of power, which in turn are ultimately backed by supremacy in the means of coercion over a territory. The separation of the capitalist from direct control of these means entails the emergence of a third social subject, whose specificity is the exercise of coercive supremacy. This third social subject is state institutions. They tend to enforce this guarantee of social relations (including the capitalist relations of production) when the virtual and underlying promise of support for them is invoked to make it effective. Here we enter territory where we must proceed with caution.

A distinction must be made between the genesis and the conditions of the validity of the capitalist relations of production.[223] In both, we can find the specificity of capitalist society, but in different ways. In terms of genesis, the seller of labor power is free, not only in the sense of being dispossessed of the means of production, but also in that he is not brought into this relationship through coercion, which is very different from the situation of the slave and the serf. What draws them into the relationship is economic coercion resulting from the fact that, lacking the means of production, their only way of securing a livelihood is to become wage workers. This economic coercion is also diffuse: state institutions do not compel the sale of labor power, nor can capitalists, either on their own or through these institutions, impose this obligation on any specific social subject. The need to do so, therefore, is not imposed by anyone; society is "simply" structured in such a way that workers who lack the means of production could not otherwise survive. The absence of coercion to sell labor power is a necessary condition for the (formal) appearance of equality between the parties. Furthermore, along with diffuse economic coercion, this is one of the main roots of ideological control derived from the opacity of domination in capitalist society, again in contrast to other historical experiences in which economic and physical coercion are transparent in themselves and in the social subject that applies them.

In this genetic sense, economics and economic coercion are paramount in capitalist relations of production. On the other hand, however, once labor power is bought and sold, an agreement is entered into that

---

223 Regarding this point, I draw on Marcelo Cavarozzi's reflections on an earlier version of this work.

formalizes relations that are also constitutively imbued with non-economic aspects, including those of a political-state nature that concern us here. The coercive guarantee of the relationship is constitutive of it; this, along with the necessary dispossession of the capitalist from direct coercion,[224] leads to the separation of a third social subject that concentrates these resources and has the capacity to mobilize them. That subject is not the "entire" state, but the part that crystallizes or objectifies itself in institutions. The fundamental point is that if this is the case, the state—as an aspect of these relationships and as an objectified plexus of institutions—is the guarantor of these relationships, not of the social subjects that are constituted through them. This implies that the state does not directly support the capitalist (either as a concrete subject or as a class) but rather the social relationship that makes them such. Another implication is that the state is primarily coercive, in the sense that not only is physical coercion the ultimate *ratio* of that guarantee, but also that the separation of the capitalist from the means of coercion is the origin of the capitalist state and its institutions. This (genetic) primacy of coercion in the state is analogous to the primacy—also genetic—of economics in capitalist relations of production; this does not imply that these relations are purely economic or that the state is only coercion. What does this mean?

First, if the emergence of a third party that ultimately provides a coercive guarantee is inherent in capitalist relations of production, then the state is already, on that basis alone, a capitalist state, before we even ask whether it benefits or is manipulated by this or that class or fraction. Second, the objectification of this split in state institutions also necessarily implies that they must not be or act as a concrete capitalist who, as such, has been separated from the coercive resources controlled by those institutions. Capitalist relations of production presuppose a third social subject that appears and acts as a non-capitalist, even though it is the objectification of a state that is, for that very reason, capitalist. Third, if the state is the guarantor of the relations of production, then it is the

224 By definition: a society in which this dispossession is not predominant is not capitalist.

guarantor of both social subjects that are constituted as such through those relations. The state is the guarantor of the existence and reproduction of the bourgeoisie and the wage worker as classes, since this is necessarily implied by the validity and reproduction of those social relations. The state is the guarantor of the wage worker as a class, not only of the bourgeoisie. This implies—logically and practically—that in certain instances the state is the protector of the former against the latter. But not as a neutral arbiter, rather to restore it as a subordinate class that must sell its labor power and, therefore, reproduce the social relationship that the state guarantees.

While state institutions are the crystallization of coercive resources that the capitalist does not control, they appear as non-capitalist and, moreover, only indirectly guarantee the classes linked to the relations of production by supporting the continuous replacement of capitalists and wage workers as classes. This implies that the state is an expression of a more general interest than that of the social subjects from whose relationship it emanates. But that interest is not neutral or egalitarian; it is the reproduction of a social relationship that articulates society in an unequal and contradictory way. This is equivalent to saying that the state as a whole—as an aspect and as an objectification—is also a form of organizing those social subjects. In this sense, the state is a generality (with respect to the particularity of those subjects and their interests), but it is a partial generality (due to the structural bias of the mode of articulation between those subjects). This, in turn, implies that the state is a mediation embedded in, and emanating from, a relationship between other social subjects. This is why the state, as well as being coercive, is usually a consensual mediation that connects social subjects, but I will explore the state as an organization of consensus in the second section.

To sum up: at the origin of capitalist relations of production lies a diffuse economic coercion that cannot be attributed to specific capitalists or state institutions; it can only be understood as a general mode of social organization. For their part, once the relationship has been established, not only does the capitalist not exercise coercion, but neither the capitalist nor state institutions can coercively compel the worker to continue selling their labor power; the wage worker is always free not to do so.[225] Finally, the state appears as an institutional objectification that concentrates control of ultimately coercive resources and as a non-capitalist that only guarantees the classes through its support of the social relationship that constitutes them as such.

We should add two clarifications to what we have covered so far. The first is that when we speak of capitalists and wage workers, we are not referring to relationships between individuals, but rather of social classes.[226] This allows us to understand the significance of the genetic primacy of the economic in relations of production and of the coercive element in the state. This primacy is neither historical nor concrete, but rather analytical, because at every moment in capitalist society, as a totality immersed in historical time, the two planes of the genesis and effective validity of those relations and of the state converge. Indeed, there would be no sale of labor power without economic coercion. On the other hand, there would be no fundamental classes of capitalism (and, therefore, no capitalist society) if that sale were not already taking place. At the same time, these relations are not only economic; we have already seen that they include other dimensions, among them the state, as co-constitutive. As for the capitalist state, it is capitalist because it emanates from a social relationship that involves the separation of the means of coercion by the capitalist; on the other hand, its status as guarantor of the relationship and not of specific social subjects makes it a phenomenon that is not only coercive. Therefore, the respective genetic primacy of the economic and the coercive is analytical, not a historical or ontological factor that precedes the other co-constitutive dimensions of the relations of production and of the capitalist state.

---

225 This is, of course, another key difference with respect to other historical experiences. The capitalist is also free to terminate the relationship, thereby retaining a fundamental means of economic coercion.

226 Every wage worker can hope to cease to be one. Although statistically low, the probability of upward social mobility in capitalism is another difference from other historical experiences that helps—as an expectation of individual escape from that class position—conceal its aspect of domination. On the other hand, beyond this individual level, capitalism presupposes the existence of a class of "free" buyers and sellers of labor power and another class of buyers.

The second clarification is that the political in the true sense is an inherent aspect of relations of domination, including the capitalist relations of production. However, the effectiveness of the guarantee entails the emergence of a concrete subject, state institutions, which appear in non-capitalist form, more general and external to the direct subjects of those relations. To the extent, then, that the implicit guarantee is usually only made effective on certain occasions and that the modality of it is originally linked to the social relationship and only indirectly to the capitalist as a social subject, state institutions appear as an external and more general interest than those of the parties directly involved in the relationship.

We can now systematize the following assertions. I have noted that the political is a co-constitutive aspect of certain social relations, including capitalist relations of production. I also noted that, to the extent that the political or the state can be invoked to support that relationship—whether or not that invocation is made in each case—that aspect contributes to a crucial guarantee for the validity of that relationship, which jointly constitutes capitalists and wage workers as social classes. This, in turn, implies the organization of a system of social domination, translated into differential access to numerous resources. Furthermore, this mutual constitution as classes is the social relationship that creates capital and allows it to be dynamically reproduced as a process of accumulation. This means that the levels I have just mentioned are mutual and necessarily interrelated aspects of the social relationships that define the specificity of a capitalist society. It also implies that one of these aspects, that of the state or of politics proper, is simultaneously a guarantee of the capitalist relations of production, of the articulation of classes in that society, of the systematic differentiation of access to resources of power (or system of domination), and of the generation and reproduction of capital.[227] This is the meaning of the assertion that the state or the political sphere is originally constitutive of these social relations and that, therefore, it is mistaken to seek this meaning "outside" or "after" them. If this is so, it also follows that the state can only be what it

---

227 Hereafter, where I refer to the guarantee that the state provides to society qua capitalist, it should be understood that I am referring to this set of aspects.

co-constitutes: an inherently contradictory social relation. I will return to this point later.[228]

The above-mentioned guarantee operates within a network of social relations that unfolds in a historical time frame. This leads us to another corollary: this guarantee exists in relation to and is part of the dynamic reproduction of the whole formed by the capitalist relations of production, class structure, the system of domination, and the creation and accumulation of capital. By "dynamic," I am referring to two things: that these relations are reproduced in a changing way over time and that, as far as the reproduction of capital is concerned, this is a process of accumulation.

4. Organization

The state is an aspect of certain social relations. This is its fundamental characteristic, on which its other attributes depend. Because the capitalist relations of production presuppose that the ruling class does not possess the means of coercion, the state tends to objectify itself in primarily coercive institutions. In terms of concrete social subjects, the capitalist-worker relationship entails the separation of a third party: state institutions. But the level of the state as an aspect is crucial, because confusing the state with these institutions is to subsume a broader phenomenon into its concretely objectified part. Based on this confusion, the capitalist-worker relationship appears to be only "economic," while, as a result, the state appears to intervene in this relationship from the outside and only occasionally. The split that thus occurs between society and the state, and the mutual externality to which it condemns them, is the main basis for the concealment of the state as the guarantor of domination in society and for the opacity of that domination. These are the topics we will now explore in greater depth.

---

228 We can also put it this way: as an analytical manifestation of a contradictory class relationship, which its objectifications guarantee and—as we shall see—help organize, the capitalist state is one of the social arenas of that contradiction and, at the same time, exhibits a continuous tendency to conceal it.

I must now elaborate on something that was simply implied in the preceding pages. As the guarantor of society qua capitalist, the state is the architect and organizer of society, beyond its role as the coercive enforcer of certain relations of domination. In an initial sense, the state, as a guarantor of these relations, is the negative limit of the socially destructive consequences of their reproduction.[229] That is, the existence of the capitalist in competition with other capitalists, all subject to the needs of accumulation, means that individually they would tend toward excessive exploitation (from the point of view of concealing their domination and reproducing the labor force), and they would also be thrown into "excessive" competition that would eliminate a significant portion of capitalists from their class, thereby exacerbating the antagonisms implicit in the reproduction of capital. On the other hand, competition based on the accumulation of capital means that entrepreneurs do not concern themselves with the decisions and investments necessary for the achievement of the social conditions that allow, among other things, the reproduction of the class system, accumulation, and the resolution of certain general problems: typically, the tasks of the liberal state in education, health, and infrastructure, as well as the directly "economic" interventions of the modern capitalist state. Unlike the previous ones, these are not negative limits on the actions of capitalists, but rather a conditioning of the social context in which "someone" must take action.[230] Note that both the imposition of negative limits as well as regulatory interventions appear to actors as external to their "private" relations, which parallels the apparent externality of the state with respect to the relations of production. Furthermore, as these are decisions, unlike those of the capitalist, that are not usually aimed at generating profits for their actor, they appear as an expression of a rationality

229 For more on this aspect, see E. Altvater, "Remarques sur quelques problèmes posés par l'interventionnisme étatique" in N. Vincent, ed., *L'Etat contemporain et le marxisme* (Maspero: Paris, 1975), 135–170.

230 I do not believe it is possible to expand much further on these methods of intervention at the general level at which I have situated myself here; of course, the differences between these methods are highly significant when studying specific historical cases.

different from that of the capitalist. Additionally, the more they are imposed as a negative limit or as conditioning of the social context, the more they embody a more general, and in this sense "superior," rationality to that of each individual capitalist. Finally, the introduction of negative limits may be experienced by certain capitalists (or perhaps even all of them) as not only an external act but also a hostile one on the part of that "someone" who is imposing them. In particular, many of the negative limits specific to each country are the result of struggles by the dominated classes, for whom they represent victories that are experienced inversely by the bourgeoisie.

The "someone" who deals with these plans is the state institutions. The existence of these institutions and their notable weight in society is one of the reasons for the perception of the state as external. We have already seen other reasons, but this is a point worth emphasizing. This appearance of exteriority is based on the concealment of the domination that underlies the capitalist relations of production, which means that the state only appears (as an institution) when it is called on to back them. But it is also based on the fact that, especially in their imposition of negative limits, state institutions appear as the embodiment of a more general, non-capitalist rationality. Although we still need to examine this mode of action, it allows us to understand why the state tends to appear to the capitalists themselves as an external force driven by a foreign rationality. Based on its primary role as the guarantor of a relationship, the capitalist state is not directly the state "of" the capitalists, nor, for the reasons I have just pointed out, does it tend to be experienced this way by them.

But the objectifications are not only institutions embodied in complex and bureaucratic organizations. They can also be formalizations that crystallize typical social relations. The contract for the buying and selling of labor presupposes the formal equality of the parties by means of a legally defined status—worker/employer—that disregards the actual conditions of each party.[231] The outcome of this relationship is embodied

231 This does not imply disregarding the complexity introduced by modalities such as collective bargaining or state policies aimed at protecting workers. These shift the plane of formal equality from interpersonal relations between worker and capitalist to the whole of both, without altering the assumption

in goods that circulate with the mediation of money. Money can only be a means of circulation as a generic equivalent of commodities. This implies that every subject must be considered "equal" in relation to money, whose possession gives them the right to access commodities "only" limited by the amount they possess and not by their class position. On the other hand, in order to be a commodity, labor power must appear as one among other commodities exchanged for money, for which formally equal and free social subjects (in other words, subjects who did not enter into the contract through coercion) come together and, as such, uphold the validity and enforceability of the contract they enter into.

The formal equality of the social subjects with respect to money and in the contractual relationship (including the sale of labor power) are exact parallels. The exchange of goods mediated by money is a crucial element in the circulation of capital. Mutual consent between formally equal subjects is a key element in the state's organization of capitalist society. Its objectification is modern law—rational-formal in the Weberian sense—which enshrines the social subject as a legal subject on a level of equality corresponding to that of the circulation of capital. Money and rational-formal law are real abstractions, in the sense that they stem from a social relationship that they transform, on the one hand, and on the other, they are at a level that is not purely mythical and that, in a contradictory way, is linked to the former.

Rational-formal law emerged and expanded alongside capitalism. This is the expression of a profound relationship: this law is the formalized codification of domination in capitalist society through the creation of the legal subject implied by the appearance of free and formally equal relations in the buying and selling of labor power and, in general, in the circulation of goods. Like the other aspects we are considering, rational-formal law contains ambiguities that are an expression of its contradictory ties to the deeper levels of society. On the one hand, this law makes the wage worker what a serf or a slave is not: that is, a subject who, on certain levels, has equal rights—including the right to invoke

of formal equality that underlies the sale of the commodity—labor power—which is thus partially and distortedly "collectivized" under the abstract and formalizing logic of capital.

state institutions to enforce them—that differentiate them from other subordinate classes. On the other hand, the legal subject created by rational-formal law is an abstract entity—stripped of all attributes other than formal equality—who freely and therefore validly sells their labor power. Furthermore, the law also codifies domination by enshrining and coercively enforcing private property rights, especially those related to the means of production appropriated and used in a market integrated by these abstractly equal legal entities. This in turn implies formalizing the structuring of society in such a way that the dispossession of the means of production by the worker is enshrined and the worker is then forced, without the need for coercion, to sell their labor power.

This right is the most formalized crystallization of the state's contribution to society qua capitalist. This is not only because it creates the stark social subject implied by capitalist relations and the private appropriation of the means of production. It is also because, as a cognizable formalization, it preventively teaches the parties the limits of their rights and obligations and therefore reduces the need for ostensible intervention to ultimately invoke the coercive guarantee of the state. As a result, this guarantee appears to be mobilized not by actors in a system of domination but by legally equal subjects who "only" demand compliance with what they have freely agreed upon and based on situations abstractly typified in legal norms.[232]

For this reason, rational-formal law is more than just preventive teaching and a regulated path for the effective enforcement of the state's coercive guarantee. By crystallizing the planes that correspond to the sphere of circulation and making them predictable as frameworks of rights and obligations, law is also a fabric that organizes society and the domination that structures it. This abstraction corresponds to the

232 It should also be noted that, for this very reason, the law appears on the one hand as the foundation and, on the other, as a mechanism for restoring a certain "order," a socially valued regularity in the organization of society, when that order is threatened with disruption. For more on the immense implicit weight of the "order" guaranteed by the state, see Norbert Lechner, "Poder y order: La estrategia de la minoría consistente" (mimeo) (Santiago de Chile: FLASCO, 1977).

emergence and reproduction of a relationship of power—that which ties the capitalist to the worker—in which the dominant party has detached itself from direct control of the means of coercion. The exploitation that takes place through the capitalist relations of production is thus concealed by a twofold appearance: that of the (formal) equality of the parties and that of the free will with which they may or may not enter into the relationship. Capitalism presupposes both the separation of the worker from the means of production and that of the capitalist from the means of coercion. Both are requirements for the underlying relationship to be transmuted into a relationship of exchange between abstract equals, mediated by the universal equivalent of money. Regulated by law in this way, the relationship may appear to be solely economic: an exchange, like that of other commodities, mediated by money.

Since the fundamental social relations of capitalism appear detached from all coercion, it is hard to recognize in them their primarily coercive aspect: the state. For this reason, the state tends to be understood in a derivative and secondary way: in its objectifications as law and as a set of institutions. These then tend to appear as the entirety of the state and, to the extent that they are moments of the objectification of a social relationship that is no longer visible, also as a force alien to social subjects and driven by a rationality that is foreign to them. What is primarily an aspect of relations of domination is reduced to its objectified surface in institutions. In other words, the reification (or objectification) of the capitalist state in its institutions is the typical modality of its appearance, which is why the critique of that state must begin by uncovering it as an aspect of domination in society. Like money and goods, state institutions are a fetish. Both an emanation and at the same time a concealment of the underlying contradictory relationship, the fetish does not appear solely as an external power. It is also a determinant of ordinary consciousness: its modality of externalization tends to govern a perception of the social world that is itself a concealment of the underlying reality.

This apparent split between society and the state is another specificity of capitalism that—it bears repeating—has a real foundation in the differentiation of a third social subject that provides primarily coercive support. It implies a parallel split between the "private" and the "public"; the subjects of civil society are the "private" parties, while state institutions are the embodiment of the "public." This is another area in which the law is of fundamental importance. In effect, it is the law that places social subjects as private parties opposite state institutions. Civil society and the subjects that constitute it are thus reduced to what they appear to be in capitalist relations of production: agents who, unconditioned by any coercion, reproduce relations of exchange driven by a rationality limited to the economic sphere. On the other hand, state institutions remain as the higher mediating authority in these relations. Thus, the subject of the law is the same as the apparent surface of capitalist society: the "private" sphere, reduced to the daily reproduction of the fundamentally economic, as opposed to the public sphere of a fetishized state.

Before turning to other issues, I will briefly summarize some of the main points of the argument. This may be necessary because too often the theory of the state remains trapped in the "fetishized" appearance of the capitalist state. As a result, a series of false problems and dilemmas cannot be overcome. The key is to first understand the state as an analytical dimension in civil society, and only then (as a consequence of the necessary separation of a third social subject imprinted in the specificity of that aspect) as a set of objectifications.

5. Exteriority

The fact that the social subject that enforces coercive guarantees has been differentiated (and that its institutional realization is therefore external to the parties at this level, but only at this level) does not prevent the social relationship from being jointly and originally constituted by various aspects, including the state or political aspect in the strict sense and physical coercion. These are questions that must be carefully disentangled. To reiterate, then: relations of domination—including those between capitalists and workers—are not purely economic. They are also inherently political and, assuming a certain "normality," ideological as well. The concrete level of objectification in social and institutional subjects is secondary and derivative (although it has important effects of its own) of the interweaving of those aspects as jointly constitutive of a social relationship. This has several consequences. One is that if social subjects are constituted in and through their status as bearers of social relations, classes are not solely an economic phenomenon, because the capitalist relations of production that shape them are not. Another is that if the state, or the political in the proper sense, is an aspect of social relations of domination, the opposition between the "private" and the "public" or state is false. And it is in the specific sense that not only is the "private" sphere permeated by the political-state sphere, but also because, as a constituent part of the social sphere, it is an (analytically distinguishable) part of the latter. In other words—and although this reiterates previous reflections, it is key—the state or political sphere is not "outside" society; it is an intrinsic part of it.

On the other hand, we know that the state derives from a social relationship that involves the separation of a third social subject. We also saw that this subject is not only the objectification of the effective validity of the coercive guarantee underlying these relationships. It also organizes domination through negative limits and the conditioning of the social context, which is undertaken by state institutions, as well as through its objectification as law. In addition, however, law is the consecration of the apparent exteriority of the state with respect to social subjects. We saw that capitalist relations of production generate a subject—state institutions—that appears as a non-capitalist external to the direct subjects of the capitalist relations of production. We also saw that this third party is not a direct guarantor of the classes but of the relations that constitute them as such. This is the origin of the apparent split between state and society or, likewise, between the political and the economic. This split is apparent because it is an emergence of the inherent interweaving of the political and the economic (as well as other planes) as aspects of those relations. But it is also real in its own way because, at the level of concrete social subjects, a third party emerges that is neither capitalist nor worker, nor does it act with the rationality of either. This, in turn, is the basis for a transformation that conceals the capitalist state as a form of domination. First, it subsumes these institutions under the "whole" state. Second, it gives the appearance that they only intervene occasionally and without systematic bias in social relations. When the state is no longer seen in its primary role as a guarantor of social relations of domination (especially capitalist relations of production), its coercive component disappears and everything seems to be due to a diffuse economic coercion. Furthermore, when that primary role is erased, the resources concentrated in state institutions (including the capacity for coercion) may appear to be linked to a general and abstract interest. In other words, the sale of labor to those who lack coercive resources requires control by a third party who, since coercion has been removed from that relationship, can then appear to apply it neutrally. The sum of these two movements is negative: domination and its coercive backing tend to disappear from both society and the state. What remains is a legally crystallized "order" to which all subjects, free and equal, can appeal, and are subject to coercion only when they attempt to violate it.

6. Limited Rationality

The capitalist state is a fetish insofar as it appears subsumed in its objectifications and, therefore, detached from its fundamental embeddedness in society. But this does not prevent us from considering the immense importance of what its institutions do and do not do. At the level of analysis we are concerned with, the main issue is whether it is correct to assert that these institutions, as moments of the objectification of the full reality of the state, express the inherently capitalist condition of the state in their own right and, if so, in what ways. This topic has given rise to too many simplifications and false dilemmas for us not to examine it carefully. We must begin by criticizing the claim of truly superior rationality that is often postulated by these institutions.

Margaret Wirth raises the following pertinent question: "The argument according to which the state must guarantee the reproduction of social capital poses as a problem *firstly* the way in which the state becomes aware of the conditions of global reproduction, distinct that is from the way in which individual capitals do. The state bureaucracy 'knows' as little as the individual capitalists of the measures 'objectively' necessary in any given circumstance."[233] This statement is based on a reality: whether or not they are at the top of the state's institutional system, human beings are subject to acute cognitive limitations regarding

233 Margaret Wirth, "Towards a Critique of the Theory of State Monopoly Capitalism," *Economy and Society* 6, no. 3 (1977): 305.

their own shortcomings and the multidimensionality of the social world. This determines that theirs is a "bounded rationality": that is, they cannot really seek or find optimal solutions. Their attention span is limited; the list of problems they can address is short; the search for information is becoming increasingly costly; the criteria that guide that search are biased by unconscious factors and operational routines; and the information has little influence.[234] As a result, the typical method used for decision-making is through trial and error, based on finding non-optimal (simply "satisfactory") solutions that assume a rudimentary theory of the causal connections governing the problems to be solved.

These data are not consistent with the Hegelian self-image of the bureaucrat, which coincides with that of some misguided critics. Nor do they fit with the view that some fraction of the bourgeoisie "controls" the state as a shrewd instrument serving its interests. How, then, is it possible to answer in the affirmative the question that opens this section? The state guarantees and organizes the reproduction of society qua capitalist because it is in a relationship of "structural complicity" with it.[235]

As an aspect of society, the state is a part of even the capitalist relations of production. Because of this, the state is already capitalist, without the need for the decisions and volitions of its agents for it to become so. Capitalist society is a systematic and habitual bias toward its reproduction as such; the same is true of the state, which is an aspect of

---

234 The references to cognitive limitations that I will make in this section are based mainly on the research of Herbert Simon and his collaborators; see in particular James March and Herbert Simon, *Organizations* (New York: Wiley, 1958); and Richard Cyert and James March, *A Behavioral Theory of the Firm* (Englewood Cliffs, NJ: Prentice Hall, 1963). Also relevant, though it is hard to agree with them as normative models, are the "incrementalist" conceptions (see the preliminary works of Charles Lindblom, "The Science of Muddling Through," *Public Administration Review*, and Aaron Wildavsky, *The Politics of the Budgetary Process* (Boston: Little Brown and Co., 1964); and on "bureaucratic politics," G. Allison, *Essence of Decision: Explaining the Cuban Missile Crisis* (Boston: Little Brown, and Co., 1971).

235 The concept comes from C. Offe, "Structural Problems of the Capitalist State" in K. von Beyme, org., *German Political Studies*, vol. I (London: Sage Publications, 1974).

that society. In what ways? First, as law, as the codified crystallization of formal equality and private property. Second, as the tacit presence of resources of power ready to be put into action if the relationship of domination they support for some reason "fails." Third, as one of the anchors for the ideology of a capitalist society that erases itself from ordinary consciousness as domination and exploitation. Fourth, the plausible separation of the state as an institution from capitalist society is in itself a plane of its structural complicity because it rounds off the apparent surface of capitalist society as a socially real abstraction, and in doing so it conceals it and conceals itself as domination. These reasons make the state the structural accomplice of the validity and reproduction of capitalist society, of which—it bears repeating—it is a co-constitutive aspect.

Where have these reflections taken us? To the realization that the state, or the specifically political, is the same bias with which society tends to reproduce itself as capitalist. This is a different problem from what state institutions do and do not do (more precisely, what people in roles that allow them to "speak" on behalf of the state and mobilize its resources do and do not do). This level is derived from the one I just referred to since it can only be properly understood from the perspective of the state as a co-constitutive aspect of society. However, this is the arena in which the discussion of the question we have raised is usually placed; but if my reflections on the fetishization of the state are not mistaken, it is not surprising that, at this level detached from its underlying reality, there is no possible answer to that question.

These institutions act specifically on the systematic bias toward guaranteeing and reproducing their society qua capitalist, which is already imprinted on the state of which they are an objectification. When and how do they act? Basically on two occasions: first, as a bureaucratic administration that performs routine tasks of the general organization of society; second, in response to situations perceived as "crises." What do these institutions do and how do they do it? Let's start with routine administration. This, together with the law (with which it largely overlaps, insofar as the latter is part of these routines and, on the other hand, much of this administration is carried out through the application of legal norms), is the usual and largely invisible fabric of the many daily decisions that sustain and organize society. This functioning, despite its inefficiencies and inconsistencies, systematically presupposes—in its real content and in the daily aggregation of the impacts of those decisions—society to be class-based and composed of abstractly equal legal subjects capable of privately appropriating the means of production, that is, a capitalist society. And by presupposing it, it tacitly but decisively ratifies it, through the myriad decisions with which the bureaucratic Penelope re-weaves, day after day, a fabric that is the image and likeness of that of the previous day (where every previous day was capitalist). This "natural" repetition as an obvious extension of the past is, like the routines of work (and it is no coincidence that it is part of them), one of the fundamental contributions of the state, objectified in bureaucracy, to the reproduction of capitalist society. The framework of support and the state organization of society is also woven by its institutions into daily routines that presupposes society as capitalist. While understanding the state as an aspect required analytical effort, the repetition of these routines is like an opaque hum that is not easy to detect.

Another level at which state institutions operate is in response to (and, sometimes, in an attempt to prevent) a "crisis"[236] or "issues."[237] But what is a crisis? Something that for some reason is perceived as "going wrong" and that a state institution is responsible for "resolving": a general strike, an excessive inflation rate, a fall in the investment rate, or demands that certain economic resources of the state be allocated to program A rather than program B. More generally, crises and issues appear in political terms as disruptions of "order" and in economic terms as obstacles to the accumulation of capital. In other words, what constitutes a crisis is not determined neutrally: crises are crises insofar as they are crises of society qua capitalist.

Crises and issues are defined as such based on certain basic conceptions of what, in contrast, constitutes "normality." So, for instance, labor exploitation is hidden as normality unless an excessive rate threatens

---

236 This point is emphasized by Margaret Wirth in "Towards a Critique."

237 On the emergence, development, and resolution of social problems or "issues," see Oscar Oszlak and Guillermo O'Donnell, "Estado y políticas públicas en América Latina: Sugerencias para su estudio," CEDES/GE-CLACSO, *Documento*, no. 4 (1976).

the reproduction of the workforce or for any reason generates "disorder." Only then is it brought to the attention of the subjects and tends to generate corrective and/or coercive actions. In the same way, the dynamics of capital accumulation mean that the bourgeoisie continually devours and reconstitutes itself. But this only appears to be a problem when a group demands, under conditions that allow it to be heard, that these effects be limited and that it be supported in order to survive as capitalist (or when certain officials take the initiative to protect this or that group). There is no need to insist with further examples. What is important is that the very definition of crisis or issue presupposes an "order" (which we already know is a relationship of domination) and a "normality" of capital reproduction (which is a reality of exploitation sustained by that order). In other words, there is an implication of the naturalness of society as capitalist, which must be dynamically restored through the "solution" to each problem. This is another level of structural complicity translated, first, into Penelope's routine and, second, into the reconstruction of a "normality" in which the fractures arise from the underlying contradictions that that "normality" helps conceal.

I have noted that contrary to the illusions of technocrats, human beings confront the problems they come up against with an attention span, availability of time, and capacity for information processing that are extremely limited. The expansion and differentiation of state institutions, as well as the growing complexity of the law, are attempts to allocate these and other scarce resources to the large number of issues raised by the contradictory development of society. Just as individuals "factor" problems—dealing with them "one at a time" and isolating them by means of the *ceteris paribus* clause of dimensions outside the rudimentary causal scheme they use—the growth and differentiation of state institutions are the collective *ceteris paribus* of issues and crises.[238] Similarly, the creation of bodies of coordination and command are always insufficient attempts to overcome some of the negative consequences of the resulting institutional dispersion. This is consistent

238 These are some of the other reasons indicated by the authors cited above in showing that decision-making corresponds to bounded rationality and not to "optimals."

with the fragmentation of society. In this sense, the map—the distribution and density—of the state institutions in each historical case is that of the sutures in the areas in which the underlying contradictions have scratched the surface. These institutions are not there due to some grand design of rationality, nor do they act in accordance with it, as they would be more familiar with the conditions of their reproduction than the capitalists. The institutional architecture of the state and its decisions (and non-decisions) are, on the one hand, an expression of its structural complicity and, on the other, the contradictory result of the equally contradictory mode of the existence and reproduction of its society. Limitations with respect to attention and information processing mean that, in order for state institutions to take care of an issue, someone has to propose it "from the outside," or someone "from within" has to define it as such. "Everything that matters" is far from being in the consciousness of social subjects, and even further from being on the agenda of state institutions. The ability to raise an issue or define a situation as a crisis is power. More precisely, it entails having significant resources of domination at one's disposal. Workers can exercise their power collectively, for example by imposing severe sanctions through a strike, although this may lead to a reactive mobilization of resources that result in even more severe sanctions being imposed on them. Of course, in terms of the great differentiator of access to resources that comes with being the ruling class, capitalists tend to have an even greater capacity to raise "their" problems, with less likelihood of retaliatory sanctions. Likewise, the control of resources and of sources of information, as well as the "authority" that comes with speaking from a position that is consistent with the normality of society qua capitalist, allows them to raise issues and define crises in a privileged way. Furthermore, only a grossly instrumentalist view of the state can find it surprising that through its own institutions it can take the initiative to raise these issues.

But what are the issues that make it onto the agenda of state institutions, how are they defined as such, who are the parties that are "authorized" to debate them, and how are they resolved? This is the result of struggles in which the importance of the foundations of domination at play are constantly challenged in complex ways. They are also the silent result of other struggles that are suppressed before they reach the consciousness of individuals due to the opacity of social domination and the structural complicity of the state. This is why the state is, like any social relationship, a relationship of forces. And this is also why its law and its institutions, despite the facade of neutrality that they continually reconstruct, are permeated by the struggles and contradictions of society.

If the state is—in addition to what I have discussed in the previous sections—these planes of structural complicity, and if the crises and issues that reach the agenda of its institutions have been filtered, those problems will tend to appear under the guise of their most immediate effects and causes. A particular business association demands a subsidy because without it its companies would operate at a loss; there is a strike at a particular factory; a particular locality demands that a future road be planned nearby. The problem is presented in terms of its immediate effects, and the causes that give rise to it tend to be understood in their closest connections.[239] Conflicts, too, with their triumphs and defeats of the dominant and dominated classes, tend to be woven around a limited and biased radius of their causes and consequences. Almost everything happens on the surface of society, where, as we know, it is hard to get at the underlying causes that, with the noise of their manifestations as "crises," overwhelm the attention span of individuals and do not appear

239 According to Margaret Wirth in "Towards a Critique," 305, "Such deficiencies appear not as 'social' but rather as particular: . . . the cause of this crisis, immediate or otherwise, is not obvious; . . . the linear chain of cause and effect is bypassed by the contradictory structure of the causes of crises." These observations are confirmed by empirical studies of organizations; cf. the above quotations, to which it should be added that both the attribution of causes as "issues" and the attribution of possible consequences of decisions aimed at solving them are often "simplistic" and based on information "that is frequently hard to obtain and of uncertain reliability" (Richard Cyert and James March, *A Behavioral Theory of the Firm*, 80–81). This reinforces the tendency to operate within a "basic" causal framework, even when it comes to limiting oneself to causal connections that are very close to the problem detected. For organizations that do not usually "choose" their problems but rather jump "from one crisis to another" (ibid., 102), this means that they can usually only scratch the surface of these crises.

as what they truly are: the contradictory mode of reproduction of capitalist society.

The measures adopted may or may not be "appropriate"; they may mitigate or fuel the specific conflict they were intended to resolve or prevent; they may or may not be implemented; and they may be more or less ostensibly inconsistent with those that were taken previously or adopted by another state institution. The fragmentation of the state's institutional system and the bounded rationality of its agents mean that these dilemmas tend to be accurate in the overall picture of what this set of institutions does and fails to do.

The structural complicity of the state and the unequal base of resources with which each individual can make themselves heard by state institutions mean that many decisions are guided by the intention to favor this or that fraction or group of the bourgeoisie. But, as I hope to emphasize, this is just the tip of the iceberg: the decisive factor is that the usual treatment of problems (already filtered, moreover) in their most superficial and immediate form implies reaffirming the texture of society qua capitalist. This, along with Penelope's task, is what allows us to understand why, through a cacophony of inconsistencies and of failures and successes that are always partial and precarious, state institutions tend to contribute to guaranteeing and organizing the reproduction of society as capitalist.[240]

Therefore, the answer to the initial question is that the state, objectified in institutions, backs and organizes the reproduction of society qua capitalist through the apparent chaos of decisions and abstentions that, framed by a bounded rationality, tacitly presuppose and tactically ratify the deep texture of that society. No magic anoints its agents with superior rationality. Quite simply, because the iceberg is part of the deep

---

240 Therefore, nothing could be more misguided than the view of the state as a monolithic entity, which prevents us from recognizing, on the one hand, that its institutions tend to internalize the relative weight of the subordinate classes and, on the other, that this is not only not an obstacle but a condition that enables the mosaic of institutions, decisions, and non-decisions that give concrete form to the structural complicity of the state.

reality of the sea, it tends to travel—almost never in a straight line, and without a map or sextant—in the direction of the current.

We can now connect the above with what has been said about the non-capitalist rationality that appears to guide state interventions. It is clear that the claim to a "superior" rationality is false. But it remains true that, although the rationality of the civil servant is as limited as that of the capitalist, his motivation is not immediately capitalist insofar as it is not usually oriented toward profit per se. However, decisions that renew the tacit vow of loyalty to society qua capitalist tend to occur amid clashes of "individual" interests. These are the concrete terms in which the conditions for the reproduction of society are proposed and resolved. When faced with them, state officials tend to make decisions based on more general interests. Of course, this is not a truly general interest. But the verisimilitude of this belief (and, derived from it, the belief of a state that stands above a society over which it arbitrates impartially and sovereignly) is rooted in the greater generality of the motivation, which is not immediately capitalist, with which state officials tend to process the fragmentation of society.

On an even more abstract level, the image of the state official as an agent of the general interest is confirmed on the tacit but fundamental level I discussed above: despite their bounded rationality, the aggregation of state decisions and abstentions tends to contribute to the general interest of reproducing society qua capitalist. State institutions thus complete their imposition on society. Not only are they the fetish of the apparent split between state and society (albeit founding real characteristics of society), but they also—despite their bounded rationality—appear to be above society. Indeed, they are the publicly and coercively backed organization of a surface that conceals, partially pieced together by state institutions, the rifts that constitute it for what it is. This is how the state, reified in its institutions, is the "mask of society," an appearance of external force driven by a superior rationality that presents itself (and is believed to be) the embodiment of a just order that it serves as a neutral arbiter.

7. Contradiction

The state is inherently contradictory. Such is the case because it is essentially an analytical part of a contradictory social relationship. But that is not enough. The state has its own specificity, which allows it to be distinguished as a constitutive aspect of global society because it introduces its own contradiction into that relationship. What we explored in the previous section will allow us to begin to address this issue. The capitalist mode of production presupposes the emergence of a third social subject. This exteriority, as a moment of its full meaning, is the basis for its usual perception as an actor detached from that relationship, and this, in turn, is the origin of the fetishization of state institutions. This allows the capitalist relations of production to appear as non-coercive and purely economic, while the coercion of state institutions disappears in their inherent connection to those relations. The split between the public and the private is a condition of possibility for the capitalist relations of production, because it is only thus that they can appear as free agreements between equal subjects and not as inherently backed by the coercive power of the state. This, however, generates the need for mediation between the public and the private, or between the state and civil society. How can we extricate civil society subjects from their fragmentation and everyday lives in such a way that, without exposing them as domination, state institutions can continue to base themselves on the plausible argument that what they do and do not do is guided by a more general interest than that of "private" parties?

How can coercion be legitimized and justified even against the dominant classes, and, ultimately, how can the political obligation to obey the "order" of which the state is the guarantor and organizer be justified? We have already seen that the real foundation of the power wielded by state institutions is external: it comes from the capitalist relations of production as a guarantee of those relations. In the same way, the fetishized state must owe its legitimacy to a foundation other than civil society: for the simple reason that this fetishization has reduced it to the private sphere as a fundamentally economic everyday opacity.

The gap between the state and civil society must be bridged so that the power wielded by the former does not reveal itself as such and ultimately functions as a guarantee of domination over the latter. If state institutions were unable to routinely obtain obedience from social subjects, and if they did not have some generally accepted authority to apply the *ultima ratio* of coercion, then they would not be the guarantee that they are objectively considered to be. But if that obedience and authority were based on the relationship that secures them, they would be exposed, just as those institutions cannot appear as the foundation of their own power without abdicating their own legitimacy and exposing themselves as domination.[241] The capitalist state must appear as a fetish split off from civil society, but neither the former nor the latter could conceal themselves as domination if that split were not overcome through mediations that ground state power outside its institutions and domination in society. The contradiction of the capitalist state is that it is both a hiatus from and a need for mediation with civil society. These mediations, which we will examine in the second section of this essay, are the ambiguous and ultimately contradictory expression of this.

Furthermore, the foundation of power is not necessarily its referent (the subject or collective interest it is supposed to serve). In reality, the capitalist, as a class, is the indirect beneficiary of the state guarantee since it lends itself to the social relations of production and these, in turn, entail the continuous replacement of a class of capitalists who buy labor power from a class of formally free workers. Nor does the ruling class tend to appear as a direct beneficiary of the fetishized state. Just as in deep reality, the beneficiary in this case must be a more general referent than those mentioned above. But the marginalization in the private and fundamentally economic sphere that this split determines for civil society means that it cannot be the referent to which state institutions can attribute the generality of the interest they appear to serve.

The only possibility for the power wielded by state institutions to have a foundation and a referent is for this split to be overcome, but this is the negation of the necessary split between the state and capitalist

---

241 In other words, the state is a remarkable concentration of domination, but in order to truly function as such—that is, beyond mere coercion, which is unsustainable except perhaps in the very short term—it must not appear as such in its institutions, in the law, or in the social relations from which it actually emanates.

society. Out of the profound falseness of this split emerges the necessary impulse to overcome it. This brings us to the second section, in which I will address the main mediations between the state and society. Here we will find other components of the capitalist state that, although they depend on the fundamental level we have already analyzed, are also indispensable for fully understanding it. After considering these mediations, I will attempt to recover some of the key aspects of the totality that comes from the vector we have just explored and that we will address in the following pages.

Before proceeding, however, a clarification is necessary, prompted by the original motivation for these reflections. The historical cases that these reflections evoke are characterized by the suppression of the mediations that I will analyze. Contrary to "normal" cases, in which the capitalist state also organizes consensus when these mediations are in force, in these cases there is a clear combination of class domination with the coercive guarantee of the state. In these cases, the capitalist state shows that it is first and foremost a capitalist state rather than a national, popular, or citizens' state. Its coercive element linked to class domination is, as I have tried to show, the underlying scaffolding that structures the state, exposed when social consensus and state legitimacy are sacrificed to save that domination. The product of a contradictory relationship, the capitalist state is intrinsically that same contradiction, even expressing and "returning" with its own specificity the changing balance of power with which it historically occurs.

Furthermore, the capitalist state also necessarily tends toward a false transcendence, concealing this contradiction, except at conjunctures in which the nonnegotiable core is at stake: the very survival of the social relations of which it is an intrinsic part. There, for its own salvation, state and social domination must take the enormous risk of exposing itself as such, the exact opposite of its occasional victories.

III. Mediations Between State and Society

1. Introduction

We know that the state is primarily an aspect of certain social relations and that "public" institutions and the law are its main objectifications. We also saw that the true embeddedness of the state is with these relations and, only through them, with its social subjects. This implies that the state is a more general entity than those subjects, referring to an interest that, because it maintains those relationships, is also more general to them. This characteristic of the state is transposed to its appearance in ordinary consciousness, where it does not emerge as a generality that is systematically biased toward a relationship of domination, but rather as an undifferentiated and impartial generality. This is what we will explore below.

The state's role as a guarantor and organizer of society qua capitalist tends to be denied by mediations that reconnect the state and society in ways that ignore class divisions and confine society to the "private" and fundamentally economic sphere. These mediations are generalizing mechanisms, superimposed on the fragmentary nature of society like a curtain that hides the clutter that should not be shown on the grand stage of politics. Inter-bourgeois competition and the dismantling of the subordinate classes tend to generate systems of solidarity that are inferior to those that the state, seeking to rule over a territorially limited population, cannot fail to implicate. Whether through the myriad groups and coalitions that arise from the fragmentation of society, or through alignments that express its deepest divisions, the groupings that emanate directly from society cannot forge solidary ties that cover the entire population.

Furthermore, to the extent that the main alignment was based on class divisions and was not encompassed by any type of more general solidarity, the contribution of the state to society qua capitalist would become apparent; this does not mean that such a state is necessarily unfeasible, but it does reduce ideological control and, correspondingly, exposes it as coercion.

Every state involves a political community in the sense that it is a necessary condition for consensually accepted domination and that its continuous reconstitution tends to be one of the goals that state institutions strive for. By political community, I mean collective solidarities, prevalent among a large part of a population that is territorially delimited by a state, resulting from the belief in a shared set of core values and interests, and that it is possible to establish common goals attributable to those values and interests. Just as, at its deepest level, the state is a more general entity than the subjects constituted by the social relationship of which it is an aspect, the link between the state and a political community is another form of generality: a mode of organizing subjects in a territory in ways that make them a level of generality equivalent to that of the state.

State institutions exercise power when they back their decisions with the ability to impose severe sanctions (not only coercive ones). On what grounds can such power be claimed? Furthermore, on what grounds can it be claimed that each individual must fulfill the political obligation to adjust their behavior (even obeying explicit commands) without the need to invoke this power of coercion? This is, of course, one of the classic themes of political theory. But this has not always been the case. Rather, it became an issue when power could no longer justify itself as a traditional right to rule, as the expression of the intangible rights of the monarchy or as the secular arm of a higher spiritual power.

The capitalist state is the first state with a need to base its power on something outside itself. Two closely related processes—the expansion of capitalism in Europe and the successful demand to obey only a consensually formed power—raised the crucial issue of political obligation. Hobbes, Locke, and Rousseau each offered different answers, but the practical outcome was that its foundations had to be rooted in the idea that, in some way, the subject appears to be shaping the same will to which they adapt their behavior and/or because it is in their rational interest to do so.

By foundation of the state, I am referring to the basis of its control over the resources of domination and its claim, backed by those resources, to be routinely obeyed. By referent of the state, I am referring to the subjects and their social relations whose interests in validity and reproduction it serves. The capitalist state, in its deepest reality, is neither its own foundation nor its referent. Both are external to it. They are located at the—analytical—level of society, the foundation and referent of the state.

As we have already seen at other levels, this deep reality has an impact on the way the state appears in ordinary consciousness. Indeed, just as the state often appears reified in institutions, the foundation of its right to command and coerce, as well as its expectation of widespread obedience, are also external. Similarly, the "for whom"—the referent that these institutions appear to serve—tends to appear external to them.

The possibility of the widespread acceptance of control over resources of domination by state institutions demands that the foundation and referent for this capacity be external to them. But society does not tend to appear as that foundation or referent either. First, because its fragmentation is not sufficient to generate collective solidarity at the level implied by the state, which is a generality encompassing the population within a territory. Second, if society were the foundation or referent, the state would appear as the guarantor and organizer of the class domination it wields, in which case the state would not conceal that domination and would directly reflect back to society the fundamental contradiction from which it emanates. This foundation and referent, which are neither society nor the state as embodied in its institutions, are other methods of the constitution of collective subjects, in which solidarity tends to be rooted at a level of generality corresponding to that of the state. These are the mediations between state and society that we have begun to analyze.

Many of the actions of state institutions and of what takes place through the rule of law entail the interweaving of these mediations and, with them, the consensual organization of the structures of society. This being the case, the capitalist state is a crucial factor in the cohesion of global society:[242] its role as the guarantor and organizer of society qua capitalist is complemented by consensus in society and its correlation with the legitimization of the state fetishized in institutions. The result is broad ideological control, or hegemony, the full but covert exercise of domination in society backed by a state that appears as the essence and custodian of a shared sense of living together, accepted as natural and ethically just.

---

242 By global society, I am referring to society, the state, and the mediations that we are discussing in this section as a whole.

It is through these mediations that the capitalist state reflects back to society its own specific contradiction. I pointed out at the end of the previous section that the state is both an apparent split from society and a tendency to overcome it. More specifically, its own contradiction is that its "normal" way of establishing these mediations is a postulation of equality—abstract and concrete, as we will see—in its foundation and in its referent, while at the same time it is unable to cease being a systematic bias toward the validity and reproduction of the contradictory social relations from which it emanates. That is why the capitalist state is a permanent oscillation between hegemony and the discovery of its true embeddedness in society.

Another characteristic of these mediations is that they are the recovery of the privacy and fragmentation of being-in-society, modes of constituting collective identities. The social subject, a synthesis of depoliticized privacy, thus returns to the political and public sphere, but does so predetermined by identities that are different from what they are in their primordial reality as subjects shaped by the relations of domination in society. After depoliticizing society, cornering it into the economic and private spheres, the state, the condensation of the political, re-creates it—partially and distortedly—in its ties with mediations that deny the founding primacy of society. These mediations develop identities that are linked to the "public" sphere as part of the collective foundations and referents of the state. The worker, employee, and homemaker also tend to be citizens and members of the nation; in other words, they are positioned as something more than what they are in their daily lives, in ways that are the negation of that daily life. Like the state, the mediations we are concerned with are generalities, but particularized generalities that can only be understood at the primordial level—society—which they deny in their deep reality.[243]

243 At the level of this work, I am only able to address the most general forms of mediation and not other, more specific and historically variable ones, such as corporate organizations or political parties. However, my hope is that, from the perspective I propose, it is clear that the meaning of these other forms depends to a large extent on the more general mediations on which I focus here.

2. Citizenship, Foundation of the Capitalist State

The capitalist state was the first form of political domination that posits its foundations on the equality of all subjects within its territory. These subjects are citizens, and the capitalist state is normally a state of citizens. A citizen is someone who has the right to fulfill the acts that lead to the constitution of the power of state institutions, to elect leaders who can deploy those institutions' resources and demand obedience, and to claim recourse to preestablished legal procedures to protect themselves from interference they consider arbitrary. Historically, citizenship developed alongside capitalism, the modern state, and rational-formal law. This is no coincidence: citizens are precisely the legal subjects capable of freely entering into obligations. The premise of this right is the abstract equality of subjects, regardless of whether they own anything beyond their labor power. Capitalism must generate subjects who are free and equal before the law, contracts, and money, since without them, its seminal act—the sale of labor and the appropriation of value—could not exist. This freedom, which is effective (in the abstract sphere in which it is placed) and illusory (in relation to class position), has as its parallel the abstract equality of citizenship. And not only in logical terms: in practice, efforts to limit membership in the political community (and therefore citizenship) to "property owners" were quickly defeated. Those who must appear abstractly equal in order to enter into contracts tend to appear abstractly equal in order to constitute political power; the free subject in the market mediated by capital-money is the exact counterpart of the voter. This has made the capitalist state the first that must tend to appear founded on some plane of equality among all subjects.

This equality represents immense progress compared to the non-belonging of slaves, metics, and serfs to the political community, as well as contemporary regressions in the validity of citizenship. On the other hand, as a postulation of an abstract equality that would be the main foundation of the state, citizenship is the negation of domination in society. Citizenship is the highest possible abstraction in the political sphere. Every citizen, regardless of class position, contributes to the formation of state power embodied in law and institutions. This abstraction thus becomes the foundation of a power that is skewed toward the reproduction of society and the class domination that shapes it. If each person, as a citizen, appears to constitute the power of state institutions and to decide which leaders should deploy their resources, then the basis of political obligation is joint participation in the shaping of the will expressed by those institutions. This implies that democracy is the normal form of political organization in capitalist society. The freedom of citizens to exercise their right to choose their leaders presupposes the existence of options that are feasible under limited but genuinely pluralistic conditions. The mobilization of resources of power by the state can then be carried out with the understanding that the right to do so has been conferred by all citizens. In addition, the competitiveness between parties, involving citizens and their corollary of political democracy, allows for the expression of interests which—although filtered in the sense mentioned in the previous section—support a belief that is key to the legitimacy of state institutions: the idea that there are no interests that are systematically denied by these institutions. This, in turn, is a correlate to the lack of belief that a ruling class exists.[244]

Citizenship is the most consistent foundation of the state as it appears on the surface of capitalist society. This is because it is the most abstract form of mediation between the state and society. However, it is for this very reason that citizenship cannot be a referent for the state. Why? Because what state institutions do and do not do must be related to some general interest (which has a real basis in the fact that the state is a more general interest than that of the subjects it helps associate as an aspect of their relationship). That interest cannot be attributed to the abstract entity of the citizen, except insofar as it continues to exist. In other words, if the totally disembodied condition of citizenship is what allows it to be the egalitarian foundation of the state, it is also what prevents it from being attributed a general interest in the concrete sphere of what state institutions do and do not do.

One of the differences between the state and capital is that the latter appears in the abstract moment of money; the state, on the other hand, is embodied in institutions that, although they postulate an abstract

244 For more on this point and its crucial contribution to ideological control, see Perry Anderson "The Antinomies of Antonio Gramsci," *New Left Review*, no. 100 (1976).

foundation, cannot cease to be, in their actions, omissions, and impacts, a concrete sphere that is usually perceptible as such. A disembodied subject cannot be the bearer of concrete interests. That is why citizenship, an attribute of belonging to the political community, is a creature of capitalist society on the same level on which it presents itself to ordinary consciousness: that of the abstract equality implied by the circulation of capital, but only as a foundation. This indeed involves the enforcement of rights that pertain to the dominated as citizens, including the right to organize politically and thus exert greater influence in society and within the state apparatus; on the other hand, it contributes to ratifying the apparent texture of capitalist society and thus to reproducing it.

3. The Nation, Referent of the State

What interests of what generality—reflecting the population of the territory they cover—do state institutions appear to serve? Those of the nation. The nation is the arc of solidarities that unite the "we" defined by a shared belonging to the territory delimited by a state. The state demarcates one nation from others on the international stage. This demarcation tends to generate a "we,"[245] defined through contrast with or difference from the "they" in that scenario. In other words, the state tends to be coextensive with a nation.[246] Normally, this is a factor of cohesion based on the recognition of that "we" as an acceptable claim to real validity.

---

245 What interests me here is not the genetic question of whether this or that state preexisted the nation or vice versa. The point is that the state tends to postulate the nation, either by recognizing its preexistence or by "inventing" it as a postulation when it does not yet exist. Of course, the degree to which the nation is effectively such has significant consequences, but I am unable to go into that level of specificity here.

246 The existence and/or the possibility of plausibly positing a nation does not depend (even if it makes it more or less difficult) on a community of language, religion, race, a shared past, or other factors that some have attempted to identify. There are plenty of examples to show that none of these factors is a necessary or sufficient condition for the emergence of a nation.

For its part, the state, reified in its institutions, appears as a state-for-the-nation. This is true in two respects. First, as a delimitation of the nation vis-à-vis other states. Second, within its territory, as a claim, ultimately backed by its coercive supremacy, to be the privileged agent for the safeguarding, interpretation, and achievement of the general interests of the nation. The referent for state institutions, the community whose interests they would serve, is not society but the nation. The invocation of the interests of the latter is the justification for imposing decisions against the will of individuals, even against segments of the ruling classes, for the sake of preserving the homogenizing meaning of the nation. Therefore, the imposition of the state before and above society is completed when it is transposed to the level of the nation. From there, state institutions seek to embody a rationality that, far more than the conditions of the reproduction of society, only their agents could achieve. That rationality could not belong to the "parts" of a society that can now appear fragmented without contradicting its apparent surface. In contrast, this fragmentation is a condition that allows the fetishized state to rise above society while speaking of and to the nation. This overlap between state and nation allows us to understand the Hegelian position of state agents. They are more than mere guardians of the general interests of the nation; they are its active synthesis because the members of the nation, who are themselves subject to the particularization of society, are ill-equipped to decipher those interests. We saw that the state is the transmuted secretion of society; we now understand that when the state becomes connected to the nation, society can be cornered into "private" and economic spheres. This inversion dispossesses society of its significance as the fundamental level of global society and, therefore, as the foundational place of domination. For the same reason, the political vanishes from society (as a state and as a struggle for the control of the state resources of domination), to remain tied to the homogenizing and undifferentiated level of state and nation.

The postulation of the nation as a community that is superior to the particular interests of society facilitates the fundamental task of not ignoring inequalities that remain evident but rather denying them in a way that is the most problematic for the reproduction of the system of domination: denying them as contradictions. The validity of national solidarities that would take precedence over society is the denial of these contradictions as such. Furthermore, the conjunction between state and nation sacralizes what continues to be undeniable: social inequalities and "imperfections" do not result from certain interests being systematically denied (because everyone's interests are included under the homogenizing arc of the nation) but are part of the nation's "way of being" that can, in any case, be corrected but not denied. Demands and interests—however "justified" they may be—must conform to these parameters, since not doing so would be to deny the prevailing reality of the nation. Every "private" interest must yield to the higher collective interests derived from the fact that each one is-in-the-nation. How could the interest of any of the "parties" prevail over the interests of all, that of the nation? But, of course, the sacralization of the historical mode of being of the nation also tends to be the reproduction of society qua capitalist.

I insist. State decisions invoke the interests of the nation and condense them into a symbolism that constantly recalls the nation. By jumping over the rifts in society and denying it as inherently contradictory, this presupposes—and therefore ratifies—society qua capitalist. Thus, the nation occupies the space vacated by the sidelining of society and positions itself as the main referent of the state. The state consequently appears as a state-for-the-nation, not as a state of and for society. The state is the "official summary," the majestic facade of society when it distances itself from it and reappears as an active synthesis of the nation. Therefore, insofar as the nation denies the structural rifts in society, it is analogous to citizenship. But if the latter is an abstract mediation, the nation alludes to the concrete acts, omissions, and impacts of state institutions. The consequences of defending a particular position in an international forum, allocating resources to alleviate a disaster, subsidizing certain activities, or modifying labor regulations affect subjects who are members of the nation. For the reasons analyzed above, it is hard for them to fully grasp the causal connections and the range of relevant impacts. However, this does not mean that these activities are not perceived as having significant consequences for the specific interests of those subjects.

Citizenship is an optimal foundation but cannot be a referent because it is an abstract generality. The nation, on the other hand, is a concrete generality, which makes it possible to attribute the general interest that is the referent of the reified state to it. To say that it is a concrete generality is equivalent to two things. First, that it is an undifferentiated homogenization with respect to the divisions in society. Second, that the social subject to which it refers, the member of the nation, is not the disembodied subject of citizenship and rational-formal law. To be a member of the nation is to see oneself as part of a collective identity that transcends class divisions. But it also means sustaining the expectation that one's interests will not be systematically denied, that one is entitled to benefit—concretely and recognizably—from the general interest that state institutions claim to serve. In other words, the consequences of what state institutions do and do not do presuppose a collective identity that, on the one hand, continues to deny the rifts in society and, on the other, is not abstract. This is a way of restating the contradiction that the state returns to society: it cannot be entirely subsumed into the abstract equality of citizenship but must appear mediated by a referent that is the postulation of a concrete generality. State institutions are a systematic bias that must reflect a general interest that presupposes the non-existence of that bias.

The discourse of state institutions is therefore egalitarian and homogenizing insofar as it refers to citizens and members of the nation, while the aggregate impact of their actions and omissions is the practical negation of that discourse. This contradiction (not always or necessarily obvious) is a consequence of the fact that the state cannot have a foundation or referent in society—lest it expose itself and be exposed in the domination that it actually is—and, on the other hand, that its optimal foundation—because it is entirely abstract—cannot, therefore, be its referent. For this reason, if the state does not already find it there, it must postulate it for the nation, inventing it: the capitalist state tends to be a national state.

If the fetishized state is credible as a state-for-the-nation and as a state of citizens,[247] it is therefore, in addition to coercion, an organizer

247 The connection between one level and the other stems from the fact that those who are members of the nation are usually, by virtue of that title, citizens. The subject of the political community normally postulated by the capitalist state is the foundation (citizenship) and referent (nation) of the state. Or, conversely, it is an abstract generality and a concrete generality placed at the same

of consensus. I have already mentioned that its correlate is the legitimization of state institutions and its more general consequence is hegemony. But this is only one possibility that, moreover, has no point of equilibrium: despite the mediations of citizenship and nation, society can impose its own systems of solidarity. Even before that, the capitalist state tends to associate itself with a mediation that is less palatable than the previous ones: the *pueblo* or *lo popular.*

4. The *Pueblo*, Ambiguous Foundation and Referent of the State

In this section, I will shift the level of analysis. I will focus on the *pueblo*, or *lo popular*, another form of collective solidarity that tends to mediate between the state and society. According to the definitions I will propose, this dimension tends to be present to some degree in every capitalist state, but its relative importance has undoubtedly been greater in the Latin American cases addressed in these reflections than in the core capitalist countries. I will argue later—and develop this further in a future work focused directly on the bureaucratic-authoritarian state—that this greater importance has been closely linked to the lesser validity of citizenship as an effective mediation between state and society. This, in turn, appears to be a function of a less extensive and dense form of capitalism, which did not manage to round out, as it did in the core countries, the set of abstract appearances of which, as we have seen, citizenship is one of the components.[248]

In any case, since the element of *lo popular* is always present in every case, I believe it is worth discussing briefly. Members of the nation are entitled to share in the consequences of the achievement of the general interest of the nation. But these consequences are distributed in

---

all-encompassing level as the state and mediating—in a real but covert way, as we are seeing—between the state and its foundation and deep referent, society.

248 Norbert Lechner insists on this point in "La crisis," as does Marcelo Cavarozzi in his work in progress on the historical origins of the question of democracy in Latin America.

an obviously unequal manner. This often gives rise to demands for substantive justice, whereby citizens and members of the nation, based on the discourse of equality implied by the capitalist state and society, seek to have these inequalities remedied. The undifferentiated postulation of the general interest of the nation fails to cover up the evidence of inequality. This often leads to demands that state institutions act in an equalizing way: that is, favoring or protecting the relatively dispossessed. The poor, the common people, the underprivileged are, when collectively recognized as such, the *pueblo* or *lo popular*.

We immediately encounter an initial ambiguity in the concept of *lo popular*. On the one hand, it tends to create a sense of solidarity that transcends class divisions, as it broadly encompasses those who identify as dispossessed. On the other hand, the demand for substantive justice that is specifically aimed at benefiting them can only be made in opposition to those who are also part of the nation: the rich, the powerful, those who have more, and, in some cases, state institutions that appear to be excessively biased toward them. The extent to which part of a population recognizes itself as the *pueblo*, as well as its simultaneity with the validity of citizenship and the nation, is a variable that must be analyzed in specific historical situations. But whenever *lo popular* is effectively valid, it is a sphere of solidarities that is less comprehensive than that of the nation. *Lo popular* is often a field of political struggles defined by its counterpart: the non-popular, which unites at least a portion of the ruling classes.[249] At their most extreme, the struggles over *lo popular* carry with them the claim that their sphere is that of the "true" nation, a fusion of the national and the popular: those who place themselves outside this field are not "really" part of the nation. Furthermore, their demands may affect the limits of the reproduction of society qua capitalist. This may touch on and expose contradictions that the capitalist state cannot resolve nor accept as such.

The fundamental point is that the confrontation between the egalitarian and impartial discourse of the capitalist state and the evidence of inequalities—even if their root causes are not uncovered—continuously

---

249 For an analysis of *lo popular* as the main camp of political struggle, see Ernesto Laclau, "Towards a Theory of Populism" (mimeo) (University of Essex, 1977).

raises the possibility of a resurgence of *lo popular.* This is its second ambiguity. On the one hand, while it continues to bring together social subjects for reasons other than their true condition of being the dominated and exploited in society, it is another means of concealing this condition. Furthermore, to the extent that—depending on contexts and historical periods—a not insignificant part of these demands can be absorbed without exploiting the parameters of society qua capitalist, the state can appear to be embracing *lo popular.* Additionally, the state presents itself to the classes as the guarantor and organizer of the social relations that constitute them as such, which is why—as we saw in the first section—it is also the guardian of the subordinate classes. Similarly, at a fetishized level, the state's acceptance—or anticipation—of demands from the relatively dispossessed who invoke their condition as such facilitates their reproduction as subordinate classes. First, by making the claim to be a state "for all" seem plausible, and even that of being a state that is benevolently biased—in its most notable and publicized decisions—toward the nation's dispossessed. Second, by promoting living conditions for the subordinate classes that are roughly compatible, in each historical case, with the prevailing relations of production and the accumulation of capital.[250] State institutions can thus appear, in cases close to the center of hegemony, not only as an active synthesis

---

250 Even violating the assumptions of the abstract equality of rational-formal law. Typically, this occurs in the regulation of certain labor relations, where it implies the social desirability of some form of state protection for workers. However, just as typically, these departures from the pure assumption of rational-formal law begin by placing the subordinate classes as such, only to then protect the conditions of their reproduction, again as subordinate classes. This is encompassed by a discourse that denies the social relationship thus protected as contradictory. In reality, the benefits derived from this and other forms of protection, and the not infrequent conflicts they provoke with segments of the dominant classes, are one of the main anchors of the legitimizing belief in a state that does not systematically deny any interest and that, moreover, promotes substantive "social justice" over the dominant classes. I hope it is clear that this is true, but in the limited sense that, in accordance with the profound meaning of the state as the guarantor and organizer of a social relationship of domination, it occurs within the limits of the replacement of the subordinate classes as such.

of the nation but also as dedicated—albeit chronically unsuccessful—guardians of the subordinate classes.

However—and this is the other aspect of the ambiguity—, the tendency toward the continuous rethinking of substantive justice issues predefines the non-popular as the adversary, thus diminishing the comprehensive and homogeneous nation that is the ideal referent for the state. Furthermore, the eventual impossibility of satisfying the demands raised, along with remedial actions that fail to close the gap between egalitarian discourse and observable inequalities, can place an "excessive" burden on capital accumulation. Furthermore, this may be one of the fields of social practice in which the subordinate classes understand themselves as such. That is why *lo popular* is at the same time a veil over the profound reality of society (and, consequently, of the state) and a possible point of transition toward its discovery.

That is also why *lo popular* is a less palatable mediation for the capitalist state, and for the domination in which it is embedded, than citizenship and the nation. *Lo popular* is not the abstract mediation of citizenship nor the concrete but undifferentiated mediation of the nation. Its contents are more specific than those of the latter. They are also less generic, since the arc that covers the *pueblo* is more limited than that of the nation, which claims to offer solidarity to the entire population. On the other hand, the contents of *lo popular* are more generic and less concrete than those derivable from class position. Ambiguously positioned between citizenship and the nation on the one hand, and class on the other, *lo popular* can be both the foundation and the referent for state institutions.

The authority to command and coerce may appear to be conferred by the *pueblo*, not only (and sometimes not as much) by the abstract generality of citizenship.[251] The state then appears as a state based mainly

---

251 To reiterate a previous point, this has happened in certain cases in Latin America in periods prior to the emergence of BA. This seems to be the norm in late and dependent capitalist economies (in many cases with the additional complication of strong ethnic and regional solidarity). In these societies, capitalism coexists with other historical forms and reproduces itself in a particularly unequal manner, with the result that the abstract surface of capitalist

on the relatively dispossessed. When they are the foundation, they also tend to be the postulated referent for the state: what its institutions do and do not do would mainly serve the *pueblo*, the dispossessed who are in greatest need of their tutelary concern. But the capitalist state can only really be a popular state in very special and short-lived historical circumstances.[252] That state cannot fail to be what is determined by its profound reality: the emanation, guarantor, and organizer of a relationship of domination that structurally biases what its objectified moments, laws, and institutions bring to bear on society.

5. Concealment and Rupture

No society is purely capitalist, even if its capitalist nature tends to overshadow its other dimensions. In particular, the state's control over a territorially defined population in the name of the nation often includes, to varying degrees, other divisions—ethnic, linguistic, regional, religious—whose connection to class must be carefully assessed on a case-by-case basis. This, along with the reasons explored in the preceding pages, reinforces the tendency to obscure the emergence, as a central issue in the consciousness of individuals, of civil society (including the state as an analytical part of it) as the founding plane of global social reality. In particular, the mediations discussed above tend to cast an integrating veil over the structurally torn background of civil society and sustain the imposing architecture of a fetishized state. However, we have seen that these mediations—each in its own way—are also an expression of and a way of reflecting back to civil society the fundamental contradiction from which the state emanates and the contradiction

society (with its correlate of citizenship) does not cover the whole of social relations.

252 That is, as a plausible postulation of a foundation and popular referent, whose aggregate social impacts are not too inconsistent with that postulation. Not every invocation of the *pueblo* makes the state, in the terms I am laying out here, a popular state.

derived from this that the state, in its reification, creates for itself by appearing split from its origin.

On the other hand, citizenship, nation, and *pueblo*, each in their own way, are contradictory, beyond what we have already seen as the specificity of each, because their concealing effect cannot exist without them being—and helping make the law and the state apparatus—arenas for the practical presence of the subordinate classes. Transcending their everyday fragmentation in civil society, in these spheres—even though they are biased toward concealment and, therefore, toward reproducing the existing "order"—these classes can recognize and constitute themselves, politically and ideologically, as such. This, in turn, opens up the possibility for them to discover the foundation of their condition. From this point on, we enter a level of specificity that exceeds the scope of this discussion.

IV. A Few Conclusions

In the preceding sections, we explored two vectors that are essential to understanding the capitalist state. In the first, we dealt with the crucial point: the state as an analytical aspect of society, partially crystallized by law and institutions. There, we understood it as primarily coercive. But we also saw that the tendency toward the fetishization of the state and toward an apparent split between it and society leads to a necessary tendency toward the generation of mediations between the two. I therefore dealt with the main ones in the second section: citizenship, nation, and *pueblo*. There, we saw that the state is also, normally, an organization of consensus insofar as it constitutes collective solidarities that tend to veil the structural rifts in society and the systematic biases of the state. This often leads to the legitimization of state institutions, which find in these mediations a generally credible foundation and referent.

While this is often the consequence of such mediations, they are also the way in which the state expresses its own contradiction, reflecting a society whose fundamental contradiction at the level of the relations of production is a co-constitutive aspect. The capitalist state cannot fail to have, in the aggregation of its impacts over time and across society, a structural bias that reproduces the capitalist society of which, in its deepest reality, it forms a part. But for these mediations to be effective—and not just empty rhetoric—they must be based on an ideology of equality: abstract in terms of citizenship, concrete but undifferentiated in terms of the nation, and eventually more concrete and less undifferentiated at the level of *lo popular.* The correlate is the postulation of the state as an arbiter and impartial guardian. In its most attenuated expression, the contradiction appears as a perpetual incongruity between postulated foundations and referents, on the one hand, and the evidence of profound inequalities, on the other. This does not necessarily imply that these are understood in their root causes, that is, as contradictions. But evidence of such inequalities places the state in the irresolvable tension of having to be both structurally biased and a proponent of equality. This tension produces, in addition to the reasons I noted in the first section, advances and setbacks, as well as attempts by state institutions to remedy inequality. These attempts may serve as an anchor for their legitimacy, but they also provide an opportunity to recognize them as contradictions that are inherent to capitalist society. What seems evident—if these reflections are not too far off the mark—is that the second possibility lies fundamentally in the realm of politics and ideology and that, despite the imposing weight of the fetishized state, the decisive locus for the reproduction and potential transcendence of domination is society.

Last, there is no metaphysical need for the mediations in question to exist. But their non-existence or possible suppression means that, although the state no longer reflects back to society the contradiction I have just pointed out, it reveals its entanglement in the fundamental social contradiction much more directly. It then falters as an organization of consensus and reveals its primary component—coercion—and its fundamental role as the source and guarantor of the main relations of domination in society. Stripped of its "normal" components of mediation and consensus, this state, which is authoritarian in several ways, shows that it is first and foremost a capitalist state rather than a national, popular, or citizens' state. But the imposing face of coercion is its failure to organize consensus and, therefore, to legitimize its institutions and contribute to the hegemony in society.

I hope that these notes, focused on assumptions of domination tending toward the pole of consensus and capitalism as a broadly imposed historical form, have paved the way for future attempts to understand, through contrast, cases of capitalist states in which these assumptions are absent or were drastically eliminated.

About the Author

Guillermo O'Donnell (1936–2011) was for nearly four decades the most influential social scientist studying contemporary Latin America. At the time of his death in his native Buenos Aires, he was professor emeritus of political science and senior fellow at the Kellogg Institute for International Affairs at the University of Notre Dame. He had previously served as the Helen Kellogg Professor of Government and International Studies (1982–2005) and founding academic director of the Kellogg Institute (1982–97) at the University of Notre Dame, and director of the Centro de Estudios de Estado y Sociedad (1976–79) in Argentina. He received his LLB from the Universidad Nacional de Buenos Aires in 1958 and his MPhil and PhD in political science from Yale University in 1971 and 1988, respectively. Among many distinguished positions, Professor O'Donnell served as president (1988–91) and vice-president (1982–88) of the International Political Science Association and vice-president of the American Political Science Association (1999–2000). He was visiting fellow or visiting professor, in chronological order, at Princeton University; the University of Michigan; the University of California, Berkeley; the Instituto Juan March (Madrid); Stanford University; the University of Cambridge; and the University of Oxford; and he held honorary doctorates degrees from two universities in Argentina as well as institutions in Chile, Germany, and Peru. He was named a member of the American Academy of Arts and Sciences in 1995. In 2003, LASA awarded him its highest honor, the Kalman Silvert Award for lifetime achievement. In 2006, he was the inaugural recipient of the International Political Science Association (IPSA) Prize for Lifetime Achievement. In 2014, LASA established the Guillermo O'Donnell Democracy Award and Lectureship to honor his distinguished career and pioneering intellectual leadership. This annual association-wide award recognizes either outstanding scholarship in the field of democracy studies or particularly meritorious public service that promotes democracy and democratic values in Latin America and the Caribbean. In 2025, his alma mater, the University of Buenos Aires Law School, awarded him a posthumous honorary doctorate.

Index

B

E

R

S

About LASA Press

LASA Press is the open-access publishing house of the Latin American Studies Association (LASA), dedicated to academic research related to Latin America. It seeks to contribute to the dissemination of knowledge through the publication of new research and translations of fundamental works on Latin America from a variety of disciplinary perspectives. It gives priority to proposals that are relevant to the region as a whole, contribute to defining the public agenda, and serve as a bridge between cultures, languages, and academic traditions, thereby extending the impact of Latin American knowledge throughout the world.

www.ingramcontent.com/pod-product-compliance
Lightning Source LLC
LaVergne TN
LVHW041113080826
845145LV00007B/1792

* 9 7 8 1 9 5 1 6 3 4 6 6 7 *